A Short Introduction to the U.S. Census

John D. Carl
Rose State College

Boston Columbus Indianapolis New York San Francisco Upper Saddle River
Amsterdam Cape Town Dubai London Madrid Milan Munich Paris Montreal Toronto
Delhi Mexico City Sao Paulo Sydney Hong Kong Seoul Singapore Taipei Tokyo

DEDICATION

To my family. . . I love you all!

Editorial Director: *Craig Campanella*
Editor-in-Chief: *Dickson Musslewhite*
Senior Acquisitions Editor: *Brita Mess*
Editorial Assistant: *Seanna Breen*
Executive Marketing Manager: *Kelly May*
Marketing Assistant: *Janeli Bitor*
Senior Production Project Manager: *Roberta Sherman*
Editorial Production and Composition Service: *Words and Numbers*
Manufacturing Buyer: *Megan Cochran*
Cover Administrator: *Joel Gendron*

Library of Congress Cataloging-in-Publication Data
CIP information not available at time of publication

10 9 8 7 6 5 4 3 2 1 RRD-OH   15   14   13   12   11

www.pearsonhighered.com

ISBN-10:   0-205-21325-1
ISBN-13: 978-0-205-21325-2

Contents

1 History and Science of the Census   1

2010 Census Sparks House Realignment   2

History of the Census   2

   The Historical Origins of the Census   2

   Early Census Methods   3

Legal Basis for the Census   4

   The Census Bureau   5

Changes in the Census over Time   6

   A Changing Country   7

   Evolution of Census Philosophy   8

   Technology and the Census   10

Census Methodologies   11

   Breaking down the Census   11

   Twentieth-Century Census Efforts   11

   Undercount   12

   2010 Census   14

What Can the Census Bureau Data Show Us?   14

   Economic Changes   14

   Racial Changes   14

   Gender   14

   Age   15

   Marriage and Family   15

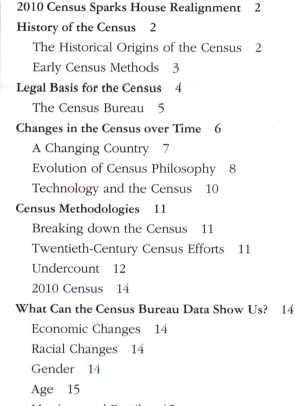

2 Economic Trends and Employment   17

Income Inequality Worsens across the United States   18

Social Class and Stratification   18

   Wealth and Poverty in the United States   19

   Social Classes and Outcomes   20

   Economic Inequality   21

Historical Perspectives on Economic Trends and Employment   23

   History of Income Inequality in America   23

   Race, Gender, and Immigration   24

Recent Economic and Unemployment Trends   26

   Income   26

   Employment and Unemployment   27

   Poverty   28

   Inequality   29

State-by-State Comparison   29

3 Issues of Race   33

Population Changes in Post-Katrina New Orleans   34
Historical Background of Race in America   34
  The Concept of Race   35
  Race Definitions for the Census over Time   35
  Historical Variances in Census Racial Definitions   37
Immigration to the United States   38
  What Is Immigration?   38
  Who Migrates and Why?   39
  Foreign-Born Residents   39
2000 Findings on Race   40
  Non-Hispanic White   40
  Black   41
  Asian   42
  Native American or Alaska Native   42
  Hispanic or Latino   42
2010 Findings on Race   43
  Non-Hispanic White   43
  Black   43
  Asian   44
  Native American or Alaska Native   44
  Hispanic or Latino   44
2000 Findings on Foreign-Born Population   45
2010 Findings on Foreign-Born Population   45
State-by-State Comparison   45

4 Demographic Changes in America—Gender   51

A Larger Pool of Men and Women   52
The Concept of Gender   52
  Patriarchy and the Census   52
  Gender Roles   53
Sex Ratios and the Census   54
  Applying the Sex Ratio   54
Women in the 21st Century   58
  The Gender Bias   59
  Changing Roles for Women at Home   59
  Education   59
  Employment   60
State-by-State Comparison   62

5   Demographic Changes in America—Aging   67

Rising Young Hispanics in Texas Poised to Pick Up Aging Tab   68

The Impact of Aging Populations on the Nation   68

Historical Trends: The Graying of the United States   69

    Worldwide Aging Trends   69

    Aging in the United States   70

    Aging and Demographic Change in the United States   71

Coping with Aging Generations   73

    Health Care   73

Aging in the Recent Censuses   74

    2000   74

    Beyond the 2000 Census   75

    Geographic Age Distribution   76

6   Marriage and Family   79

The New American Family   80

The Changing American Family   80

    Unmarried Adults   81

    Age at First Marriage   82

    Divorce   83

2000–2001 Findings in the Family   83

    Marriage and Divorce   84

    Marriage and Race   85

    Characteristics of the Married Population   87

    Cohabitation   89

2005–2009 American Community Survey (ACS)   90

    Race and Marital Status   92

    Parenting   93

    Cohabitating Couples   93

    State-by-State Differences in Marital and Cohabitation Patterns   93

7   Using Census Data   97

A Fresh Way to Explore the Census   98

The U.S. Census: Your Source for Data   98

    American FactFinder   99

    Social Explorer: Simple Access to Census Data   104

    Make the Most of It   105

Appendix I: Selected Population Data by State   107

Appendix II: 2010 Census Questionnaire   138

Endnotes   140

Index   147

Preface

We are all consumers of data. Whether it is the latest data on radiation leaking from Japan, or the newest numbers on the birth rates of Americans, we are bombarded each day with numbers. But, from where do we get all these numbers? When I decided to write this book, *A Short Introduction to the U.S. Census*, it was because I was searching for a brief primer on the data produced by the Census Bureau for my students to use. As I dove deeper into the work, I realized that many of my colleagues in a variety of fields also sought such information. Thus, this book is designed to help the reader understand the largest single source of data on the United States, those data gathered in the decile census, as well as the vast array of other data gathered by the Census Bureau. It is my hope that this book will be useful to the reader regardless of whether he or she has an interest in sociology, political science, history, or some other discipline.

As a college professor and demographer, I believe that population data are vitally important to understanding a field. In my teaching, I noticed that my students knew almost nothing about the history and purpose of the U.S. census. Most of them simply thought that the census was something we did every 10 years for reasons that few actually understood. They knew even less about the variety of data available from the decile census and/or the many surveys conducted by the Bureau on a regular basis. While it is true that volumes have been written about the history of the U.S. census, such information is not available in a brief and inexpensive text. Furthermore, these books tend to incorporate only the history of a particular topic and do not bring the reader up to the current day. This book hopes to do both by providing the reader a brief background to the topic of the chapter and by leading her to the most recent data available.

The book begins with a brief overview of the history and science of the decile census, and the more recent sampling survey's completed by the Census Bureau, such as the American Community Survey. Here, the reader will gain an understanding of the constitutional purpose of the census, as well as the variety of methods used to gather such data throughout history.

The next five chapters address data gathered by the Census Bureau on a variety of topics. In the second chapter, income and inequality data are reviewed. While the decile census does not include such data, the Census Bureau has kept track of poverty and income data for a number of years. These data provide the reader with a solid understanding of the United States and the official statistics collected by the bureau to illuminate the topic of inequality.

The third chapter reviews issues of race and immigration. Race is a subject that has deep roots in census history, being one component that has been asked on every census since 1790. The various definitions of race are reviewed. Data from the decile census as well as other bureau products are provided to help the reader understand the racial changes in the United States. In addition, this chapter provides an overview of the foreign-born population in the United States and the transitions of this population throughout our history. The reader will gain an understanding of changes in racial characteristics in the United States and how immigration has affected these.

The fourth chapter considers the issue of gender. Like race, gender has been an important part of the decile census since its inception, despite the fact that women were not given the right to vote until 1920. Sex ratios throughout time are explained, as well as income and educational differences between men and women. This chapter covers data relating to these issues throughout the history of the census.

Chapter 5 looks at the demographic issue of aging. The decile censuses as well as more recent survey data are provided to help the reader understand the phenomenon of aging in the United States. With a population that is getting increasingly older, the United States is similar to most other industrialized nations, and yet has a considerably different possible future because of our birth rates, which remain higher than most other industrialized nations.

In the sixth chapter, the issue of family in America is reviewed. Here again, the decile census data is often lacking as it relates to this topic, but numerous census studies provide a snapshot of marriage and divorce as well as family issues in the United States.

The seventh chapter concludes the book with a hands-on tutorial for two programs designed to help students and researchers use data from the Census Bureau and other sources. The American FactFinder from the Census Bureau is a search engine that provides the researcher with access to a variety of data gathered by the Census Bureau. Access to the website, Social Explorer is also reviewed. In both cases, exercises and explanations of how to use these websites are described.

The appendix of the book provides a detailed state-by-state comparison with tables providing the details of all 50 states.

This book was written with valuable input and insight from Andrew Beveridge, PhD professor of sociology at Queens College and the Graduate School and University Center of the City University of New York. Dr. Beveridge is an analyst of census data and developer of an interactive application and Web-based set of maps entitled Social Explorer (www.socialexplorer.com). We are fortunate to include some of these maps in this text and thank Dr. Beveridge for his kind support of this project.

Acknowledgments

No book of any kind is written only by that author. The process of writing involves many talented people, who use their talents to support and improve the text you see before you. This book is no different.

When Pearson agreed to publish this text, I realized that I would, once again, lose precious time with my family and, in particular, with my children. I am sorry that so often it seems I must work late into the nights writing. I owe a debt of gratitude to my wife, Keven, who supports me unconditionally and willingly steps in to fill the holes I leave while writing. This text would not exist had she not been so selfless.

In my demographic training, I was schooled at the feet of Craig St. John, who has provided me not only knowledge, but also a true appreciation for the reality that population changes are the most important things to understand about any society. It is with that understanding that I hope this book can help readers to learn about the needs and trends of American society.

I would like to thank the many people involved for their support and assistance in writing this book. The team of professionals who bring you this text are an amazing group of people who are almost too numerous to mention. However, special thanks go to Dickson Musslewhite and Maggie Barbieri who led me through this process yet again. Special appreciation goes to Andrew Beveridge for his wise counsel and assistance with data allocation. Others include Roberta Sherman at Pearson and Michael Egolf and Ally Brocious at Words & Numbers. Each of you helped shape this text and I am grateful for that assistance.

I am also exceedingly grateful to work at Rose State College, where the administration supports faculty goals and encourages scholarship. I am indebted to the college leadership for its support of me during this project.

Sincerely,

John Carl, PhD

About the Author

John D. Carl holds a PhD in Sociology from the University of Oklahoma. Born in Nebraska, John has spent most of his life in Oklahoma, living for brief periods of time in Texas, Indiana, and Mexico.

John continues to enjoy his life as it unfolds, striving always to continually be curious about life and interested in a wide range of topics. In particular, he finds support with many friends at work, church, the golf course, and "the studio." John lives in Oklahoma with his family, wife Keven, and daughters Sara and Caroline. In his free time, he gardens, throws pottery, plays his guitar, and occasionally finds a golf course on which he loses a few balls.

220 years and counting!

The U.S. Census is the largest mobilization of resources undertaken by our government. First conducted in 1790, and taking place every 10 years as required by the Constitution, the Census counts every resident in the United States.

Though it takes the form of a brief questionnaire, the Census has a big impact upon our communities. The data collected helps determine the number of seats for each state in the U.S. House of Representatives. And, over $400 billion in federal funding—for schools, hospitals, job training centers, senior centers, public works projects, and emergency services—will be allocated based on the results of the 2010 Census.

Q: How many questions were on the first Census in 1790?

A: The first Census, managed by Secretary of State Thomas Jefferson, included just six questions: name, gender, race, relationship to head of household, name of head of household and, sadly, the number of slaves.

Highlight contemporary issues using 2010 Census data.

The release of the data from the 2010 Census is an exciting opportunity for you and your students to explore the history, methods, and application of one of the largest and longest-running sociological studies ever conducted. It also provides a topical impetus to highlight key contemporary issues in your course.

Q:

What was the population in 2000? What is the 2010 projection?

A: In 2000, total population was calculated at 281,421,906, a 13% increase over the population in 1990. The 2010 Census is projecting a population of more than 310 million, an increase of approximately 10% since 2000.

Encourage class discussion, and illuminate important sociological concepts, by raising the following Census-related questions in the classroom:

- How will reallocation of resources affect different groups, regions, and communities across the United States?

- How will public policy change as a result of increased and decreased representation in the House of Representatives?

- How will our government reallocate resources for those living in low-income households—the group with the most to gain from participating in the Census?

- Will families living on or near military bases see an increase or decrease in resources?

- How will the Census impact the family—particularly in lower-income or immigrant households which rely on nutritional, health care, and educational resources from social services and foundations?

- How will shifts in public funding affect local housing communities?

Pearson's 2010 Census Update Program—
the best way to incorporate

Pearson's 2010 Census Update Program helps you incorporate 2010 Census data into your course—simply and easily. The components of the Census Update Program are as follows:

Census Update Editions feature fully updated data throughout the text—including all charts and graphs—to reflect the results of the 2010 Census. These editions also include a reproduction of the 2010 Census Questionnaire for your students to explore in detail.

Q:

At its peak in 2010, how many Census workers did the U.S. government hire?

A: The Census is the U.S. government's largest peacetime operation. More than one million Census workers counted roughly 310 million people in some 120 million households. This works out to 1 Census worker for every 310 residents.

A Short Introduction to the U.S. Census presents a brief seven-chapter overview of the Census, including important information about the Constitutional mandate, research methods, who is affected by the Census, and how data is used. Additionally, the primer explores key contemporary topics such as race and ethnicity, the family, and poverty. The primer can be packaged with any Pearson text at no additional cost, and is also available via MySocLab, MyFamilyLab, MySockKit, MyFamilyKit, and MySearchLab.

Census data into your course.

A Short Introduction to the U.S. Census Instructor's Manual with Test Bank

includes explanations of what has been updated, in-class activities, homework activities associated with the MyLabs and MyKits, discussion questions for the primer, and test questions related to the primer.

The MySocLab Census Update

gives students the opportunity to explore 2010 Census methods and data and apply Census results in a dynamic interactive online environment. It includes:

- a series of activities using 2010 Census results
- video clips explaining and exploring the Census
- primary source readings relevant to the Census
- an online version of the 2010 Census Update Primer

Census Updates for MyFamilyLab, MyFamilyKit, MySocKit, and MySearchLab will also be available.

Q:

What did the 2010 Census ask people?

A: The 2010 Census was one of the shortest in history and asked name, gender, race, ethnicity, the type of residence, the number of people who live there, and whether some people live elsewhere sometimes.

1 History and Science of the Census

Up until the middle of the 20th century, the census was entirely carried out by door-to-door surveyors. (EdBockStock/Shutterstock)

2010 CENSUS SPARKS HOUSE REALIGNMENT

The statistical data about population demographics contained in census reports may have broad implications in the political arena. Most recently, the 2010 Census had good news for Republicans. The U.S. Census Bureau reported that in the past decade the nation grew 9.7 percent to 308 million people. Population growth is not necessarily a partisan issue, but in this case, the population growth was significant in the South and Southwest United States, areas where strong conservative beliefs largely favor the Republican Party. One way that census data are used is to **reapportion** congressional representation by reallocating a state or district's number of representatives in an effort to ensure that people are fairly and equally represented.

As a result of the population changes revealed by the 2010 Census, the 435 seats in the U.S. House of Representatives will be reassigned, and it is likely that Republicans will gain seats. New York and Ohio will both lose two seats; Iowa, Illinois, Missouri, Pennsylvania, Louisiana, Massachusetts, Michigan, and New Jersey will each lose one seat. Texas will gain four seats, while Florida will gain two seats. Arizona, Georgia, South Carolina, Utah, Washington, and Nevada will get one more seat each. These changes will likely impact the representatives elected to hold congressional seats in these states and the legislative actions taken as a result. The population changes will also impact the presidential elections in 2012, 2016, and 2020, because the number of Electoral College votes assigned to each state reflects the number of seats it has in Congress.[1]

HISTORY OF THE CENSUS

In the minds of many Americans, the **decennial** population and housing census is a kind of 10-year bureaucratic cycle that occurs on its own and without any real impact on daily life. However, as the congressional reapportionment example shows, the census is directly related to the political and social lives of every American. The truth is that the census affects which states gain political power, thereby influencing which representatives are elected into office. As demographics change, different parts of the country may emerge as more influential than others that once had more political power. But while these political upheavals may grab headlines every 10 years, the Census Bureau is active throughout the decade. It takes continuous study of the economy, the government, communities, and various other demographic data. The variety of information gathered has expanded throughout history and is now used by researchers, policy makers, industry leaders, and economists. These provide more information than the **enumeration**, a count or tally, of the population taken every 10 years.

The Historical Origins of the Census

The first recorded census data date back to approximately 4000 BCE, when China became one of the first cultures to count its own people.[2] The word *census* comes from the Latin word meaning "a registering of the populace and their property." Every five years, male citizens of the Roman Empire had to declare themselves, their family, their slaves, and their possessions. If they failed to take part in the count, their possessions could be confiscated, and abstaining citizens could be sold into slavery. The census was central to the social cohesion of the Roman Empire. Two elected censors conducted the count as a way to assess military potential and tax revenue.[3]

The U.S. census had ideological origins. One of the more memorable cries from the American Revolution was "no taxation without representation." A major issue that led to the break with England was that American colonists did not have equal representation with other British citizens, leaving them with little recourse to address onerous taxes and laws. In 1787, during the writing of the U.S. Constitution, the founders struggled with an appropriate way to distribute political representation among the states. They decided on two legislative branches with the House of Representatives providing political representation based on the population of that state. Therefore, it became necessary to actually know the population of each state. In addition to this, the issue of fair taxation was a motivating factor for the census, as it was the only way for the new federal government to assure state legislators that it was asking for a federal tax contribution that was within the state's means. Knowing the population of the state also helped make sure tax revenues were fairly distributed. Thus, the census made certain that population, not wealth or prestige, would be the determining method for apportionment of government power. This method sought to give the citizens from heavily populated states more political power, which was seen as somewhat fair, because that population would then incur a greater share of taxes.[4]

Equality in this instance was denied, however, to specific segments of the U.S. population. Native Americans were not supposed to be counted in the original census; they were not generally taxed, and so they were not deemed worthy of a representative voice in Congress.

When Native Americans were taxed, however, a complicated situation arose in which local municipalities ended up making the decision on how to categorize the Native populations. In 1860, untaxed Native Americans were first counted and categorized as a separate, non-white population. **Blood quantum laws**, which analyzed bloodline to determine what percentage of a person's genetic heritage was Native American, were also used in the census to determine whether the government would consider Native Americans of mixed descent as white or as members of a specific tribe.[5]

The status of African Americans during early census counts was also a complex issue. They proved to be the exception to the idea that population, rather than wealth, would determine representation. Enslaved African Americans at the time could not vote. But their presence counted both as property for the slave owners and as three-fifths of a person, allowing slave states to wield a great deal of power without actually giving representation to the enslaved. This compromise gave the illusion that African Americans were being counted and may have helped to ensure the Constitution's ratification, but in time it proved to be a divisive issue, eventually culminating in the emancipation of the slaves.[6]

Early Census Methods

When the first U.S. census was conducted, there were no professional statisticians involved or even an office of the census to handle the details of its implementation. Sixteen marshals, their assistants, Congress, and the executive branch handled the entire operation. As the foundation of a nation in its infancy, the U.S. Constitution didn't provide every detail for how official tasks should be carried out. Many government actions during this time were being figured out as they happened. Even the nation's first president was an army general before taking on the responsibilities and subtleties of executive leadership.

The inaugural census took 18 months, twice the anticipated time. The census takers were given the First Census Act as a reference. They recorded the responses to the questions in whatever kind of books they felt were appropriate. Mistakes were made and crossed out, additional information was sometimes included, and a general lack of attention to accuracy was the norm.[7]

The census of 1810 saw several changes for census takers. In an effort to improve the efficiency and accuracy of the census, Congress specified that the census takers appointed by the marshals should be from the county or civil division they were assigned to enumerate. The census takers were also charged with actually visiting the household, while previous census takers may have relied on secondhand information.[8] As the country became an industrialized nation, the census began taking manufacturing surveys, designed to provide statistics on payroll, material and operational costs, inventories, and other data regarding the manufacture of goods. At the same time, longer census forms were developed, and the job of collecting and counting began to exceed the limits of the census apparatus. Census takers sometimes wrote down information from memory, and the lack of a standardized methodology made many of the survey answers of little value. The answers to one question on manufacturing ranged from "good" to "the whole establishment ruined for want of a market."[9] The early manufacturing censuses were also carried out by the marshals, but the results were sent to the Secretary of the Treasury, who then presented the results as "an ill-assorted aggregation of unattached and unconnected items."[10]

With sectionalism dividing the country and placing increasing importance on the census numbers, the haphazard methodologies of census takers began to come under increasing criticism. These criticisms were part of the impetus for Congress to create a census board in 1849, headed by a secretary who instituted major changes. This phase of the census began the earnest involvement of the growing science of statistics in the census mechanism. The new Secretary of the Census sought the advice of statisticians on proper methodologies and modern statistical theory. As a result, the unit of the census was changed from the "household" to the "individual," and the completed census forms were to be tabulated by the census board, rather than by the marshals and their assistants. By having all of the original census forms, the census board could assure a greater degree of accuracy than in previous censuses.[11]

The immediate results of these innovations were the loss of an estimated 67,000 returns en route from California and a longer wait for the final tabulation. The surveys could only be counted after the census board received them, after which even more difficulties in the counting ensued.[12] Legislation in 1879 and 1880 created a body of 150 census supervisors who took over census control from the U.S. marshals, who had still been doing the actual collecting of the census. The 1890 Census required a staff of more than 50,000 people to handle filling out and counting more than 2,400 different forms. It was only in 1902, however, that the Census Office was made a permanent part of the federal government.[13]

Early Census Record Book

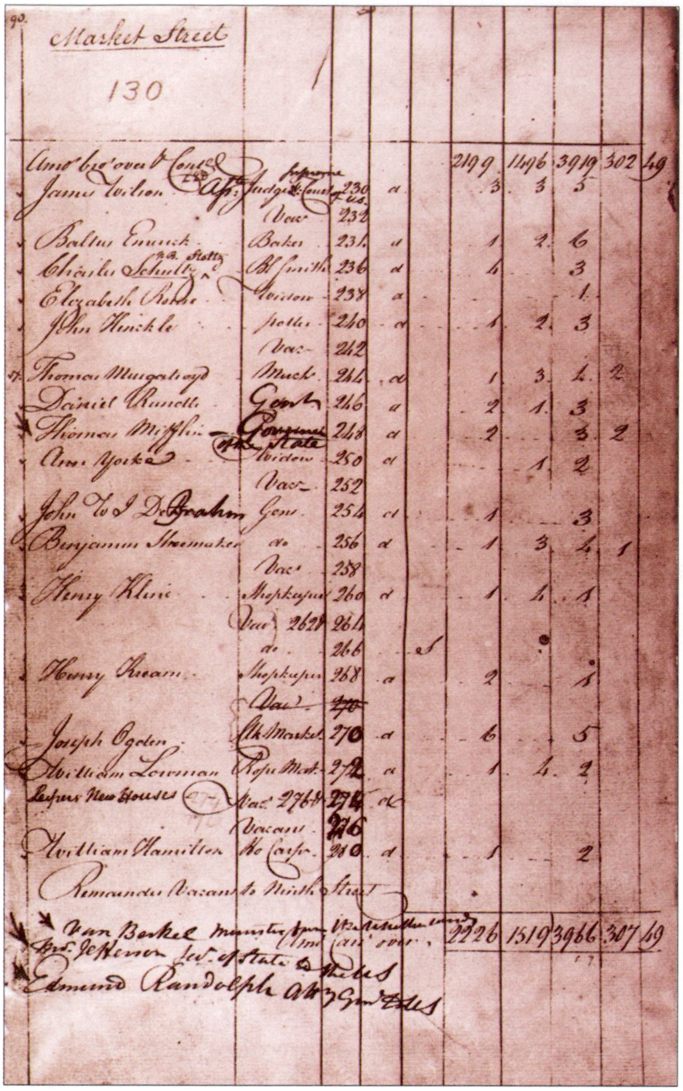

Figure 1.1 Early censuses were recorded by hand in a variety of different books.

LEGAL BASIS FOR THE CENSUS

The framers of the Constitution decided to base political representation, in part, on a state's population. Therefore, they understood the importance of having an accurate measure of the population and using it to determine this representation. Since the first census of 1790, the population had grown and migrated dramatically. Immigration from Europe pushed the boundaries of the new nation to lands that had been held by Native peoples. The history of this conquest and the repeated violation of treaties led to more and more states being formed through westward expansion.

The potential for population growth and shift in the United States made fair representation fundamental to the framing of the new government. Article 1, Section 2 of the Constitution reads,

> Representatives and direct taxes shall be apportioned among the several States which may be included within this Union according to their respective Numbers, which shall be determined by adding to the whole Number of free Persons, including those bound to Service for a Term of Years, and excluding Indians not taxed, three fifths of all other Persons. The actual Enumeration shall be made within three Years after the first Meeting of the Congress of the United States, and within every subsequent Term of ten Years, in such Manner as they shall by Law direct. The Number of Representatives shall not exceed one for every thirty Thousand, but each State shall have at Least one Representative; and until such enumeration shall be made, the State of New Hampshire shall

Shift in the Mean Center of Population over the Course of U.S. History

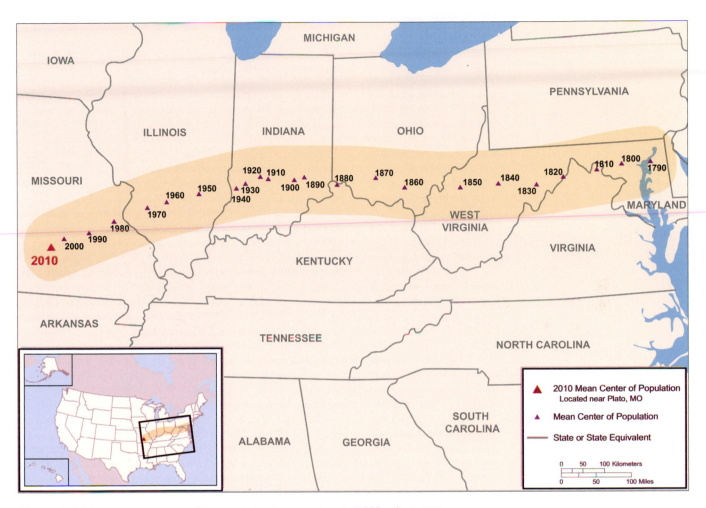

Figure 1.2 The geographic center of the population has moved nearly 1,000 miles in 200 years.
Source: U.S. Census Bureau. "Mean Center of Population for the United States: 1790 to 2010." 2010.
http://www.census.gov/geo/www/2010census/centerpop2010/centerpop_mean2010.pdf

be entitled to chuse three, Massachusetts eight, Rhode Island and Providence Plantations one, Connecticut five, New York six, New Jersey four, Pennsylvania eight, Delaware one, Maryland six, Virginia ten, North Carolina five, South Carolina five, and Georgia three.[14]

Each state had two representatives in the Senate. This allocation ensured that the states would be represented as entities on an equal footing. However, if the system had only one house, large populated states might suffer. A second branch of Congress, the House of Representatives, was added to represent the people proportionally. The House of Representatives balanced the weight of the states with the will of the population. The census was the tool for ensuring this balance.

As the case of the 2010 Census demonstrates, the founders were on the right track with their ideas about the importance of population and population changes and their effects on politics. The census can have a dramatic impact on national politics when it shifts representatives from one state to another, potentially altering the political balance of power. The census began with a legal mandate to ensure fair representation. Subsequent laws and necessities created a broader mandate for the census, making it fundamental to a number of different programs and charging it with keeping the statistical records of the entire nation.

The Census Bureau

The Census Bureau is the government agency charged with conducting the decennial census. Previously handled by local marshals, a central office for conducting the census was established in 1840 by the Census Act. The current Census Bureau's mission statement is the following:

> The Census Bureau serves as the leading source of quality data about the nation's people and economy. We honor privacy, protect confidentiality, share our expertise globally, and conduct our work openly. We are guided on this mission by our strong and capable workforce, our readiness to innovate, and our abiding commitment to our customers.[15]

It is worth noting that the Census Bureau's statement does not mention its constitutionally mandated role as an apportionment mechanism. Today, the Bureau sees itself primarily as an information-gathering agency. In an age when the Internet can reveal personal information about most of the population and gathering information seems ubiquitous and easily accomplished, it is important to understand the enormous scope of the Census Bureau. While Internet-based companies may pride themselves on their ability to track the consumer habits of online users, the Census Bureau has an entirely different task: to record information for every single U.S. household. In the 2010 Census, 74 percent of U.S. households responded with mailed census forms, and the other 26 percent were contacted directly by Census Bureau employees walking door to door.[16] In addition to the coverage requirements of the census, the data gathered must be specific to each address. As you might guess, there are some problems associated with trying to count an entire population, especially one that is estimated to be more than 300 million people.

Internet marketing companies can gain a great deal of information by gathering data through Internet-based surveys. However, the Census Bureau cannot use such surveys because not everyone in the United States has Internet access, and, of course, it is difficult to verify the physical addresses of an Internet responder. Because the Census Bureau uses physical addresses to conduct the 10-year count, Internet surveys are not open to them. The bureau must conduct the census on the basis of physical location, either by regular mail service or on a door-to-door basis.[17]

The Census Bureau is also bound by a mandate to collect *quality* data, which means it must adhere to the most modern and accurate research methodologies. These methodologies help to ensure an adequate master list of addresses for the 10-year census, as well as accurate use of sampling when it occurs in other data-collection efforts. If you think about it, trying to obtain an updated list of addresses is a sizable task; getting the addressees to respond to their mail, as well as door-to-door calls, makes the job an incredible undertaking.

Recall that the bureau conducts more frequent surveys that collect data on topics ranging from computer ownership to health insurance. The Census Bureau also collects information on economic indicators, such as new home sales and international population numbers. These statistics are often used by news organizations and pundits to give their audiences an idea of the state of the economy. They are also used by politicians to gauge the success or failure of specific economic policies.

CHANGES IN THE CENSUS OVER TIME

Although the Constitution mandated the census, the institutions and individuals charged with conducting it had to work out the details. For example, in January 1790, a committee made up of representatives from each of the 13 states presented a bill that provided the crucial details. The bill, approved in March of that same year, gave the job of conducting the census to the 16 U.S. marshals. On the first ever Census Day, August 2, 1790, these marshals, along with their assistants, set out to conduct the entire census door to door. This was a relatively simple and even enjoyable task in the more populated areas, where the census takers could treat their job as a kind of social call. But it was an often arduous process in rural parts of the new nation, where census workers were charged with tracking down every household, no matter how isolated.[18] Because there was no official list of where people lived, a complete and accurate count was unlikely.

The 1790 census bill provided for a number of details, and, with minor changes, these held fast through the census of 1840. The first census was to be conducted throughout the 13 states as well as the districts of Kentucky, Vermont, and Maine, and the Territory of the Southwest, which would later become Tennessee. The results were to be posted publicly in each jurisdiction, and the totals were to be given to the president. The 1790 Census only asked for six pieces of information from each household. It recorded the name of the head of the family and the following numbers: free white males over the age of 16, free white males under the age of 16, free white females, all other free people, and slaves. These categories reflect the two main goals of the census: to count the population for political representation and to assess the amount of taxes potentially owed to the government from the people. The final population count from the first census was 3.9 million people. Both President George Washington and Secretary of State Thomas Jefferson, under whose direction the census marshals worked, were skeptical over the accuracy of what they deemed as a low population number.[19]

A Changing Country

The U.S. census began as way to assess the growth of the country and has proven to be an enduring part of the federal government and an institution that impacts decision making at every level. The early censuses were haphazard affairs that relied on U.S. marshals to conduct the count. Congressional legislation mandated the questions, but the forms themselves varied. The results of these early censuses were often questions and became points of contention for political power and representation.[20] The current census conducted by the Census Bureau is run by statisticians who have created a means of livelihood by tabulating the numbers that indicate the state of the United States. Forms are mailed to individual addresses and read by computers. Statistical methodologies are now employed that had not even been imagined in the early days of the census.

The census documented the first century of this country, which saw an unprecedented population explosion, expanding from 3.9 million people on the East Coast to 63 million covering the entire country by 1890. The census of 1890 was used as a way to definitively mark the progress of the United States; the official report exulted, "This census completes the history of a century of progress and achievement unequaled in the world's history. The century has witnessed our development into a great and powerful nation." The idea of a nation maturing was not simply a metaphor for growth. As the censuses indicated, the median age of the population had risen from 16 to 22. The first century of the census also documented the transition from a mostly agrarian colonial-style economy in which only 5 percent of the population lived in cities, to an industrialized nation where one-third of the population lived in cities interconnected by rail lines.[21]

While the censuses of the first century of the new nation documented the rise of an urban population, the 1920 Census saw that population become the majority. The country was changing, and the count showed the United States was no longer predominantly agrarian. The censuses of the second century of the United States recorded the advances in industrial production, transportation, and communication that have become the modern landscape. They also saw massive immigration and the subsequent ethnic diversification of the populace. As the Census Bureau recorded more and more details concerning life in the United States, policy makers began to increasingly rely on the census and the bureau's other efforts at gathering data for accurate statistics on which to base their decisions. This has, in turn, increased the demand for more accurate methodologies, a goal the Census Bureau continues to pursue.[22]

★ TABLE 1.1 CENSUS-RELATED CHANGES FROM 1790 AND 2010[23] ★

The census has, not surprisingly, undergone changes in the two centuries since it began. This table gives some historical indicators of the context of the respective decades, along with some of the data that the census retrieved.

Year	1790	2010
Notable Events	• First "State of the Union Address" given by George Washington on January 8, 1790 • Washington, D.C., named the capital of the United States in 1791 • Eli Whitney patents the cotton gin in 1794	• A 7.0-magnitude earthquake devastates Haiti on January 12, 2010 • President Barack Obama formally declares an end to combat operations in Iraq on August 31, 2010 • A series of revolutions in Northern Africa ousts longtime political leaders from power beginning in late 2010
U.S. Population	3,929,214	308,745,538
Population per Square Mile	4.5	87.4
Cost/Cost per Capita	$44,000/$0.011	$12.9 billion/$47.78
Number of Census Workers	650 (est.)	635,000 (est.)
Number of Questions Asked	Six	Ten

Evolution of Census Philosophy

The United States was only the second Western country to conduct a complete census. While most censuses had previously been conducted to assess military strength and levy taxes, the U.S. census was also an integral aspect of a new form of representative government. The census became a valuable tool for assessing the growth and development of the nation. The growing importance of the census in the mind of the public and in the practice of legislators made it an institution that went through a great deal of change. By looking at several factors indicating these changes, it is possible to understand some of the motivations that drove the various phases of the census.

Throughout the 200-year history of the U.S. census, the questionnaires have changed in ways that often indicate the different purposes and philosophies behind the count and reflect the state of the nation at the time. These questionnaires are, perhaps, the most important indicator of the motivations for the census. For example, the racial classifications used by the census over the course of its history have factored into actual race relations. Various classifications speak to the many philosophies of race and the politics of ethnicity that have defined racial interactions over the past 200 years. In Chapter 3 we will discuss the issue of race specifically.

QUESTIONNAIRES Although the six questions of the first census indicate a straightforward approach to gathering data, some legislators wanted to gather a great deal more information that went beyond the necessities of representative government. James Madison, during the discussions about conducting the first census, wanted to include occupations, economic position, and men of draft age. These indicators would have been used to assess military potential and make decisions about economic policy, but the other legislators thought it would be a waste of government time and funds.[24]

The questions on the census did not remain as they were in 1790. By the census of 1800, information about draft ages was being requested, as well as greater detail concerning the location of households. As scholars and statisticians outside of the census bureaucracy attempted to document the changing demographics of the new nation through voluntary surveys, they increasingly came to rely on census figures as an accurate reference. The census numbers showed that the U.S. population was growing at a rapid rate, far outpacing European countries. The value of demographic information became apparent to both legislators and the general public, leading to the 1820 Census, which included information about the occupations of the household residents as well as the number of nonnaturalized foreigners, the first attempt to measure new immigrants.[25]

By 1840, census workers were asking for the names of each member of a household, along with their sex, age, skin color, occupation, place of birth, real estate holdings, and mental health status. As the role of government expanded, legislators called for more information so that they could adequately assess the needs of the populace. The 1890 Census included such information as marital status, employment status, education level, chronic diseases, and mortgage details.[26] Questions regarding education level could be used to indicate a need for better educational resources, while health information was valuable in assessing the state of various diseases and epidemics.

The 1940 Census reflected the increasing role of the government in combating the Great Depression. Fourteen of the questions asked about aspects of employment. The census also added 16 supplemental questions that were only asked of 5 percent of the population. The supplement included questions about the newly instituted Social Security numbers and payroll deductions. In addition to the regular census, a housing census was also conducted that targeted dwellings, asking questions about the structure and uses of buildings throughout the country.[27] This supplemental sampling reveals the ways in which the government was using the census to assess the efficiency of its policies.

The questionnaire from the 1980 Census asked a number of questions that reveal the increasing importance of the census to policy makers. Detailed questions about commuting, education, and income were tied to the usual age, gender, and racial statistics. These types of questions were not created simply to gather general information, but to assess the need for federal dollars through grant-in-aid programs that targeted local infrastructure and civil rights initiatives.[28]

The 1990 Census and 2000 Census each used two forms: a short form sent to the entire population with a minimum number of questions and a longer form sent only to a portion of the population. The long form asked detailed questions regarding English-language capabilities, past military service, income changes, and a host of other issues.[29] After the 2000 Census, the long form was discontinued. In 2005, the Census Bureau began the American Community

Survey (ACS), which samples the U.S. population by requesting information on a variety of topics and eliminated the need for the long form. The 2010 Census continued the practice of a short form and included only 10 questions.[30]

AMERICAN COMMUNITY SURVEY The 2010 Census introduced the biggest change in census methodology in more than 60 years. This census sent out a short-form questionnaire that only contained 10 questions. Previous censuses, as has been discussed, included many more questions dealing with a number of issues. As a replacement for the longer list of questions, the Census Bureau has instituted the American Community Survey, an annual survey that is sent to a portion of U.S. households. It asks many of the questions from previous censuses, including questions concerning education, occupation, race, health, and family. By conducting the American Community Survey on a continuous basis, the Census Bureau hopes to provide up-to-date demographic data to policy makers and the public to aid in decision making and to inform citizens about the nation's demographic status.[31]

LEGISLATION AND THE CENSUS Another important gauge of the importance of the census is the legislation that has surrounded it. Apportionment has proven to be one of the more controversial aspects of the census. Although the census only provides raw data, which are then used to determine the number of seats to be assigned to the House of Representatives and the Electoral College, its crucial role in the apportionment process has made it the subject of much legislative scrutiny. In 1913, the number of representatives appointed to the House became set at 435. This made reapportionment of members among the states particularly important because one state's gain of a representative results in another state's loss.

This scrutiny often occurred just before or just after a census was taken, when the impact of the census was either anticipated or felt. For example, efforts to legislatively manage the 1810 Census were made when Congress unsuccessfully tried to shorten the duration of the census from nine to five months, presumably to encourage a faster apportionment by lessening the count in rural areas.

In the 1840s and 1850s, **sectionalism**—the different and diverse cultures of the North and South—led to a great deal of scrutiny over the way the census was conducted. It became clear to those who had studied the issues that the census was by no means accurate, and many new reforms were suggested. These reforms were among the contentious debates that surrounded the census leading up to 1850. The result of these debates was the creation of a Census Board, which took over control of the census from local districts that had collected the data, made the tallies, and submitted the information to the federal government. The new legislation had the census workers simply collect the data and then send it in to be tallied. By distributing responsibilities in this way, this change represented an important step in the accuracy of the census and aimed to curb the deliberate efforts to falsify the count to increase political power.[32]

The increasing need for detailed and accurate statistics led to legislation that made the Census Office permanent in 1902.[33] Up to that point, the office had routinely shut its doors when it wasn't preparing for or conducting a census. The newly instituted Census Office functioned as an agency of statistics for the federal government, conducting various annual surveys in addition to the decennial census. By 1903, the office was renamed the Census Bureau and was moved to the Department of Commerce and Labor. The institution of a permanent office for the management of the census is a prime indicator of the increasing role that the census and statistics were taking in the functioning of the nation.[34]

As the federal government implemented policies and institutions to ward off the effects of the Great Depression, it began to rely increasingly on surveys to assess the success rate of these projects. The Works Progress Administration conducted an unemployment survey that proved to be successful enough that legislators wanted it to outlast the institution that initiated it. The survey was handed to the Census Bureau, initiating a phase of increasing responsibilities for the bureau in assessing the rates of success for an increasing number of government programs.[35]

Legislation in the 1990s made it possible for the Census Bureau to share addresses with local jurisdictions to improve mailing lists while simultaneously forbidding these institutions to use the addresses for any purposes other than surveys. This legislation exemplifies the efforts made by the Census Bureau to amass an accurate mailing list and also to ensure the privacy of the census. By ensuring this privacy, the Census Bureau sought to remove the stigma that the census held for many marginalized groups. Many illegal immigrants and others in questionable legal circumstances have balked at the idea of sharing information with a government organization. This legislation, accompanied by marketing campaigns, works to increase responses and give an accurate picture of the U.S. population.[36]

★ TABLE 1.2 RISING COST OF THE CENSUS[38] ★		
Census Year	Overall Cost	Cost Per Person
1790	$44,000	$0.011
1840	$833,000	$0.049
1890	$11,547,000	$0.183
1940	$67,527,000	$0.511
1990	$2.5 billion	$10.05
2010	$12.9 billion	$47.78

CHANGING COST OF THE CENSUS An inevitable aspect of increasing responsibilities of the Census Bureau as well as an increasing population is an exponential budget increase. The population grew from 3.9 million in 1790 to over 308 million in 2010, necessitating a monumental increase in cost: from $44,000 in 1790 to $12.9 billion in 2010. Although the need for door-to-door enumerators was cut back by the mailing of the census in 1960, the Census Bureau still employed almost 1 million part-time employees to follow up on unreturned forms. The increasing reliance of the government and the population on accurate figures from the census has made it important to fully fund the Census Bureau and its efforts to increase census response.[37] The effort to provide high-quality data while cutting costs has led the current bureau to implement the American Community Survey.

Technology and the Census

Until 1850, the census was collected and tabulated by U.S. marshals and their assistants, and the government received the final numbers from the census takers, who had counted the forms themselves. The census reform of 1850 established a census office, which created the forms and tabulated them once they were completed; centralized the process; and paved the way for mechanical counting procedures. In 1890, the census office began using punch cards that could be counted mechanically to tabulate the results. The punch-card system was developed by a former census office employee, R. Herman Hollerith, who went on to cofound IBM. This innovation was one of the earliest uses of computers for mass data processing.[39]

Technology figured largely into the advances of the 20th century Census Bureau. The first nonmilitary computer, Universal Automatic Computer (UNIVAC), was developed to tabulate the 1950 Census. Although it arrived too late for this task, it was still a revolutionary addition to the Census Bureau. The computer converted the traditional census punch cards into electrical impulses that were then recorded onto magnetic tape and tabulated.[40]

Although UNIVAC greatly sped up the tabulation process, it still relied on mechanical means to read the punch cards, making it a bit cumbersome. By the 1960 Census, UNIVAC was supplemented by FOSDIC (Film Optical Sensing Device for Input to Computers), a device that read pencil marks on surveys and transmitted the information to UNIVAC. The FOSDIC system was used up until the 2000 Census for the tabulation of surveys.[41]

The Census Bureau has used the Internet extensively in its promotional and informational functions. In 1994, the Census Bureau created a Web portal that has seen increasing use by both the private and public sectors. The Census Bureau uses the Internet as a data-collection tool as well, allowing larger companies to complete surveys and return them without the use of either traditional paper surveys or reliance on the U.S. Postal Service. More than 66,000 people used the Internet to submit their short-form questionnaires during the 2000 Census.[42]

Another innovative tool that the Census Bureau has put to use is its TIGER (Topologically Integrated Geographic Encoding and Referencing) database. This database, first used in 1990, is based on U.S. Geological Survey maps and allows the Census Bureau to find geographical information on any of its subjects. This information is useful for conducting enumeration efforts, but it can also be used to cross-reference important geographic information with sample survey results. For example, a survey that asked questions about commuting could be cross-referenced with the available rail, highway, and waterway information from the TIGER database. Analyses could then be conducted to assess the relative impact of these geographic features on the commuting habits of the survey participants.[43]

CENSUS METHODOLOGIES

Since the founding of the United States more than 200 years ago, the country has changed a great deal. The research methods used by the census takers, however, have changed very little. In essence, the government still tries to count everyone, but it no longer sends U.S. marshals door to door. The government delivers census forms via U.S. mail and then, if necessary, visits every address in the country in an effort to make the count.

Breaking down the Census

The basic form of the census is a simple survey. A **survey** is merely a questionnaire designed to help researchers gain information. Every survey needs a clear purpose. What does the survey seek to discover? For example, if a survey was developed to compare political views of liberals and conservatives, it might only include questions related to politics. However, to learn more about specific groups' attitudes about a political question, it could be wise to include questions about age, gender, race, and income so that the political views of different demographics could be compared. A specific goal is crucial to developing a useful survey.

A second task for creating a survey is to define the population to which it will be given. The population must be made up of individuals about whom a researcher wants to have knowledge. Again, consider the example of a survey on political views. If the survey wanted to know the views of the entire country, then U.S. residence would be the population. Defining the population is an important part of creating a survey. The 10-year census seeks to count the entire population of the United States, which is a daunting task. It is costly and difficult to try to contact everyone in large population.

For this reason, the Census Bureau's other data-collection efforts tend to use sampling methods. **Sampling** involves taking a subgroup of the population and studying it. Sampling must be done with care to ensure the survey finds a group that accurately represents the target population. If it does represent the population accurately, then the results can represent the opinions of the population. To accomplish this task, researchers prefer a method of randomization which assures them that every person in the population has an equal chance of being selected for the sample. A genuine random sample would select individuals from the defined population with no regard for gender, age, income, or any other aspect of the individual's demographic. When the sample is taken randomly, then the appropriate proportions of these demographic variables should be approximately the same as they are in the population. By using random samples, researchers can increase the chances of finding a group that accurately represents the population.

Twentieth-Century Census Efforts

Many professional statisticians envisioned the establishment of the permanent Census Office as the foundation of a central statistical agency for the entire federal government. This vision would have had the Census Office in charge of handling and analyzing the statistics for every agency, publishing reports that analyzed the numbers, and ensuring a consistent methodological approach. This also would have changed the role of the Census Office dramatically. The 1900 Census was accompanied by a 1,200-page report from a prominent statistician that interpreted the raw numbers, and this type of interpretation would have become a central role of the Census Office if it had been fully funded beyond the decennial census. However, other government agencies were reluctant to cede their data and authority to a central agency, and the Census Office was forced to let go of many of the workers hired for the 1900 Census, scaling back to its role as a "statistical factory" as opposed to a center for modern statistical analysis.[44]

President Franklin D. Roosevelt's New Deal and the host of governmental programs that it introduced brought modern statistical analysis and methodologies to the Census Bureau. The bureau underwent a major overhaul in personnel and organization, bringing in a number of younger professional statisticians who were eager to employ new statistical theories. On the surface, population statistics seemed like a simple operation, but when estimates of per-capita income by region needed to be deduced from various other figures, the issue became more complicated. Data for these estimates had to be taken from smaller government studies that were not comprehensive enough to justify the results. Because adding this information to the decennial census was not feasible, the bureau decided to use the new theory of sampling to find the answers it needed.[45]

THE SCIENCE OF SAMPLING The science of sampling has evolved over time, and the Census Bureau's efforts have evolved as well. When seeking data on the country, the Census Bureau has used two sampling methods. The older method, **purposive sampling**, sought out "typical" respondents, leaving the selection up to the survey taker, while the newer method, based on probability theory, takes its subjects at random. Purposive sampling was discredited as biased because the survey taker was in charge of deciding who qualified as a "typical" respondent. The **random sampling** method was used, with several important modifications. The statisticians conducting the sample had to know the characteristics of the **sampling frame**, or the area that had been defined for sampling. This information would include the number of blocks or houses within a city or precinct being sampled. The bureau pretested the sample for the first time and used the results to modify the questionnaire, randomizing the order of the questions to ensure the order would not introduce a bias. The 1940 Census included a sampling survey that was used to create a number of economic and social indicators.[46]

In the years following the 1940 Census, the bureau further refined its sample survey to reduce the error rate. The survey was increased from 5 percent of the population to 20 percent for the 1950 Census and integrated a number of research and evaluation studies designed to analyze errors. Some research studies indicated that many errors were actually introduced by the enumerators. These studies found that enumerators would often enter different information even when given the same answers. The 1960 Census attempted to deal with this by moving the majority of the questions to the sample census and sending it by mail for households to complete themselves. Doing so made it more likely that the essential questions on the short form would be completed correctly.[47]

Another important use of sampling by the Census Bureau is as a correctional method. Sampling and estimation techniques began to be used in the 1980 Census to take coverage measurement surveys. By comparing these surveys with the census figures, the Census Bureau can estimate the net over- and under-coverage in the census. The results of these surveys have been used to correct for net coverage errors in the 1980, 1990, and 2000 censuses. Sampling has also been used to institute quality assurance programs and as a way to evaluate new surveys.[48]

Undercount

It is highly doubtful that every single resident in the United States has been counted in any year's census as the task is daunting and there are many obstructing issues. Social scientists have long noted that many Americans may not reply or reply dishonestly to census count efforts. This is particularly true among those who are in the United States illegally, as well as those who doubt the stated intentions behind the census. Many people refuse to fill out the census or avoid contact with the government census workers because they fear any involvement with the government and feel that "big brother" government could use their personal information against them. These fears are likely to make census counts less accurate.[49]

Although uncounted populations had long been acknowledged as an issue, it was not until the mid-20th century, as census procedures were overhauled in favor of more accurate methods, that

Census Historical Highlights

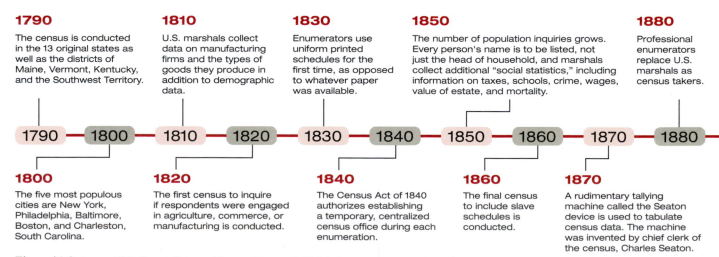

1790
The census is conducted in the 13 original states as well as the districts of Maine, Vermont, Kentucky, and the Southwest Territory.

1810
U.S. marshals collect data on manufacturing firms and the types of goods they produce in addition to demographic data.

1830
Enumerators use uniform printed schedules for the first time, as opposed to whatever paper was available.

1850
The number of population inquiries grows. Every person's name is to be listed, not just the head of household, and marshals collect additional "social statistics," including information on taxes, schools, crime, wages, value of estate, and mortality.

1880
Professional enumerators replace U.S. marshals as census takers.

1790 — 1800 — 1810 — 1820 — 1830 — 1840 — 1850 — 1860 — 1870 — 1880

1800
The five most populous cities are New York, Philadelphia, Baltimore, Boston, and Charleston, South Carolina.

1820
The first census to inquire if respondents were engaged in agriculture, commerce, or manufacturing is conducted.

1840
The Census Act of 1840 authorizes establishing a temporary, centralized census office during each enumeration.

1860
The final census to include slave schedules is conducted.

1870
A rudimentary tallying machine called the Seaton device is used to tabulate census data. The machine was invented by chief clerk of the census, Charles Seaton.

Figure 1.3 Source: U.S. Census Bureau. "Census Historical Highlights: 1790–2010." Facts for Features: Special Edition, 2010.
http://www.census.gov/newsroom/releases/archives/facts_for_features_special_editions/cb10-ffse02.html

substantial attention was paid to the **undercount**. Studies of the 1940 and 1950 censuses indicated that as much as 3 percent of the population was not counted. Even more problematic was the fact that the uncounted population was not randomly distributed. Minorities, young men, and those living in poor areas were the majority of those missed by the census. The 1960 Census attempted to deal with this issue by developing procedures for hard-to-enumerate groups, such as homeless populations. Special instructions were given to enumerators if individuals could not be reached at their homes. Despite efforts to diminish the undercount, the 1970 Census missed 1.9 percent of the white population and 7.7 percent of the black population.[50]

Despite continuing efforts to address the undercount, high-quality sampling methods repeatedly show that total counts from the official census are actually lower than the population estimates made with samples. Furthermore, these undercount issues seem to be getting worse over time. President Bill Clinton proposed that the 2000 Census be done using samples, which would lower the cost of the census to taxpayers and provide better accuracy. The speaker of the House, Newt Gingrich, opposed this move, suggesting that the use of samples was not intended by the founders. Generally, the arguments over the issue of undercount grew into a public policy debate with Democrats favoring sampling methods on the grounds of accuracy and Republicans opposing the use of sampling on the grounds of constitutionality. This eventually found its way to the Supreme Court, which interpreted the Constitution as requiring a total count, effectively ending the attempt to use sampling methods to determine the U.S. population.[51]

IMMIGRATION AND THE UNDERCOUNT Immigrant communities have been central to many debates concerning the undercount. Many immigrants, documented or not, are not counted in the census. Undocumented immigrants are even less likely to respond to census questions for fear of deportation or social persecution. One of the most important demographics in this category is the Latino community. This demographic became the largest minority group in the United States around the turn of the millennium, and an estimated 8 million members are undocumented immigrants.

The dual roles of the census make this demographic especially problematic. The census is used to determine funding for many federal programs that give aid to poor immigrant communities. If the census undercounts these populations, then states are left with the economic burden of coping with issues that federal programs were designed to alleviate. With this problem in mind, Latino community leaders engaged in an unprecedented media blitz to encourage their community members to participate in the 2010 Census.[52]

Because of the census's role in determining congressional apportionment, in 2011, a group of Texas plaintiffs introduced a lawsuit in federal courts claiming that the 2010 Census numbers should be reduced to account for the estimated numbers of undocumented immigrants. Local and national politics play an important role in this lawsuit. The plaintiffs are from northeast Texas, an area that would lose influence to the southern districts of Texas if undocumented

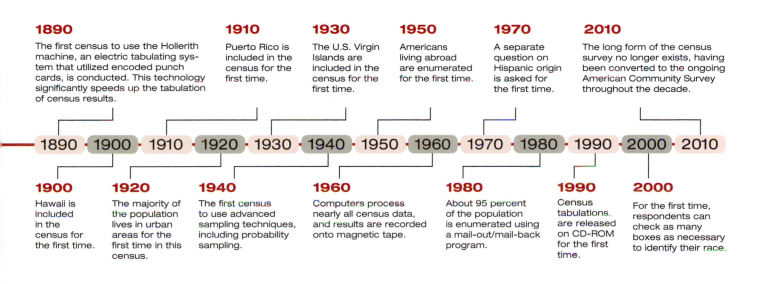

1890
The first census to use the Hollerith machine, an electric tabulating system that utilized encoded punch cards, is conducted. This technology significantly speeds up the tabulation of census results.

1910
Puerto Rico is included in the census for the first time.

1930
The U.S. Virgin Islands are included in the census for the first time.

1950
Americans living abroad are enumerated for the first time.

1970
A separate question on Hispanic origin is asked for the first time.

2010
The long form of the census survey no longer exists, having been converted to the ongoing American Community Survey throughout the decade.

1890 · 1900 · 1910 · 1920 · 1930 · 1940 · 1950 · 1960 · 1970 · 1980 · 1990 · 2000 · 2010

1900
Hawaii is included in the census for the first time.

1920
The majority of the population lives in urban areas for the first time in this census.

1940
The first census to use advanced sampling techniques, including probability sampling.

1960
Computers process nearly all census data, and results are recorded onto magnetic tape.

1980
About 95 percent of the population is enumerated using a mail-out/mail-back program.

1990
Census tabulations are released on CD-ROM for the first time.

2000
For the first time, respondents can check as many boxes as necessary to identify their race.

immigrants were included in the apportionment count. Similarly, states that have a smaller number of undocumented immigrants would lose political power to the states that traditionally have larger immigrant populations. The lawsuit alleges that only those who can vote should be counted for apportionment purposes. However, this would also eliminate anyone under the age of 18 from being counted as well. The issue promises to be an important one as immigration issues and the accuracy of the census become increasingly debated.[53]

2010 Census

Throughout the first decade of the 21st century, the Census Bureau has continually tried to update its Master Address File (MAF), an inventory of addresses for the entire U.S. population. The increasing reliance of the decennial census on mail-out surveys makes an accurate address list an essential aspect of conducting the census. The MAF was first created by combining the 1990 Census Address Control File and the Postal Service's Delivery Sequence File (DSF). The stated goal of the MAF is to "ensure that each housing unit in the United States is included in the Census." The Census Bureau has attempted to ensure the accuracy of the MAF by integrating Global Positioning System data with a biannual update from the U.S. Postal Service.[54]

With only 10 questions, the 2010 Census questionnaire was one of the shortest in history. The simplicity of the census form and the supplement of an extensive marketing campaign were part of an effort by the Census Bureau to ensure greater response rates by the public. The marketing campaign included advertising across many forms of media, school educational programs, a promotional road tour, and a Web site devoted specifically to the 2010 Census.[55]

WHAT CAN THE CENSUS BUREAU DATA SHOW US?

The census has evolved into an essential aspect of legislation and resource allocation in the United States. The information that the Census Bureau provides to the public is a valuable tool for understanding the ways in which the nation has changed and continues to change. The following chapters in this book will illustrate the ways in which the census has documented changing demographics and their impact on the country.

Economic Changes

Chapter 2 deals with the decennial census and other data gathered by the Census Bureau that discuss economic trends. The census has provided a valuable historical record of the ways in which economic trends have impacted the sociocultural fabric of the nation. In a nation without a defined ruling class, such as an aristocracy, social classes are linked directly to income and wealth. Since the Great Depression, the Census Bureau has increasingly sought information on the economic status of the country in order to help the government design programs geared toward helping the less fortunate. Figures from these censuses are often used to analyze the effects of political policies and the overall economic health of the nation. Correlating demographic trends with economic ones raises important questions about the nature of the U.S. economy and the mechanics of social mobility.

Racial Changes

Chapter 3 deals with the census and racial issues. The census has had a generally peripheral role when it comes to the demographics it studies. It is primarily a tool to document rather than influence cultural definitions of gender, age, and social class. In regard to racial definitions, however, the census has had a historically active role. This introductory chapter discussed some of the terminology used to differentiate between races. Terms such as "African American," "Native American," "American Indian," "Latino," and "Hispanic" are often politically charged, and the census has relied on them throughout its history to evaluate changing racial demographics.

Gender

Chapter 4 deals with gender issues and the census. Gender has been recorded in the census since the first enumeration. As subsequent censuses have become more detailed, various realities of gender in the United States have also become more visible. Census data have allowed researchers to assess the ways in which gender affects employment and social roles in various demographics across the country. Studies based on this data have led to a number of initiatives that attempt to rectify gender inequalities.

Age

Chapter 5 deals with aging and the census. This chapter discusses the ways in which the early censuses indicated that the median age in the United States rose from 16 to 22 over the course of the first century. Age estimates are essential for understanding the public educational needs of various areas. For example, if the population of 1- to 4-year-olds rose dramatically in a particular district, more funding could be allocated to anticipate the rise in the elementary school-age population. Age demographics can also anticipate health care needs in an aging population. This information is useful for both the public and private sectors because it allows both government and industry leaders to anticipate needs in a community and act accordingly.

Marriage and Family

Chapter 6 deals with the census and family demographics. Many different groups use census data to assess the social fabric of the nation, including how the population defines and understands marriage and family. While it was a fairly rare occurrence to find single mothers in the earlier censuses, this kind of family is much more common today. Divorce rates and marriage rates tabulated by the census are the subject of punditry, religious initiatives, public policies, and general discussion across the population. Other data have shown changes in the median age of married couples, indicating a changing concept of marriage and a changing set of values in younger generations.

KEY TERMS

Reapportion is the adjustment of a state's allocation of seats in the House of Representative as a result of the population count.   *2*

Decennial is recurring every 10 years, such as the population census.   *2*

Enumeration is a count or tally.   *2*

Blood quantum laws were a way of identifying a person's race as classified by the census based on analyzing bloodline to determine a person's genetic heritage.   *3*

Sectionalism refers to the different, and often divisive, cultures of the American North and South.   *9*

Surveys are investigations of the opinions or experiences of a group of people by asking them questions.   *11*

Sampling is surveying a subset of the population as representative of an entire population.   *11*

Purposive sampling is selecting a group of subjects by choosing who appear to be typical representatives of the larger population.   *11*

Random sampling is selecting a group of subjects arbitrarily from a defined population, so that every member of the population has an equal chance of being selected into the sample.   *12*

Sampling frame is the area defined for sampling.   *12*

Undercount is the percentage of the population not counted in a survey.   *13*

CHAPTER QUIZ

1. The census was originally undertaken in order to
   a. assess demographic trends.
   b. help lawmakers create public policy.
   c. document historical changes within the country.
   d. allocate seats in the House of Representatives.

2. _____ were counted as three-fifths of a person in the first census.
   a. Native Americans
   b. Slaves
   c. Free blacks
   d. Undocumented immigrants

3. The 2010 Census used one of the shortest questionnaires in history, at only 10 questions, supplemented by
   a. a sample taken of 10 percent of the population.
   b. a long form mailed to 25 percent of the population.
   c. the American Community Survey.
   d. the Dual Systems Estimation Survey.

4. In 1902, the Census Office
   a. transferred its responsibilities to U.S. marshals.
   b. became a permanent part of the federal government.
   c. was renamed the Census Bureau.
   d. was eliminated in favor of state-run offices.

5. Statistical sampling is often used to determine
   a. the undercount.
   b. apportionment.
   c. the MAF.
   d. the total census count.

Answers: 1. d; 2. b; 3. c; 4. b; 5. a

ESSAY QUESTIONS

1. Describe how and why the U.S. census has been different from other censuses throughout history.

2. Discuss how the introduction of the American Community Survey has changed the census process.

3. Consider the dramatic budget increase the census has received over time and argue for or against scaling back the Census Bureau to a strict apportionment role.

4. Analyze the role of the census and the undercount in public policymaking.

5. Discuss the ways in which different kinds of sampling can skew a survey's results.

SOURCES FOR FURTHER RESEARCH

Census statistics by state:
http://quickfacts.census.gov/qfd/index.html

Census history:
http://www.census.gov/history/

Bureau of Labor Statistics:
http://www.bls.gov/home.htm

Historical Census Browser:
http://mapserver.lib.virginia.edu/

Current social and demographic trends:
http://census.pewsocialtrends.org/

Population Reference Bureau:
http://prb.org/

Access to TIGER database files:
http://www.census.gov/geo/www/tiger/

History and current activities of the American Statistical Association:
http://www.amstat.org/

General census resources:
http://hcl.harvard.edu/research/guides/census_us/index.html#fourth

2 Economic Trends and Employment

Income inequality in the United States is at its highest point since the Census Bureau began reporting this statistic in 1967. (Anyka/Shutterstock)

INCOME INEQUALITY WORSENS ACROSS THE UNITED STATES

In the spring of 2010, many Americans were reeling from the global financial crisis and subsequent recession. Recent college graduates, unable to find jobs, were moving back in with their parents in record numbers. Faced with declining investments, many older Americans were delaying retirement or picking up second jobs. Even those who once believed their jobs to be secure found themselves out of work and struggling to find new positions in a highly competitive job market. Yet, at an art auction hosted by Christie's, someone spent $106.5 million—the highest price ever paid for a piece of art—for a Pablo Picasso still-life painting.[1]

The fact is, while the economic meltdown and slow recovery touched the lives of millions of Americans, the pain was not dispersed equally. In fact, the wealthiest 5 percent of Americans (those with incomes over $180,000) made a bit *more* money in 2009 than the year before, according to the U.S. Census Bureau. At the same time, the share of Americans making up the poorest poor was growing. In 2009, a record-high 6.3 percent of Americans were making do on half the federal poverty level—$10,977 annually for a family of four. The average American didn't do much better; the median household income also slipped slightly that year.[2]

As older workers delayed retirement, fewer jobs were available for younger workers just entering the workforce and for experienced workers recently laid off. The hardest-hit group, according to 2009 Census Bureau statistics, was lower-skilled adults aged 18 to 34. The tough employment outlook meant that many young adults moved back home. Half of young Americans aged 18 to 24 were living with their parents, while 30 percent of those 25 to 34 did as well.[3]

These figures point to a potentially troubling trend: the growth of income inequality in the United States. According to the Gini index, an international measure, income inequality is the highest it's ever been since these statistics were first measured in 1967. If all the income generated in the United States each year was one huge pie, the richest 1 percent would get a disproportionately large slice—24 percent. That means 99 percent of Americans are splitting the remaining three-quarters.[4] And it's not just the recession that's the problem; inequality rose during the tech bubble of the 1990s and continued to rise during the more recent economic downturn. As Timothy Smeeding, a professor at the University of Wisconsin-Madison, puts it, the United States is increasingly moving toward a "winner-takes-all economy."[5]

These census figures were released in the months leading up to the 2010 midterm elections, adding fuel to the already heated debate about whether to extend the George W. Bush-era tax cuts. Republicans argued for extending tax cuts across all income levels, while President Barack Obama advocated extending the cuts only for individuals earning less than $200,000 a year. Eventually the Republicans would win and, upon taking over the House of Representatives in the elections of 2010, they pushed through, as their first agenda item, extending the tax breaks to the wealthiest 1 percent. The president agreed to extend the cuts despite only 40 percent of Americans supporting tax breaks to the richest people in the country.[6]

This is just one example of how census data both affect and are affected by governmental policy. Tax cuts for the wealthiest Americans contributed to the rise in inequality (a subject discussed in greater detail below), while at the same time census data were used as political ammunition from both the left and right.

Political sound bites often reduce complicated issues to simplistic talking points; the realities are often far more complex. How do these governmental policies affect Americans on all levels of the income spectrum? How do poverty, wealth, employment, and inequality intersect? In this chapter, we'll explore how employment in the United States got where it is today and what trends may continue into the future.

SOCIAL CLASS AND STRATIFICATION

In a text about the 10-year census, it's important to state that, in general, the census does not measure anything related to income and/or social stratification. The Census Bureau collects data on such things, but the measuring of income share, poverty rates, and unemployment rates are not relevant to the 10-year count of citizens in the country. Such things, however, are incredibly relevant to understanding the United States, and for that reason policy makers and other government agencies have repeatedly called on the Census Bureau to gather and collate data related to social stratification and social class.

It's hard to say what the "normal" American family looks like, at least from an economic perspective. Many people throw around terms like "working class," "upper class," and "middle class" in day-to-day conversation, but most would be hard-pressed to come up with a precise definition of exactly who fits into which category, or even where they themselves fit. According to a Pew research study from 2008, 53 percent of Americans consider themselves middle class; when those who self-identify as "upper-middle" or "lower-middle" are included, that number rises to 91 percent. The study's authors point out that 4 in 10 Americans earning less than $20,000 a year self-identify as middle class, but so do a third of those earning more than $150,000."[7] Clearly, our understanding of what makes up "the middle" (as well as the top and the bottom) is a fuzzy concept that begs closer scrutiny.

Almost every known society has some level of **stratification**, or division of groups into separate and distinct parts. These divisions can be based on objective criteria, such as income, or more ineffable qualities, such as power, prestige, or status. **Social class** is a kind of stratification that divides people into groups based on similar economic and social positions. Members of different classes may dress or speak differently; may have different access to education and employment; and may differ in terms of values, family structures, and even legal rights. In feudal societies or caste systems, the divisions between people may be based on inherited roles. In Western capitalist societies, class is more mutable—and difficult to define precisely. An individual's place in society is related to income, education, occupation, and wealth. Adults may end up in the same class as their parents, or they may move up or down the social-class ladder.

There is no one way to conceive of social class in the United States. Some use the broad divisions of upper, middle, and lower class. We might tend to think of social class as it relates to economics: The richest people make up the upper class, the poorest are the lower class, and everyone else is somewhere in between. But it's also important to note that status, wealth, and power often—but don't always—intersect. For example, in the years leading up to World War II, some Jewish merchant families in Europe were wealthy but still suffered political marginalization and persecution. Nonetheless, in the United States higher incomes do tend to correlate with higher social class—and vice versa. And although the majority of Americans may consider themselves middle class, it's also important to take a look at the extreme ends of the income spectrum by examining the role of wealth and poverty in the United States.

Wealth and Poverty in the United States

The introduction to this section noted how incomes in the United States are becoming more unequal. **Income** is money received through work or gains on investments; weekly paychecks and dividends from stock options are both examples of income. It's important to distinguish between income and **wealth**, which refers to all the assets or resources in a person's control. A home, a car, property, and a retirement or trust fund all might constitute a person's wealth, or net worth. A college student from a wealthy family may have little income—because he or she does not work, or only works part time—while having significant inherited wealth.

If wealth is a measure of resources and assets, **poverty** refers to the lack of resources. Although there is no objective guideline to resolve whether a person is wealthy, there *is* a way to determine if someone is in poverty according to the standards of the U.S. government. The **poverty line** is a specific national standard set by the federal government to help allocate resources. In 2011, a family of four earning less than $22,350 or a single individual with an income under $10,890 was considered to be in poverty, according to the Office of Management and Budget (OMB) definition.[8] The Census Bureau uses this official OMB definition in its research. Those living below the poverty level are considered unable to meet basic needs of food, shelter, and medical care. The official definition of poverty is based on pretax cash income and does not include capital gains or benefits such as food stamps or Medicaid.[9]

The United States first defined poverty in the 1960s. After finding that households usually spent about a third of their incomes on food, the federal poverty level was fixed as three times the cost of an economical but healthy food plan. The calculations have been modified somewhat since then but are still based on the changing cost of goods. Since the guidelines were first established, poverty levels have fluctuated mildly; generally, 13 to 17 percent of Americans live below the poverty line at any given time. The poverty level does not take into account income from government programs, such as food stamps.[10]

Some critics have argued that this method of determining the poverty threshold is outdated, as it does not take into account the rising costs of things like child care, housing, and medical expenses. Furthermore, geographic differences are not taken into account. In this way, a one-size-fits-all definition of poverty is both useful and oversimplified. Consider how the cost of living varies greatly across the United States. For example, the average price for a two-bedroom apartment without a doorman in Manhattan in February 2010 was $3,704 a month—nearly four times as expensive as the average two-bedroom apartment in Kansas City, Missouri, which rented for $992.[11] While a national poverty standard simplifies calculations for the federal government, it leaves out some of the nuanced ways that wealth, income, and cost of living vary across the United States.

In taking a closer look at poverty in the United States, it is apparent that there are many different gradations of what it means to be poor. For one, 58 percent of Americans will spend at least one year living below the poverty line. For some, this is only a temporary status, and for others, it is a chronic circumstance that is passed down from generation to generation.[12]

The government uses annual income to give poverty a concrete definition, but poverty can also be a relative state. **Relative poverty** applies to those who feel poor when compared to the people who surround them. Recently, a University of Chicago law professor wrote a controversial op-ed titled "We Are the Super Rich." After noting that his household income was over $250,000, he went on to argue why he considered himself far from rich:

> Like most working Americans, insurance, doctors' bills, utilities, two cars, daycare, groceries, gasoline, cell phones, and cable TV (no movie channels) round out our monthly expenses. We also have someone who cuts our grass, cleans our house, and watches our new baby so we can both work outside the home. At the end of all this, we have less than a few hundred dollars per month of discretionary income. We occasionally eat out but with a baby sitter, these nights take a toll on our budget. Life in America is wonderful, but expensive.[13]

What do you think of the notion of relative poverty as outlined in this excerpt? When reading the author's rundown of the seemingly necessary expenses of "life in America" one must wonder: What is the cost of his home? What kind of cars does he own? What type of groceries does he buy? One would guess that the author's standard of living is much higher than that of a family making one-fifth of his annual income. Such a family most likely owns a less expensive home and car, buys a lower quality of groceries, and does not use lawn care, house cleaning, and one-on-one child-care services. Because the author's standard of living creates lofty expenses, he considers himself far from rich, but a family that brings in one-fifth of his annual income might think otherwise.

Another useful term in discussing poverty is **near poor**, which is used to describe people who live just above the poverty line. These people may have a difficult time making ends meet, but they do not qualify for government services offered to those in poverty. The near poor are typically qualified as those who live between the poverty line and 25 percent above that line. According to the Census Bureau, about 19 percent of the U.S. population was poor and/or near poor in 2009.[14]

Social Classes and Outcomes

Most Americans exist somewhere between extreme wealth and extreme poverty. Because vague terms like "middle class" and "lower class" are problematic, to get a clearer picture of how income is distributed in the United States, it might be helpful to look at some precise figures. Sociologists and economists divide the population into five equal segments called **quintiles**, each group accounting for 20 percent (one-fifth) of the population. Ranking U.S. households based only on income reveals some interesting facts. In 2009, the richest 20 percent of Americans, for example, accounted for just over 50 percent of total income, while the poorest quintile accounted for only 3.4 percent.[15] In between these two extremes, the second-lowest quintile accounted for 8.6 percent, the middle quintile 14.6 percent, and the second-highest for 23.2 percent of all income. The richest of the rich—the top 5 percent of all earners, making $180,000 or more per year—accounted for 21.7 percent of the nation's aggregate income.[16]

Put a different way, while the median household income in 2009 was $49,777, one in five households (the bottom quintile) made do on an income below $20,453. The second quintile's incomes ranged from $20,454 to $38,550; the third, which contains the median income, from $38,551 to $61,801; the fourth, from $61,802 to $100,000. One-fifth of American households earned more than $100,000.[17]

As you can see from this graphic, the progression of what group gets which percentage of income is moving from bottom to top. In other words, the poorest 20 percent of people in the United States lost income share, while the top 20 percent gained about 8 percent. Note that the richest people in the country, the top 5 percent, gained the most income share in this period.

This 40-year perspective shows that the highest quintile (including the top 5 percent) has a history of taking the largest piece of the proverbial pie of available income. Because the pie is only so big, the division of income creates somewhat of a reverse Robin Hood effect in which the income share of the rich has increased by assuming some of the income share of poor. But

★TABLE 2.1 SHARE OF INCOME BY QUINTILE, 2009[18]★

In 2009, the highest-earning quintile earned a greater share of the nation's total income than it did in 1968; all other income groups saw their shares decline.

	2009 Share of Income Received (Percent)	1968 Share of Income Received (Percent)
Lowest quintile	3.4	4.2
Second quintile	8.6	11.1
Third quintile	14.6	17.6
Fourth quintile	23.2	24.5
Highest quintile	50.3	42.6
Top 5 percent	21.7	16.3

why exactly do some people seem to get ahead while others stay behind? Some classic arguments illustrate some of the explanations often give as to why income inequality exists.

DAVIS AND MOORE VS. TUMIN In the United States, is everyone offered an equal chance? Is success a result of hard work or good luck? Many of the questions that come up during discussions of inequality were raised more than 50 years ago by social scientists Kingsley Davis, Wilbert Moore, and Melvin Tumin. According to Davis and Moore, inequality isn't such a bad thing; in fact, it may be inevitable or even necessary in American society. Since systems tend toward equilibrium, Davis and Moore argue, there will always be both rich people and poor people. Indeed, some level of stratification is necessary for society to function smoothly. We need people to fulfill a wide set of roles, from teachers to surgeons to garbage collectors to CEOs. Income inequality comes about because the distribution of rewards (in this case, money) matches up with the difficulty of the job and the training or skills it requires. Doctors need to have highly specialized knowledge and must go to school for many years; it makes sense, then, that they receive high incomes.

Davis and Moore's argument is founded on the assumption that the United States operates as a **meritocracy**—a system where rewards are based on merit. The rich have gotten ahead because of their superior skills, effort, talent, or hard work. Tumin questions this assumption. While Davis and Moore argue that more money naturally goes to those fulfilling difficult or important roles in society, Tumin wonders who decides which jobs are the most difficult or important. What makes the job of an investment banker, for example, more difficult or important than the job of a police officer or teacher? Tumin suggests that it isn't the nature of the job but influence over industry and public policies that allows people working in high-status jobs to have disproportionate earnings. Additionally, Tumin believes that not everyone has an equal chance at filling those high-paying, high-status jobs; instead, social inequality makes access to certain types of education and occupation likelier for some than others. If you consider the income inequality of the data presented in this book, can you imagine the advantages given to a boy who happens to be born into a family earning $200,000 a year as opposed to those available to a child born into poverty? Who do you think has an easier road to success?

Economic Inequality

After the popular uprisings that toppled dictatorial regimes in Egypt and Tunisia in early 2011, some commenters claimed not to be surprised. They pointed to these countries' high levels of income inequality as an obvious source of tension between the struggling masses and the small, über-wealthy elite. In Tunisia, a young, college-educated man sold vegetables on the street illegally because he could not find a job and needed to earn some kind of income to survive. When the police confiscated his wares because he lacked a permit, he set himself on fire in protest. In contrast, the Tunisian president's family flaunted their wealth by keeping pet tigers and having ice cream flown in from Saint-Tropez, France. As these countries show, high levels of **income inequality**—the degree of difference between high- and low-income households in a population—can lead to economic, political, and social instability within a country. If trends continue, could the United States be heading down this road?

Inequality is a useful measure because it doesn't only look at individuals at the bottom of the income ladder; instead, it's a way to examine how the distribution of wealth and income affects the entire population. It is also a helpful way to compare countries that may have very different levels of wealth or resources. Wealthy countries and poor countries may have very similar levels of equality, or inequality, depending on how their income is distributed.

THE GINI INDEX   According to at least one measure, income inequality is *higher* in the United States than either Tunisia or Egypt. The Gini index measures income inequality using a scale that ranges from 0 to 1. A Gini index value of 0 represents perfect equality in which every person receives an equal share of total income; in contrast, a Gini index value of 1 represents perfect inequality in which only one person controls 100 percent of the income. The higher the Gini index, the higher the level of inequality. Internationally, countries' Gini coefficients range from 0.23 (Sweden) to 0.70 (Namibia). In 2009, the United States had a Gini index of 0.468, meaning that the gulf between the rich and poor was greater than in Canada or the United Kingdom—and also greater than in Egypt, Tunisia, and Mauritania. That same year, the 400 richest Americans saw their combined net worth climb 8 percent, at the same time as the poverty level was reaching 15-year heights.[19]

Nonetheless, comparing data from countries that are very dissimilar in terms of industry, development, and economic policy can be misleading. It may be more fruitful to compare the United States to countries that are similar in that they are also democratic, capitalistic, and developed. According to the Gini index, the United States lags behind most Western countries, including Denmark, Norway, Sweden, Finland, Germany, France, and Canada.

Another way to look at inequality is the decile ratio. The **decile ratio** measures the distance between income groups in the top 10 percent and the bottom 10 percent. These numbers can be calculated by taking the average income of the highest group and dividing it by the average income of the lowest group. By this measure, the United States has a significantly higher level of inequality than other wealthy industrialized and free countries. Of course, it's important to remember that the decile ratio of less wealthy countries is often much higher than in the United States, because usually there is a very small wealth leadership group; still, when compared to other wealthy, industrialized nations, the United States has the worst income inequality.[20] The table below presents some comparison data for you to consider.

EFFECTS OF INEQUALITY   Income inequality has been shown to have damaging effects on society. Worldwide, higher inequality correlates with increased homicide, infant mortality, depression, and obesity. It may also destabilize the economy, so it's worth considering that the last time inequality in the United States was this extreme was in the 1920s. After the 1929 stock market crash, inequality decreased, but this trend has been reversing itself since the 1970s.[23]

Income inequality affects not only individuals, but also society as a whole; while poverty affects one set group, the consequences of income inequality are spread out across society. In other words, everyone is affected. Researchers have found that inequality may erode some of the social cohesion that holds groups together. In places with higher levels of equality, people are more likely to trust one another; they are also more likely to be involved with their communities.[24] Consider what happened here after Hurricane Katrina destroyed New Orleans. Looting,

★ TABLE 2.2 INCOME INEQUALITY: HOW DOES THE UNITED STATES MEASURE UP AGAINST OTHER INDUSTRIALIZED, CAPITALIST NATIONS? ★

	2004 Gini Index[21]	2000 Decile Ratio[22]
United States	0.47	5.7
United Kingdom	0.36	4.6
Australia	0.35	4.2
France	0.33	3.4
Germany	0.28	3.4
Sweden	0.25	3.0
Japan	0.25	4.2
Denmark	0.25	2.8

crime, and violence erupted. Contrast this to the recent tsunami and earthquake in Japan. Despite the turmoil, there were no reports of widespread looting and crime in Japan. Could this be related to the fact that Japanese inequality is not as extreme as that in the United States? Social scientists Kate Pickett and Richard Wilkinson would likely answer "yes." Their research suggests that social relations are more strained in societies where some are very rich and others are very poor.[25]

Some critics of the above studies point out that looking at income inequality is only one way to examine the extent of inequality in a society. However, the extent of inequality in the United States becomes even more extreme when wealth, including residencies and stocks, is taken into account. By this measure, the wealthiest 1 percent controls more assets than the bottom 90 percent combined.[26] In other words, approximately 3 million people hold more total wealth than around 270 million combined.

ATTITUDES ABOUT INEQUALITY It's important to note that income inequality is not the same thing as inequality of opportunity. In the United States, it is theoretically possible for the poorest of the poor to attend college, or even to become a Supreme Court justice or a millionaire. Implicit in the American dream is the idea that class distinctions aren't fixed and that our egalitarian society rewards hard work, skill, and perseverance. Indeed, a 2005 *New York Times* poll showed that 40 percent of Americans were optimistic about **social mobility**, or the possibility of moving from one class to another. This 40 percent thought that the possibility for social mobility had gotten better over the past 30 years, but another 35 percent thought it had not changed. This optimism may be unwarranted, though; the *Times* also found that social mobility declined from the 1970s to the 1980s, and then declined further from the 1980s to the 1990s.[27] Furthermore, the poorest quintile showed the least mobility; more than half of Americans born into the bottom 20 percent stayed there.[28] According to a study by the Brookings Institute, only 6 percent of children born into low-income households ended up in the highest-earning quintile as adults; more than two-thirds of them continued to earn below average incomes when they grew up.[29] In other words, while class isn't necessarily inherited, economic roles that you inherit at birth are not likely to change much in your lifetime.

Although the nation's egalitarian self-image indicates otherwise, Americans may actually be more accepting of inequality than their European counterparts. One poll found that nearly two-thirds of those in the United Kingdom thought that social policies should be used to reduce inequalities; in America, the number was less than half that, at 28 percent. This may be because Americans perceive their nation as a place where social or economic benefits go to the most worthy. A recent poll conducted in 27 nations found that nearly 7 in 10 Americans agreed that "people are rewarded for intelligence and skill"—more than any other country. But by some measures, there is less real social mobility in the United States than in many other nations, including Sweden, Denmark, Spain, France, Canada, Germany, and Australia.[30]

HISTORICAL PERSPECTIVES ON ECONOMIC TRENDS AND EMPLOYMENT

When considering today's levels of employment, income distribution, and inequality, it can be easy to feel as though the march toward high inequality was inevitable. This is one reason a historical approach is vital; it allows us a broader glimpse of the trends that got the United States to where it is today.

History of Income Inequality in America

Today's high levels of income inequality are not unprecedented in the history of the United States. In fact, Americans living 90 years ago might find them rather familiar. The early 20th century was the era of the wealthy industrialist in which a small percentage of the population was able to capitalize on the changing market. During this period, it was common to see one man possessing not 10 times but 1,000 times the wealth of his neighbor.[31] The additional factor of low social mobility helped push the gulf between the rich and poor to an all-time high.

In the 1930s, the economic challenges and changes in public policy helped eliminate some inequalities in the United States. The stock market crash of 1929 and the subsequent Great Depression damaged the income share of the country's highest earners and narrowed the gap between the rich and the poor. Additionally, post-World War II policies increased social mobility for the poor by way of the GI Bill, which gives financial assistance for education to

★**TABLE 2.3 DISTRIBUTION (IN PERCENTAGES)
OF EARNED INCOME ACROSS QUINTILES: 1967 TO 2005**[36]★

	1967	1970	1975	1980	1985	1990	1995	2000	2005
Lowest quintile	4	4.1	4.4	4.3	4.0	3.9	3.7	3.6	3.4
Second quintile	10.8	10.8	10.5	10.3	9.7	9.6	9.1	8.9	8.6
Third quintile	17.3	17.4	17.1	16.9	16.3	15.9	15.2	14.8	14.6
Fourth quintile	24.2	24.5	24.8	24.9	24.6	24.0	23.3	23.0	23.0
Highest quintile	43.8	43.3	43.2	43.7	45.3	46.6	48.7	49.8	50.4

U.S. military service members, many of whom might not have otherwise been able to afford schooling. In the postwar decades, incomes rose across the board, with people at all levels seeing their incomes grow about 3 percent a year.[32] The United States was basking in an era of income growth for both the rich and poor, creating the sense that each generation would be economically better off than the one that came before.[33]

The trend toward greater income equality ended in the 1970s. Since then, inequality has marched steadily upward, both when the economy was struggling, such as during the inflation and wage stagnation of the 1970s, and when it was booming, such as during the tech bubble of the late 1990s. In fact, the richest 1 percent of Americans have seen their share of the nation's income more than double since 1979 even in the wake of the most recent economic recession.[34]

Between 1980 and 2005, labor productivity grew by 71 percent—much faster than it had in the postwar years—but median weekly wages went up only 14 percent, but this economic growth did not benefit low- and middle-wage workers. So to whom did the gains from increased productivity go? Since the mid-1980s, they've mostly gone to the very top earners; in fact, more than 80 percent of all the income gained from 1980 to 2005 went to the top 1 percent.[35] In this same period, only the top-earning quintile saw its share of the total income increase, meaning that 80 percent of Americans saw their share of the total income go down. The group that saw the biggest decline was the middle quintile, which gave up 2.8 percent of its income share between 1970 and 2009, while the top quintile added 7 percent. These may not seem like dramatic changes, but their aggregate affect is staggering.

There are many theories to explain why inequality has risen so sharply over the past 40 years. Some economists point to a decline in union membership; others point to governmental policies that benefit corporations at the expense of individuals. Another explanation banks on the increasing importance of technology and a shift in how big money is earned. Recent years have seen a shrinking demand for low- and moderately skilled workers, in part due to increased automation and the exportation of factory jobs to underdeveloped countries where labor is cheaper. The increased importance of technology has led to a demand for more educated and skilled workers, leaving lower-skilled workers to face increasing unemployment and declining wages. Below, we'll consider the effects of race, gender, and immigration on income inequality. It's important, though, to remember that none of these factors exists in a vacuum; instead, they are interrelated in complex ways.

Race, Gender, and Immigration

The middle decades of the 20th century were marked by significant social movements, namely the labor union, civil rights, and women's rights movements. This was also a period of sharply increased immigration. Changing policies and social attitudes all had an impact on incomes and employment for various groups.

Throughout the century, women earned less than their male counterparts, and black families earned less than white families.[37] These seemingly simple facts have a host of complex sociological, political, and economic contributing factors, and the data show how these trends have changed, or not, in recent decades.

GENDER In 2009, the median income for women working full time was 23 percent lower than for similarly employed men. While the persistent **wage gap** was troubling, there were some encouraging trends. For one, the gap between men's and women's earnings has shrunk significantly; in 1979, women's median income lagged men's by 40 percent. However, these gains were mostly made in the 1980s and 1990s and have stagnated somewhat since then.

Some of the credit for closing the wage gap goes to college-educated women; these days, in fact, 57 percent of those enrolled at U.S. colleges are women. According to the Census Bureau, white, black, and Latina women are earning more advanced degrees than men; among Asian men and women, however, there's little statistical difference.[38]

These degrees pay off—literally. In 2008, the average income for a person with a high school diploma was $31,283 and for a person with a bachelor's degree was $58,613. With a graduate degree, that number jumped to $83,144.[39] In other words, more women getting advanced degrees means women's median income will rise. The results of this trend have been apparent in recent years. While most groups didn't see increased productivity translate to increased wages between 1980 and 2005, college-educated women did. In fact, they were the only major group that saw their income grow in line with productivity during this period.[40]

At the same time as college-educated women are closing the income gap, an increasing number of heads of households are women; in non-census speak, they might be referred to as single mothers. The percentage of single-parent households, which tend to be run by women, has more than doubled since 1970; now, more than a quarter of children in the United States are raised by one parent. Children in these families are four to five times more likely to be poor.[41] As the share of these households increases, they push the poverty level up both for women and for the nation overall.

RACE The income gap between black and white households is even greater than that between men and women. As of 2009, black households' median income was 38 percent lower than that of white households. Put another way, in 2009 the average black household made $22,000 less annually than the average non-Hispanic white household. And while women have made strides in closing the income gender gap, the past 30 years have seen troublingly little progress made in the racial gap. On the whole, blacks have a higher incarceration rate and a lower rate of participation in the workforce, two factors that contribute to the black-white wage gap.[42]

Between 2000 and 2008, all racial groups saw inflation-adjusted incomes decline an average of 4.3 percent. Non-Hispanic whites saw incomes shrink the least, at 2.7 percent, from $57,059 to $55,530. Asian Americans, who have the highest median income, saw a decline of 5.8 percent, from $69,713 to $65,637. Black households, with the lowest median income, lost 7.8 percent, from $37,093 to $34,218, and Hispanic households saw median incomes shrink by 8.6 percent, from $41,470 to $37,913, twice the national average.[43]

IMMIGRATION In 1965, Congress passed the Immigration and Nationality Act, loosening restrictions on immigration. The results of this legislation were significant. In 1970, the foreign-born population (those who were not U.S. citizens at birth) made up 4.8 percent of the U.S. population; by 2009, that figure had more than doubled, to 12.5 percent.[44] While some of these immigrants were highly skilled, on average they had lower incomes and lower levels of education than native-born Americans.

In 2003, the Census Bureau noted that 88 percent of native-born Americans had a high school diploma compared to only 67 percent of foreign-born Americans.[45] Both groups, however, had an equal share of college graduates—27 percent. In 2008, 23.3 percent of noncitizens lived below the poverty level. These numbers were even higher for immigrant children, more than one in three of whom lived in poverty.[46]

Some theorists believe that increased immigration led to depressed wages on the lower end of the income scale, thus increasing inequality. Harvard University economist George Borjas points to the fact that native-born workers without a high school degree, who roughly correlate to the poorest 10 percent of the job market, saw their incomes decline by 7.4 percent between 1980 and 2000.[47] During the same period, native-born workers with a high school degree, but no college education, saw a smaller effect, a decline of 2.1 percent.[48]

At the same time, highly skilled immigrants contributed to a decline in inequality at the higher end of the income scale, leading former Federal Reserve Chairman Alan Greenspan to theorize that the United States has created "a privileged, native-born elite of skilled workers whose incomes are being supported at noncompetitively high levels by immigration quotas." If we sought to increase the immigration of highly skilled workers, Greenspan claimed, we "would, at the stroke of a pen, reduce much income inequality."[49] Again, though, it's important to remember that inequality does not have a single cause. While immigration policies may have contributed to rising levels of inequality, they did not create them.

RECENT ECONOMIC AND UNEMPLOYMENT TRENDS

According to the National Bureau of Economic Statistics, the current recession began in December 2007; the financial crisis hit in the fall of the following year.[50] In the years that followed, many different sectors of society felt the fallout of a wounded economy in terms of income, poverty, unemployment, and inequality. An earlier recession in 2001 had already slowed the economy. Through comparing figures from before the 2001 and 2007 recessions, it is possible to get a sense for how the U.S. economy has changed—and is still changing.

Income

In 1999, the median household income was $42,164. The census region with the highest median income was the Northeast, at $45,581; the South region of the United States, at $38,790, had the lowest. Considering that 2008's median income was $50,303 a year, it may seem like Americans on the whole were better off. Once inflation was factored in, however, it turns out that the U.S. median income sank by 4.1 percent between 1999 and 2008.[51] In other words, over the past 10 years, inflation grew more quickly than median income. A household making exactly the median income would have seen its income decline by more than $2,000 by the end of the decade.

The regions that saw the sharpest decline in income were the South and the Midwest. When comparing **real median incomes**, figures adjusted for inflation, these regions saw a 9 percent decrease between 1999 and 2008.[52] The metro areas with the sharpest increases in poverty were concentrated in the Midwest; the Detroit metro area saw a more than 17 percent decline in median income in this period.[53] Some metro areas, however, bucked the trend; the largest increase in income was in Worcester, Massachusetts, where incomes grew 8.2 percent during this period.[54]

Throughout the decade, a racial income gap persisted. By 2008, the median income for black households was almost $17,000 less than the median for all households; for a Hispanic household, it was $11,000 less. White households had a median income of nearly $5,000 above the average, and Asian households' median income outstripped the overall median by $18,000.[55]

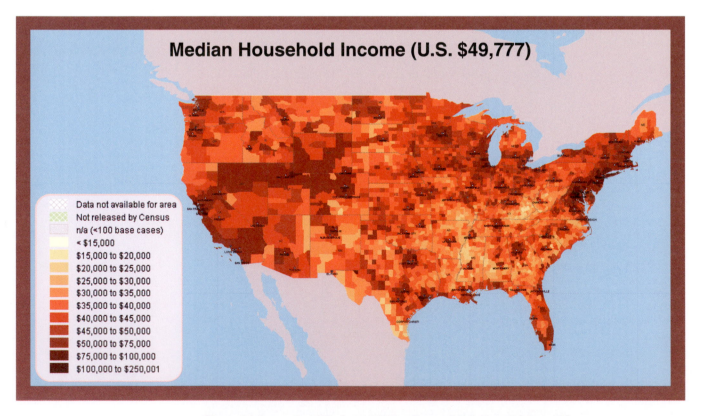

Figure 2.1 Source: Social Explorer, "1790 to Present," *U.S. Decennial Census Files*, http://www.socialexplorer.com/pub/home/home.aspx

Figure 2.2 Source: Social Explorer, "1790 to Present," *U.S. Decennial Census Files*, http://www.socialexplorer.com/pub/home/home.aspx

Employment and Unemployment

Jobs were one casualty of the ongoing recession. By the end of 2009, 138.1 million Americans had jobs, but millions more were still looking for work.[56] There were actually 5.8 million fewer employed people than the year before. The job loss affected some groups more than others, with young people aged 25 to 34 and men being hit especially hard. Men had a slightly higher unemployment rate than women (6.8 percent versus 6 percent). The unemployment level for Americans aged 18 to 65 in 2009 was the highest since the 1960s, at 12.9 percent. Compounding the job crunch, many older people stayed in the workforce, making competition for jobs even fiercer. In 2009, 27.1 percent of Americans over 60 were working, compared to 26.7 percent the year before.[57]

To be clear, the Census Bureau defines people as **unemployed** if "they do not have a job, have actively looked for work in the prior four weeks, and are currently available for work."[58] While young adults had the trickiest time finding jobs, even younger people found themselves struggling with unemployment as well. Teen unemployment—which measures those who are age 18 and younger and looking for work—was the highest on record. Perhaps this is because so many older workers had taken the traditionally teen jobs. The dismal job market may have encouraged more young people to opt for school instead of work, as 2009 saw the proportion of high school graduates who enrolled in college continue to rise.[59]

Although unemployment rates were higher for less-skilled workers, college graduates felt the crunch as well. As a consequence, many college graduates found themselves with changing priorities when searching for postcollege employment. Instead of aiming for lucrative jobs in the financial industry, for example, an increasing number of recent graduates turned to the public sector for jobs. In 2009, 16 percent more college students were working for the federal government than the previous year; the number of graduates working for nonprofits also grew by 11 percent. While the private sector traditionally pays higher wages, the public sector was where the jobs were. Over the past three years, the private sector lost 7 percent of its jobs, while the federal government added 3 percent.[60]

Ten years ago, a college graduate, or anyone else, would have faced a very different job market. Most significantly, the national unemployment rate was much lower—5.9 percent. There were some regional disparities; unemployment was highest in the West region (6.5

percent) and the lowest in the Midwest (5.1 percent).[61] By January 2011, however, each of these regions had seen a rise in unemployment. Again, the highest levels were in the West (10.9 percent), followed by the South (9.2 percent); the lowest unemployment was in the Northeast (8.4 percent), followed by the Midwest (8.5 percent).[62] Thanks in part to the decline of manufacturing jobs and the struggling automotive industry, the steepest changes came in the Midwest, where the unemployment rate was 40 percent higher than it had been a decade previously.[63] The Rust Belt continued to struggle into 2010, when the states with the greatest rises in unemployment between January 2010 and January 2011 included Michigan, Illinois, Indiana, and Wisconsin.[64]

Poverty

Although the recent recession intensified poverty in the United States, it was an issue even during times that weren't so economically taxing. In fact, between 1999 and 2008, the poverty level grew almost twice as quickly as the population did. The recession only made this trend worse, as the poverty level continued to rise to 14.3 percent in 2009, up from 13.2 in 2008; that meant that 3.7 million more Americans were added to the poverty rolls within just one year.[65] This was the largest increase since the federal government first began tracking poverty data 51 years ago.[66] One in seven Americans lived below the poverty line, meaning that they earned less than about $11,000 for an individual or $22,000 for a family of four. Nearly all racial groups were hurt by the recession; the only group to emerge relatively unscathed was Asian Americans, who also boasted the highest median income of all racial groups.[67] And once again, young people felt the crunch; while poverty levels worsened for working-age adults (aged 18 to 64), Americans over age 65 saw their poverty levels drop, thanks in part to increased Social Security benefits.[68]

Although these numbers were daunting, they were far from the highest poverty levels on record in the United States. In the mid-1960s, 22.4 percent of the population lived below the poverty line.[69] However, other troubling trends were emerging, including the rise in households with very low incomes. In 2009, the poorest poor—those making less than half the poverty threshold—made up a record-high 6.3 percent of the population.[70]

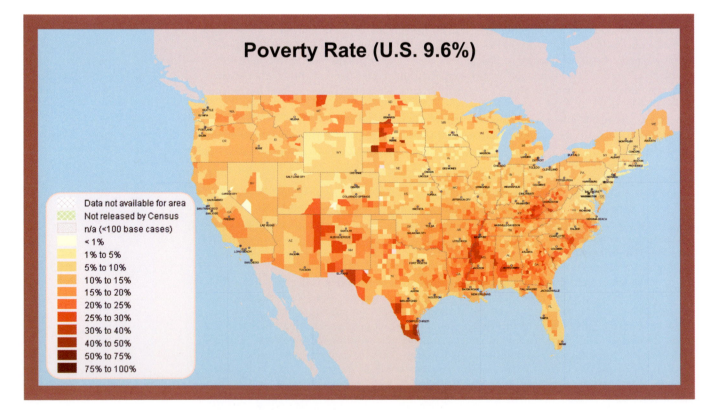

Figure 2.3 Source: Social Explorer, "1790 to Present," *U.S. Decennial Census Files*, http://www.socialexplorer.com/pub/home/home.aspx

As with unemployment, various regions were affected to various degrees. For some, especially the Midwest, the past decade has had a staggering impact. For example, during the past 10 years, Illinois saw poverty levels rise by 24 percent; by the end of 2009, 36 percent of Detroit's population lived below the poverty level.[71] In 2009, five counties had poverty rates above 39 percent; four of those were Native American reservations in South Dakota.[72]

Poverty impacted all age groups, but those most affected were children. In 2008, children made up 35.3 percent of the poor, but only 24.6 percent of the total population. Nineteen percent of Americans under age 18 were in poverty, or a total of 14.1 million people. This was an increase of 2.4 percentage points from 1999, when 16.6 percent of children (11.7 million people) were in poverty.[73] The poverty rate for people aged 18 to 64 was 11.7 percent in 2008, up 0.6 percent since 1999. Those aged 65 and older had the lowest poverty rate of all the age groups—9.7 percent, up 0.2 percent since 1999. In short, the majority of people added to the poverty rolls over the past decade have been children.[74]

Americans coped with growing poverty in different ways. Some cut back on expenses by moving in with friends and family. In 2010, there were 15.5 million multifamily households—an increase of 11.7 percent since 2008—accounting for 13.2 percent of all households.[75] Others turned to governmental programs that provide assistance for food, housing, or utilities. One striking result was that in 2010 more Americans than ever before received food-stamp benefits—approximately 1 in 10 U.S. households.[76] The states with the largest increases were Nevada, Arizona, Florida, and Wisconsin. It's important to keep in mind that food stamps and other cash-equivalent assistance are not counted in calculating incomes. Considering the extension of these benefits to many U.S. households, some researchers argued that if food-stamp benefits were factored into income calculations, 3.5 million Americans would have been lifted out of poverty, making the official poverty rate a slightly more encouraging 13.2 percent.[77]

Inequality

As the economy struggled, inequality in the United States reached record-high levels. The bottom quintile of earners received 3.4 percent of all the income generated in 2009, whereas the top quintile took 49.4 percent—14.5 times as much. In 1968, top earners made 7.69 times as much as the lowest earners.[78]

The poverty gap between young and old also widened. Thanks in part to Social Security benefits, older Americans actually saw their poverty rates decline this decade. By 2009, 9 percent of older Americans lived below the poverty line (compared to 10 percent in 2000). In contrast, more than a fifth of U.S. children were living in poverty in 2009 (21 percent, compared to 16 percent in 2000.)[79]

Another way to measure inequality is to look at the changing wages for workers. From 1999 to 2008, high-wage workers saw their earnings go up 3.4 percent, while low-wage workers saw their incomes drop by 8.3 percent.[80] Inflation-adjusted wages also sank for middle-wage workers, by 4.5 percent. This gap between high- and low-wage earners grew the greatest in metropolitan areas. In this time period, only three metro areas narrowed the inequality gap between high- and low-wage workers: Augusta, Ga., Syracuse, N.Y., and Tucson, Ariz.[81] In 2009, the states with the largest gaps between rich and poor were New York, Connecticut, Texas, and the District of Columbia. The states with the lowest levels of inequality were Alaska, Utah, Wyoming, Idaho, and Hawaii.[82]

STATE-BY-STATE COMPARISON

Looking at nationwide statistics helps give a sense of the broad trends in poverty, employment, income, and inequality. The United States, however, is not a uniform country, and a wide view can mask some of the differences between various states and cities. For example, while income was down nationwide from 1999 to 2008, during that same period incomes in Worcester, Mass., actually rose by 8.2 percent.[83] In 2008, the metro area with the highest median household income was Falls Church, Va., at $113,313; in contrast, a median household in Owsley County, Ky., took home $18,869. There are clearly vast differences within the United States.[84]

In 2009, New Hampshire was the wealthiest state in the nation, with a median income of $65,028. It was followed by New Jersey ($64,918), Connecticut ($64,644), Maryland ($63,828), and Alaska ($62,675).[85] The poorest state, Mississippi, had a median income of $35,693, 45 percent lower than that of New Hampshire. Just above Mississippi were Arkansas at $37,987, West Virginia at $39,170, Tennessee at $40,034, and South Carolina at $41,548.[86] By and large, Northeastern and Mid-Atlantic states boast incomes well above the national median incomes, while the poorest states are concentrated in the South. New Hampshire's high median incomes might be due in part to the state's lack of income or sales taxes, policies that set it apart from other states.

New Hampshire also boasted the nation's lowest poverty rate (8.6 percent), followed by Alaska (9.1 percent), Maryland (9.2 percent), Connecticut (9.3 percent), and New Jersey (9.4 percent).[87] Conversely, Mississippi had the highest percentage; more than one-fifth of the state's population (21.8 percent) lived below the poverty line in 2009. It was followed by Arkansas (18.5 percent), Kentucky (18.4 percent), New Mexico (18.2 percent), and West Virginia (17.8 percent).[88] Clearly, income and poverty are intimately related—Mississippi's low median income and high poverty indicate economic strife across the board. New Mexico's high poverty rate may be influenced by its proximity to Mexico and the influx of immigrants; as discussed previously, immigrants tend to have lower levels of income and higher levels of unemployment than the native born.

Average annual unemployment rates in 2010 showed a different geographical distribution. The highest rate of unemployment was in Nevada (14.9 percent), followed by Michigan (12.5 percent), California (12.4 percent), Rhode Island (11.6 percent), and Florida (11.5 percent).[89] Many of these states were hit hard by the burst of the housing bubble, especially Florida and Nevada. When the economy was booming, construction and service jobs drove the economy; with the housing market drying up, jobs became scarcer and unemployment rates shot up. The explanation for Michigan's high unemployment rate is probably due to the collapse of the auto industry, which contributed significantly to the state's economy.

The lowest unemployment rates were in North Dakota (3.9 percent), Nebraska (4.7 percent), South Dakota (4.8 percent), Iowa (6.1 percent), and New Hampshire (6.1 percent).[90] Many of these states have diverse economies that don't rely on just one industry; although many have strong, government-subsidized agricultural sectors, they have much else to offer as well. For example, New Hampshire's tourist industry, South Dakota's military bases, and North Dakota's food processing plants all contribute to healthy job markets.[91]

KEY TERMS

Stratification is the division of groups into separate and distinct parts. *19*

Social class is a kind of stratification that divides people into groups based on similar economic and social positions. *19*

Income is money received through work, such as weekly paychecks, or gains on investments, such as dividends from stocks. *19*

Wealth, or net worth, refers to all the assets or resources in a person's control, including property, retirement funds, and other assets. *19*

Poverty is the lack of basic resources necessary for survival, such as food, shelter, and medical care. *19*

Poverty line is a specific national standard set by the federal government to define who is considered to be in poverty and to help allocate resources to assist them. *19*

Relative poverty is a state in which people feel they have fewer resources than others. *20*

Near poor are people who live just above the poverty line; by one measure, those living between the poverty line and 25 percent above that line. *20*

Quintiles are equal fifths (20 percent) of a data set, such as the given population. *20*

Meritocracy refers to a system where rewards are distributed on the basis of merit. *21*

Income inequality refers to the degree of difference between high- and low-income households in a population. *21*

Decile ratio measures the distance between the top and bottom 10 percent (decile) of a data set. *22*

Social mobility is the possibility of moving from one class to another. *23*

Wage gap is the difference in average wages for two different populations, such as women and men. *24*

Real median incomes are median incomes that have been adjusted for inflation so that data from different time periods can be compared. *26*

Unemployed refers to people who do not have a job, have actively looked for work over the past month, and are currently available for work. *26*

CHAPTER QUIZ

1. How do Americans in general view social class and social mobility?
   a. Americans tend to think of themselves as upper or lower class.
   b. Americans think there is less opportunity for social mobility than there really is.
   c. The majority of Americans are optimistic about the potential for social mobility.
   d. Americans do not consider their society to be stratified.

2. How do Tumin, Davis, and Moore differ in their explanations for how income inequality functions in the United States?
   a. Davis and Moore argue that children born to wealthy parents lack strong work ethics, while Tumin believes the United States functions as a meritocracy.
   b. Tumin believes the United States is a meritocracy, while Davis and Moore think that economic rewards are unfairly distributed.
   c. Davis and Moore believe rewards are distributed on the basis superior skills, effort, talent, or hard work, while Tumin thinks that it is based on the influence and power associated with wealth.
   d. Tumin argues that inequality is inevitable and perhaps even necessary to the United States' economic stability, while Davis and Moore believe inequality is harmful.

3. Based on census data on income and employment, examining the wage gap between different groups suggests that over the past 10 years
   a. the gap in earnings between men and women has disappeared, thanks to the increased number of women obtaining advanced degrees.
   b. the gap in earnings between men and women has shrunk, while the gap between blacks and whites has remained relatively stagnant.
   c. the gap in earnings between blacks and whites has shrunk significantly, thanks to changes in educational policies.
   d. the gap in earnings between men and women has increased, due to the increase in single motherhood.

4. Over the past three decades, inequality levels in the United States have
   a. remained the same.
   b. periodically risen and fallen.
   c. risen steadily.
   d. fallen steadily.

5. According to 2008 census regional data,
   a. most of the states with the highest incomes and lowest poverty rates were concentrated in the Northeast.
   b. most of the states with the lowest incomes and highest poverty rates were concentrated in the Northeast.
   c. most of the states with the lowest unemployment rates were concentrated in the South.
   d. most of the states with the lowest incomes and highest poverty rates were spread out across the nation.

Answers: 1. c; 2. c; 3. b; 4. c; 5. a

ESSAY QUESTIONS

1. Discuss Americans' attitudes about social class, social mobility, and social stratification; how they differ from other countries; and whether you think the United States is a meritocracy.

2. Consider the advantages and disadvantages of the federal government setting the poverty line for the nation as a whole, as well as alternative approaches. Include a discussion of how the demographics of those in poverty might change with different standards.

3. In 2005, former Federal Reserve chairman Alan Greenspan said that "[high inequality] is not the type of thing which a democratic society—a capitalist democratic society—can really accept without addressing." Other economists have argued that inequality is inevitable or even necessary to a capitalist economy. Argue for or against whether income inequality is a problem for the United States.

4. Analyze regional or state-by-state economic differences and what factors might explain some of these differences.

5. Discuss how the recent recession and economic crisis have shaped the United States in terms of income, employment, and poverty, and how you think today's trends will impact Americans over the next decade.

SOURCES FOR FURTHER RESEARCH

U.S. Bureau of Labor Statistics CPI Inflation Calculator:
http://www.bls.gov/data/inflation_calculator.htm

Social class in the United States:
http://www.nytimes.com/pages/national/class/index.html

Unemployment data by state:
http://online.wsj.com/public/resources/documents/JOBSMAP09.html

Unemployment data by demographic:
http://www.nytimes.com/interactive/2009/11/06/business/economy/unemployment-lines.html

Labor force statistics:
http://www.census.gov/compendia/statab/cats/labor_force_employment_earnings.html

3 Issues of Race

Population shifts occur frequently as a result of economic boom or busts, immigration, and even natural disasters. Here, New Orleans is shown after Hurricane Katrina. (Caitlin Mirra/Shutterstock)

POPULATION CHANGES IN POST-KATRINA NEW ORLEANS

On August 29, 2005, Hurricane Katrina devastated much of the American Gulf Coast, including New Orleans, Louisiana, and surrounding cities.[1] The 2000 Census showed the population of New Orleans to be 484,674. But Hurricane Katrina caused a diaspora that brought the population of New Orleans down to only 343,829 by the time the 2010 Census was taken. That's a 29 percent decrease in just 10 years.[2]

The aftermath of such a tragic event is hard to fully assess. But a few key details are known already that dramatically affect the entire population of New Orleans. First, critical records were lost in the floodwaters. These records ranged from the deeds of homes and to historic photographs to birth records. Assessing the exact damage caused by the storm is made more difficult by the loss of these vital records. Residents who couldn't prove ownership of their homes found it difficult to access support services and file insurance paperwork.

Second, the laws of the state of Louisiana have been compromised by the population flux. Many laws on the books were written in a way that gave the city of New Orleans special privileges because of its high population numbers. Most of these legislative details were accomplished by exempting cities of more than 400,000 people from certain laws. Prior to Hurricane Katrina, New Orleans was the only city in Louisiana that qualified under these conditions. Now, no city in the state qualifies for special treatment under these criteria, and this could have enormous consequences for the economy and cultural integrity of New Orleans.[3]

Third, the population decrease affects the distribution of political power within New Orleans, Louisiana, and the entire United States. As we've already discussed, political representation is heavily based on population. The populations of certain neighborhoods in New Orleans vanished, such as in the Lower Ninth Ward, and redistricting has already affected not only legislative power but also schools, churches, health services, and other social services. In the federal government, one seat in the House of Representatives and its corresponding vote in the Electoral College were taken away from Louisiana.[4] Because it is unknown where all of the former residents of New Orleans now live, it is difficult to determine if they are being represented fairly. No states surrounding Louisiana gained representation following the 2010 Census except Texas, which picked up four seats.[5] The Houston area alone grew by about 140,000 people, and it may be the case that many from the hurricane-ravaged areas relocated there.[6]

Finally, the racial, socioeconomic, cultural, and age distribution within New Orleans has drastically changed. African-American residents have decreased from 67 percent of the population to 60 percent. This drop is most likely the result of those who previously lived in flooded neighborhoods and were forced to move in with family and friends elsewhere. Whites now account for 30 percent of the city, a larger percentage than in 2000, despite the fact that the White population in New Orleans has dropped by 24,000 residents since then. Scores of Latinos have moved into New Orleans to meet the demand for inexpensive construction labor. Many Latinos have moved to New Orleans and its suburbs, including Jefferson Parish, where the Latino population has grown by 65 percent. In addition, there are more than 50,000 fewer children in New Orleans, a drop of nearly 44 percent.[7] These statistics reflect a move within the social fabric. Whether these shifts will permanently change New Orleans or if the city will return to her former makeup remains to be seen.

Population changes related to post-Katrina New Orleans aren't as much of an anomaly as they might seem. The 2010 Census reveals black population shifts out of the Northern U.S. states as well. Since 1960, data have shown black populations steadily moving to Northern states, but 2010 data show a reverse trend. Black populations grew in the Southern United States and shrank in the North. States such as Illinois and Michigan saw declining black populations for the first time ever. More than 1 million current black residents of the South report having been born in the Northeast. That's 10 times the figure reported in 1970. While census data are helpful in tracking these trends, additional perspectives can help us evaluate why they occur.[8]

HISTORICAL BACKGROUND OF RACE IN AMERICA

To understand the significance of the racial makeup of the United States that the Census Bureau tracks, it is necessary to understand what race has meant in the American past. Like in most of the world, the United States has relied on race as a way to categorize people. These categorizations have resulted in slavery, armed conflicts, disenfranchisement, and undercurrents of racial tension since the moment European settlers landed on North American soil, if not earlier. Today, race is an important component of politics, religion, art, and many other facets of American life. A meaningful understanding of population data regarding race considers the data alongside historical and sociological perspectives.

The Concept of Race

But what exactly is race? Do biological differences actually exist among people of different races? Is there more to the differences in skin colors than there is to, say, hair or eye colors? Evolutionary biologist Joseph L. Graves sought to answer these very questions in *The Race Myth: Why We Pretend Race Exists in America*. In short, he found that genetically there is virtually no difference among people. He suggests instead that race is a social construct, not a biological truth.[9] Today, regular factors in life for Americans and people across the world, such as migration, intermarriage, and adoption, are further challenging racial categorization. Take President Barack Obama as an example. While he is identified most often as black, biologically, he is as much white as he is black. Even though his mother is white, he is considered African American by heritage because his father was Kenyan. But he experienced a life atypical to most African Americans; he was born in Hawaii, raised primarily by white family members, and lived part of his life overseas in an Asian and predominantly Muslim country. He has described himself as the embodiment of being an American "mutt," a label that illustrates just how unclear the distinctions between races have become.[10]

These issues of race raised by President Obama's biography are representative of many racial issues in the United States. To understand statistics and social scientific studies of race, it is important to know the difference between categorization by race and categorization by ethnicity. **Race** is the differentiation of people based on physical traits. The most obvious example of this is skin color, but other traits such as bone structure, hair, height, and facial features may be considered. **Ethnicity** is less physically based than race; it is the grouping of people who share heritage, be it national, linguistic, ancestral, or cultural. Because ethnic backgrounds have great variance, there are more ethnic groups worldwide than there are identified races. At the same time, there is no universal agreement on how many races exist or what they are. The same is true for ethnicity. For example, whites in the United States can ethnically be French-Canadian, Irish, Swedish, and so on, but they would likely categorize themselves as one race. And even within these classifications of ethnicity by national heritage, those from countries such as Ireland, Canada, and Cuba acknowledge subcategories of ethnicity based on other factors.[11]

As the American population continues to grow and change, traditional traits to distinguish among races, such as skin color and hair type, may become increasingly less valid. The important aspects of racial categorization, however, have less to with what the categorizations are than with what the categorizations mean for the experiences of individuals and groups of people within the United States. How does society interpret differences in appearance when determining the opportunities available to its members?

Whites currently make up about two-thirds of the U.S. population. Because of this, they are the **majority group**, meaning that they have greater representation in the population. As the majority group, whites also have the greatest access to political power and wealth, making them the dominant group as well. A **minority group** is often determined by the numeric representation among the population.[12] Minority groups have less power than the dominant group and often have a collective sense of being discriminated against.[13]

Race Definitions for the Census over Time

One of the few questions consistently asked by the Census Bureau since the first U.S. census in 1790 has to do with race. While definitions and categories of race have changed, it has always been a subject of interest for the census. It is interesting to consider why race would be so important in finding out how many people live in a state and how to divide up the House of Representatives. When looking at the issue of race in the census, the manner in which race has been defined has varied somewhat. There are essentially four phases of how the census has measured race in U.S. history.[14]

1790–1840 The first classification of race in the census dealt with race categories as they related to apportionment of government power, as well as issues of slavery. The early question for the government to answer was how to count slaves for apportionment of government power. They could not vote and had no political power, yet they were part of each state's population. Southern states stood to gain political power by counting them, but if blacks were counted as citizens, how could they continue to be enslaved? At the same time, Northern states were divided on whether or not they should count slaves at all. The 1787 Constitutional Convention settled on a compromise, known as the Three-Fifths Compromise: A slave would count as three-fifths of a person.[15]

The importance placed on race was related to the long-held belief that people of African descent and other non-whites were different from and inferior to the European colonists. Race was really only a factor in the census because the majority of slaves were black, and there were few free blacks at the time. Around the time of the American Revolution, to be a free white person was significantly different than to be a free black person or a Native American, neither of which shared the same legal rights as free citizens.[16] In fact, the 1800–1820 censuses asked for a record of all "free persons, except Indians."[17] The census in these early years asked almost no questions other than those related to population numbers based on race. It counted free white males, free white females, free blacks, and slaves.[18]

1850–1920 The 1850 Census marked a change in measuring race, as it introduced a new category of race: **Mulatto** identified people who descended from multiple races. This category was used, in part, because scientists convinced politicians that this category was warranted. In the United States, theorists held that people came from not one source genetically, but multiple sources. This was used to support the notion of different and unequal races. Because the races were distinct, a belief existed that a Mulatto would be significantly inferior to a person of "pure blood," or someone whose genealogy consisted of a single race. The inclusion of the Mulatto category served as the beginning of the use of census data by scientists. Beginning with the 1850 Census, scientists studying race would use the census for 80 years to test theories and discuss the differences among the races. There were obvious ulterior motives to counting the population based on racial categories. At the time, races weren't just considered different but were also differently valued. The notion of racial inferiority and superiority served the interests of those who wanted to hold onto slavery, as well as those who wished to support limited rights for blacks following the Civil War and eventual emancipation of slaves. Instructions for the 1870 Census included this dubious caution: "Be particularly careful in reporting the class *Mulatto*. The word is here generic and includes quadroons, octoroons, and all persons having any perceptible trace of African blood. Important scientific results depend upon the correct determination of this class." Thus, the Mulatto category was used to try to prove that mixed-race people would live shorter lives than whites in an attempt to prove a racial difference between whites and blacks.[19]

In this period, the effort to prove racial differences changed the categories for the 1890 Census again, adding Quadroon, Octoroon, Chinese, Japanese, and Indian to the preexisting categories of white, black, and Mulatto. The classification of black was used for people with at least three-fourths African heritage. Mulattos were persons who had three-eighths to five-eighths African heritage. A **Quadroon** was an individual with one-fourth black ancestors, and an **Octoroon** was a person who had one-eighth black blood. The motivating factor for these titles was the hope of proving that interracial marriage would create weak and frail people who would die more quickly than their pure-blooded white counterparts.

With the 1890 Census, all Native Americans were finally counted. Previously, only those who paid taxes, removed themselves from tribal relations, and lived as citizens in states or territories had been included, but now, the census counted all Native people living in the United States. This category was added to the census largely because there was a common belief in America that Native Americans were a vanishing race, and the census wanted to provide a count of them for historical purposes.[20]

1930–1960 The third phase in racial categorization in the U.S. census was 1930 through 1960. During this time, the Southern "one-drop" rule gained popularity. Hence, any trace of black blood would lead a person to be defined as black, and the categories accounting for mixed-race individuals were eliminated. If a person was of mixed race, the race was to be recorded as that of the non-white parent. In the 1940s and beyond, racial definitions took on an important part of the racial discussion. Nazism culminated the commonly held beliefs that ran throughout the world that races were different and whites were superior. The "one-drop" era suggested that clear differences existed between the races; however, this was not to last as a dominant belief in the United States.

The beginning of the civil rights movement in the 1950s and 1960s, as well as new scientific data, called into question the very notion of race. Issues of racism and inequality came to the forefront. But census definitions of race did not change much during this period. In fact, despite the new emphasis on race as a social construct, Census Bureau policy toward race remained relatively unchanged. However, one significant change did occur in 1960, when the census adopted the policy of self-definition of race. Since then, each person responding to the census, not a census taker, has self-identified his or her own race.[21]

1970–2010 The most recent period of census-taking saw racial and ethnic groups lobbying to be counted and considered as separate categories in the census. In the 1980 Census, for example, Hispanic origin was added in response to the efforts of Latino groups lobbying for its inclusion. The same was true for many Asian categories as well.[22] In 1977, the federal government defined Hispanic as an ethnicity, not a race. It also suggested that a mixed race/ethnicity person should select a race based on which one is most closely allied with the individual's sense of community, not merely his or her physical characteristics. Because of the increase in interracial marriage and the increase in interracial children being born, the Census Bureau reviewed this stance in the 1990s. After this review, census respondents were allowed to select more than one race for the first time in 2000. A multiracial category was instituted for the first time after more than 200 years of U.S. census taking.[23] The 2010 questionnaire listed 15 racial categories for the respondent. Here, too, the respondent could choose more than one race. As has been the case historically, Latino/Hispanic remained an ethnicity, and respondents were to select a race in addition to choosing this ethnicity.[24] The 2010 racial categories are listed in Table 3.1, along with all of the racial categories ever recognized by the U.S. Census Bureau.

Historical Variances in Census Racial Definitions

The categories of race found in the U.S. census from 1790 to the present day, as well as how race is determined, have changed many times to reflect the changes in American culture and politics. In the earliest censuses, the few racial options basically ignored those of mixed races, and it is unclear how those individuals were classified. However, their number is estimated to have been extremely small at the time. Racial definitions were based on little more than a census taker's interpretation of someone's appearance until the latter half of the 20th century.[26] When Mulatto, Quadroon, and Octoroon were not in use, a person of mixed white race was classified by the enumerator according to the non-white parent's race. This practice led to a classification of black that included a greater diversity of skin colors than the classification of white. It was not until 1960 that citizens had the right to define their own race; however, a person of two or more non-white races was identified as the race of his or her father until 1970. Because of self-identification and the newer option to select more than one race, it is difficult to accurately compare racial data from the U.S. censuses over long periods of time, especially regarding the mixed-race category.[27] A 70-year-old individual of African and Asian descent living today has likely been classified multiple ways by the Census Bureau during his or her life depending on the rules in use for each specific census.

The census continues to define Hispanic as an ethnicity and not a race. It has sometimes been defined by country of birth, parental country of birth, or native language. Prior to its

★ TABLE 3.1 U.S. CENSUS RACE CATEGORIES, 1790–2010[25] ★

Year	Categories
1790	Free White Males; Free White Females; All Other Free Persons; Slaves
1800	Free White Males; Free White Females; All Other Free Persons, except Indians Not Taxed; Slaves
1810	Free White Males; Free White Females; All Other Free Persons, except Indians Not Taxed; Slaves
1820	Free White Males; Free White Females; Free Colored Persons, All other persons, except Indians Not Taxed; Slaves
1830	Free White Persons; Free Colored Persons; Slaves
1840	Free White Persons; Free Colored Persons; Slaves
1850	Black; Mulatto
1860	Black; Mulatto; (Indian)
1880	White; Black; Mulatto; Chinese; Indian
1890	White; Black; Mulatto; Quadroon; Octoroon; Chinese; Japanese; Indian
1900	White: Black; Chinese; Japanese; Indian
1910	White; Black; Mulatto; Chinese; Japanese; Indian; Other; + write in
1920	White; Black; Mulatto; Indian; Chinese; Japanese; Filipino; Hindu; Korean; Other; + write in
1930	White; Negro; Mexican; Indian; Chinese; Japanese; Filipino; Hindu; Korean; (Other races, spell out in full)
1940	White; Negro; Indian; Chinese; Japanese; Filipino; Hindu; Korean; (Other races, spell out in full)
1950	White; Negro; Indian; Japanese; Chinese; Filipino; (Other races, spell out)
1960	White; Negro; American Indian; Japanese; Chinese; Filipino; Hawaiian; Part-Hawaiian; Aleut Eskimo, etc.
1970	White; Negro or Black; American Indian; Japanese; Chinese; Filipino; Hawaiian; Korean; Other (print race)
1980	White; Negro or Black; Japanese; Chinese; Filipino; Korean; Vietnamese; American Indian; Asian Indian; Hawaiian; Guamanian; Samoan; Eskimo; Aleut; Other (specify)
1990	White; Black or Negro; American Indian; Eskimo; Aleut; Chinese; Filipino; Hawaiian; Korean; Vietnamese; Japanese; Asian Indian; Samoan; Guamanian; Other API (Asian or Pacific Islander); Other race
2000	White; Black, African American, or Negro; American Indian or Alaska Native; Asian Indian; Chinese; Filipino; Japanese; Korean; Vietnamese; Native Hawaiian; Guamanian or Chamorro; Samoan; Other Asian (Print Race); Other Pacific Islander; Some other race
2010	White, Black; American Indian or Alaskan Native; Asian Indian; Chinese; Filipino; Japanese, Korean; Vietnamese; Native Hawaiian; Guamanian or Chamorro; Samoan; Other Asian (Print Race); Other Pacific Islander; Some other race

recognition as an ethnicity, the Latino population of the United States was recorded in very inconsistent ways. As shown in Table 1, the 1930 Census had a racial category of Mexican. This was the only year for this specific ethnic group's identification as a race. The 1940 Census dropped the Mexican classification and instructed enumerators to classify Latinos as white Spanish speakers. Other censuses used data on Spanish surnames and parental country of birth to account for Latinos.[28]

Because of these variances in methods of classification, accurate racial comparisons are very hard to achieve. Decades that shared the same methods of classification are easy to compare with each other, such as the 2000 and 2010 censuses. But it is very difficult to compare data from 1790 to 1850, 1860 to 1910, 1950 to 2000, and especially 1790, the earliest census, to 2010. But it is clear that, along with American attitudes about race, the racial makeup of the United States has changed drastically.[29]

IMMIGRATION TO THE UNITED STATES

Other than Native Americans, all categories of race have come about due to the influx of immigrants. It is true that at one point in time everyone living in this country, except for Native Americans, was an immigrant. Just as the internal migration patterns today have an impact on population data, as discussed at the beginning of this chapter, each wave of immigration to the United States has influenced the country and the way the Census Bureau has counted the nation's people. The recent addition of more racial categories is due largely to the immigration of millions of people.

What Is Immigration?

Immigration creates sharp racial and ethnic tensions. **Voluntary immigration** is the willing movement of people from one social system, often a nation, to another. Many voluntary immigrants migrate in search of jobs, freedoms, and opportunities that aren't available in their place of birth. However, the countries receiving these immigrants, and their current residents, are not always eager to welcome immigrant groups. This hostility has been a common reality of U.S. history, and different groups have borne the brunt of it at different times. The Irish, Italian, and Swedish, among many other specific European ethnicities, have been vilified upon arriving in the United States. Even though their descendants are now classified as white, they were not always accepted into the dominant culture. More recently, non-white immigrant groups have been the target of similar vilification.[30] Today, some of the strongest currents of anti-immigration are directed toward Latinos.[31] The fear that multiculturalism is watering down American culture leads to **xenophobia**, the fear of foreign groups and their customs, which exists in some form in most countries around the world.

History of Immigration to the United States

1600s–early 1700s	1820–1880	1880–1920	1960s–present
There were no significant immigration restrictions for free white men. Most immigrants came from the British Isles, with English, Scottish, Welsh, and Ulster Irish groups gravitating toward different colonies and regions. Additionally, some immigrants came from France, the Netherlands, and other areas.	About 15 million immigrants entered the United States, many to work in agriculture in the American Midwest. Generally, immigrants came from Northern Europe and Ireland.	The largest single mass migration in U.S. history occurred during this time, with most immigrants traveling from Southern Europe, Russia, and Poland. These immigrants mostly found work in cities.	During the Cold War, many refugees fleeing communism entered the United States. These included Cuban, Vietnamese, Chinese, and Russian immigrants. Latino immigration rose as well during this period, including immigrants with or without proper documentation.

Figure 3.1 Sources: Hasia Diner, "Immigration and U.S. History," February 13, 2008, America.gov, http://www.america.gov/st/diversity-english/2008/February/20080307112004ebyessedo0.1716272.html; Alejandro Portes & Ruben Rumbaut, *Immigrant America: A Portrait, 2nd Edition* (Los Angeles: University of California Press, 1996); U.S. Department of Homeland Security, *Yearbook of Immigration Statistics: 2007* (Washington, D.C.: U.S. Department of Homeland Security, Office of Immigration Statistics, 2008) http://www.dhs.gov/xlibrary/assets/statistics/yearbook/2007/ois_2007_yearbook.pdf

African Americans have often been the victims of racial hatred as well, even though the vast majority originally arrived on U.S. soil at the hands of whites through **involuntary immigration**, which is forcibly removing people from one society and bringing them to another society. Native Americans have also been the victims of involuntary immigration because they were removed from their lands against their will many times throughout American history.[32]

Because of the unique challenges presented to immigrants and their families, many live in concentrated **ethnic enclaves**, neighborhoods that are characterized by a particular culture, race, or ethnicity. Often, these enclaves allow groups who would otherwise be in the minority to exercise more power than they could in the larger society. Politically, minority groups may work together to have a better chance of influencing local, state, and even national elections. Many immigrants flock to these enclaves to minimize racial discrimination or linguistic obstacles, to use networking connections for jobs, or to live among others who share specific religious or cultural values. Usually by the second or third generation, immigrants choose to leave these enclaves and become more fully assimilated into the dominant American culture.[33]

Who Migrates and Why?

As with individuals within any group, each immigrant has a unique life story and different reasons for coming to the United States. **Refugees** are immigrants who leave their country of origin in order to avoid harm; they are often seeking physical safety, religious freedom, or political freedom. Since 1980, the United States has granted **asylum**, or shelter from harm, to individuals who can prove that persecution or physical danger awaits them at home.[34]

Unlike refugees, other immigrants come to the United States to seek work that they do not have access to in their home country. **Labor immigrants**, who migrate to find work, are very common. Many people enter the United States under work visas after going through the proper channels of obtaining work before arriving. Others enter without documentation. Regardless, immigrants tend to fill low-wage, heavy-labor jobs. Labor immigrants are vital to the U.S. economy, even though as a group they are often perceived as a problem, because they fill jobs that few want and are willing to take them at low wages. The longer they are in the country, however, the more they seek wages and jobs similar to the existing population.[35]

Professional immigrants migrate to the United States because they have special skills that are needed in the country to which they move. In the United States, these immigrants often work at universities or in technology-based businesses; they might be engineers, doctors, or professors. While the United States is enriched by their presence, one big drawback to this type of emigration is the "brain drain" it creates in their home countries. The brain drain is when the best and brightest of a nation leave and take their skills elsewhere. Nations that cannot match the rewards offered to these individuals suffer deficits of human capital within their own borders. Likewise, **entrepreneurial immigrants** take their business aspirations away from their home country and bring them to a new nation. Entrepreneurial immigrants want to start their own businesses in a different country; in the past, many came to the United States to farm the abundant and available land. Today, entrepreneurial immigrants can be restaurant owners, venture capitalists, or attorneys opening their own firms.[36]

Foreign-Born Residents

Because of the many large and small waves of immigration throughout American history, detailed records of countries of origin are extremely helpful in accurately identifying the United States' new residents. From 1820 through 1840, census enumerators were asked to note if U.S. residents were foreigners without specifying their birthplace. This lack of specification was not helpful in separating actual foreign-born residents from the children of foreign-born immigrants, who are also considered immigrants, albeit a generation removed. Beginning in 1850, the census has attempted to keep records of the birthplaces of all foreign-born residents of the United States for more accurate data.[37]

The foreign-born population of the United States has increased and decreased over time. When the first European settlers arrived in North America, the only non-foreign-born residents were Native Americans. Even the Founding Father Alexander Hamilton was foreign born. More recently, foreign-born Americans have filled some of the most powerful roles within the federal government. Madeleine Albright and Henry Kissinger, both former U.S. secretaries of state, were born in Czechoslovakia and Germany, respectively.[38] More recent trends are hard to project because it is hard to predict if immigration to the United States is currently peaking or will continue to grow. But it is clear that no matter the future trends, the United States has seen a considerable increase in immigration since 1970.

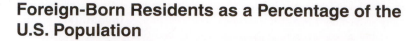

Foreign-Born Residents as a Percentage of the U.S. Population

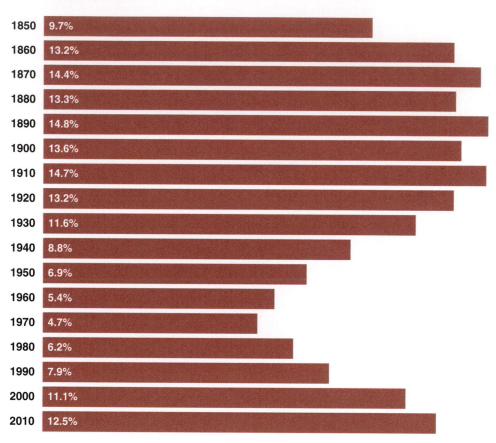

Year	Percentage
1850	9.7%
1860	13.2%
1870	14.4%
1880	13.3%
1890	14.8%
1900	13.6%
1910	14.7%
1920	13.2%
1930	11.6%
1940	8.8%
1950	6.9%
1960	5.4%
1970	4.7%
1980	6.2%
1990	7.9%
2000	11.1%
2010	12.5%

*Estimated based on 2009 America Community Survey Data. 2010 Census data unavailable at time of publication.

Figure 3.2 Sources: Campbell Gibson & E. Lennon, "Historical Census Statistics on the Foreign-Born Population of the United States: 1850–1990," in *Population Division Working Paper No. 29* (Washington, D.C.: U.S. Census Bureau, 1999); Nolan Malone, Karri F. Baluja, Joseph M. Costanzo, & Cynthis J. Davis, *The Foreign-Born Population: 2000 Census Brief* (Washington, D.C.: U.S. Census Bureau, 2000) http://www.census.gov/prod/2003pubs/c2kbr-34.pdf; Elizabeth M. Grieco & Edward N. Trevelyan, *Place of Birth of the Foreign-Born Population: 2009* (Washington, D.C.: U.S. Census Bureau, 2010) http://www.census.gov/prod/2010pubs/acsbr09-15.pdf

2000 FINDINGS ON RACE

The 2000 Census asked all respondents to provide both their race and ethnicity. A 1977 policy directive set the general categories for race as white, black, Asian, and Native American or Alaska Native. Categories for ethnicity were simply Hispanic and non-Hispanic. Respondents who selected Hispanic ethnically were also required to select a race, so the same person could be counted as ethnically Hispanic and racially white. In the 2000 Census, respondents were also allowed to select more than one race, so even more data might appear to overlap. Essentially, the 2000 data can be examined in regard to five major racial/ethnic groups: non-Hispanic white, black, Asian, Native American or Alaska Native, and Hispanic or Latino.[39]

Non-Hispanic White

In the year 2000, non-Hispanic whites made up 69.1 percent of the entire U.S. population.[40] Among them, 51.1 percent were female and 48.9 percent were male. For both white females and white males, those between the ages of 35 and 50 represent most of the population. One interesting finding was that while 1.4 percent of white women were above the age of 85, only 0.5 percent of white men were above the age of 85.[41] While the national average household size in

Region of Birth among Foreign-Born U.S. Residents

† Data from America Community Survey Data. 2010 Census data unavailable at time of publication.
* Data not available.

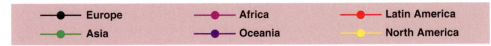

Figure 3.3 Sources: Campbell Gibson & E. Lennon, "Historical Census Statistics on the Foreign-Born Population of the United States: 1850–1990," in *Population Division Working Paper No. 29* (Washington, D.C.: U.S. Census Bureau, 1999); Nolan Malone, Karri F. Baluja, Joseph M. Costanzo, & Cynthis J. Davis, *The Foreign-Born Population: 2000 Census Brief* (Washington, D.C.: U.S. Census Bureau, 2000) http://www.census.gov/prod/2003pubs/c2kbr-34.pdf; Elizabeth M. Grieco & Edward N. Trevelyan, *Place of Birth of the Foreign-Born Population: 2009* (Washington, D.C.: U.S. Census Bureau, 2010) http://www.census.gov/prod/2010pubs/acsbr09-15.pdf

the 2000 Census was 2.6, those living in a home with a white **householder**—the person through whom all other persons on a household's census are identified, usually the owner or primary renter of the home—averaged at only 2.4 per home.[42]

In the realms of education and economics, non-Hispanic white Americans fared quite well in the 2000 Census. The highest of any racial group, 86 percent of whites graduated from high school, and nearly 10 percent of those who completed a bachelor's degree went on to earn a graduate or professional degree. This translated to the lowest unemployment rate in 2000, at 4.3 percent. This high rate of employment is reflected in the median income of white householder homes, $45,367, which was slightly above the national average of $41,994. And while Asian households boasted the highest median income in 2000, whites were by far the most likely to be homeowners rather than renters: 72.5 percent of white households were occupied by homeowners. Similarly favorable toward whites was the poverty line; only 8.1 percent of whites, roughly one out of every 12, lived below the poverty line, the lowest rate among all racial/ethnic groups. In metropolitan areas, 67.7 percent of the population was white, and whites represented 73.2 percent of the population in nonmetropolitan areas.[43]

Black

Blacks made up 12.3 percent of the U.S. population in 2000, of which 47.5 percent were male and 52.5 percent female. This gender spread represents the largest discrepancy among all the races reported on the census. A disproportionately high percentage of black men fell in the 5 to 20 age range, and there was a notable sharp decline in their numbers beginning at age 50. The same was true for black women aged 5 to 20 as well, but they lived longer: 0.7 percent were over the age of 85, while only 0.2 percent of black males were over 85. Homes with black householders had an average of 2.7 occupants, slightly more than the national average of 2.6 occupants.[44]

In the realm of education and economics, blacks graduated from high school at a rate of 72 percent, and 5 percent continued beyond college to attain advanced graduate degrees. Corresponding data on employment showed that 11.6 percent of blacks were unemployed in

2000, markedly higher than the national average of 5.8 percent. This low rate of employment is reflected in the median income of black householder homes of $29,423, significantly below the national average of $41,994. Fewer than half of black homes are occupied by their owners, with the data in 2000 showing a 46.3 percent ownership rate. Nearly one-fourth of all blacks lived below the poverty line in 2000. Blacks made up nearly the same percentage of the population in both metropolitan and nonmetropolitan areas, at 12.1 percent and 11.9 percent, respectively.[45]

Asian

The U.S. population's makeup was 3.6 percent Asian in the year 2000, with 51.7 percent female and 48.3 percent male. For both Asian females and Asian males, those aged 25 to 40 were most numerous. As with Hispanics, fewer Asian Americans were above age 85 than other age groups, weighing in at 0.2 percent of men and 0.4 percent of women. Recent immigration of younger individuals could be a factor in this finding. Homes with Asian householders had significantly more occupants than the national average, coming in at 3.1 occupants per household.[46]

In terms of economics and education, Asians boasted the highest percentage of their populace who go on to complete an advanced graduate degree after college: 17 percent. Asians graduated high school at the rate of 80 percent and were employed above the national average, with only 5.1 percent unemployed. These higher-than-average rates of employment and education are reflected in the median income of Asian householder homes. Asian Americans have the highest median income, at $51,908, nearly $10,000 above the national average of $41,994. Just over half of Asian homes are occupied by their owners, with the data in 2000 showing a 53.4 percent ownership rate. Roughly one of every eight Asians, or 12.6 percent, lived below the poverty line in 2000. Asian Americans were slightly more numerous in metropolitan areas, making up 3.9 percent of the population. They represented 2.8 percent of the nonmetropolitan areas.[47]

Native American or Alaska Native

Native Americans accounted for only 0.9 percent of the total U.S. population in 2000. They were the most evenly distributed by sex, with 49.9 percent male and 50.2 percent female. Like Hispanics, Native Americans and Alaska Natives boast a very young populace; both men and women weighed in the most heavily between the ages of 5 and 20. Similarly, only 0.2 percent of Native American and Alaska Native males and 0.3 percent of females were over the age of 85. But unlike with Hispanics, the young populace is not easily explained by recent immigration trends.[48] A variety of factors could contribute to this finding, among which known health problems in the Native American community is foremost.[49] It is also possible that Native American adults identify with another race, while those under the age of 15 are racially identified by their caregivers. Homes with Native American and Alaska Native householders also had an average of 3.1 occupants, significantly more than the national average.[50]

In terms of education and subsequent economic status, data on Native Americans and Alaska Natives suggest they were struggling to get ahead in 2000. While 71 percent graduated high school, only 4 percent went on to receive an advanced graduate degree. Both of these numbers are second lowest only to Hispanics, as will be discussed in the next section, but the Native American unemployment rate was the highest of all races, at 12.4 percent, more than twice the national average. This low rate of employment was reflected in the median income of Native American and Alaska Native householder homes of $30,599, significantly below the national average of $41,994. Just over half of Native American homes were occupied by homeowners, with the data in 2000 showing a 55.5 percent ownership rate, second highest behind white ownership. But just over one-fourth of Native Americans and Alaska Natives lived below the poverty line in 2000, weighing in at 25.7 percent. While American Indians made up just half a percent of the metropolitan population, they accounted for 1.3 percent in nonmetropolitan areas.[51]

Hispanic or Latino

Those identifying as Hispanic ethnically on the 2000 Census made up 12.6 percent of the general population. The majority of Hispanic Americans were men, making up 51.4 percent, while women made up the remaining 48.6 percent. In stark comparison to whites, Latino Americans had higher numbers of young people, with the ages of 15 to 30 being the most common among

Latino men and the ages of birth through 15 being most common among Latino women. In fact, those under the age of 30 accounted for 30.7 percent of Latino men and 27.6 percent of Latino women. Those over the age of 85 only accounted for 0.1 percent of Latino men and 0.3 percent of Latino women. While these numbers could be interpreted as showing that Hispanics do not live long lives, the data available regarding recent immigration suggest another story. Hispanic immigration has been on the rise in the past few decades, and these numbers are indicative of young Latinos making their homes in the United States. Future censuses should tell a more complete story. Hispanics did boast the largest average household size, with 3.6 occupants, one whole person greater than the national average of 2.6.[52]

Educationally, Hispanics had the lowest numbers for both high school and graduate degrees, 52 and 4 percent, respectively. On a related note, Hispanics over the age of 16 suffered unemployment at 9.3 percent, significantly greater than the national average in 2000. This low rate of employment was reflected in the median income of Hispanic householder homes, at $33,676, significantly below the national average of $41,994. Fewer than half of Hispanic homes were occupied by homeowners, with the data in 2000 showing a 45.7 percent ownership rate. Roughly two out of every nine Hispanic Americans, 22.6 percent, lived below the poverty line in 2000. More Hispanics lived in metropolitan areas, where they represented 13.8 percent of the population compared to 9.1 percent in nonmetropolitan areas.[53]

2010 FINDINGS ON RACE

Although it is difficult to compare censuses with vastly different racial and ethnic categories, such as between 1790 and 2000, we can more easily consider racial and ethnic group changes between 2000 and 2010. Looking at similar data taken from the 2010 Census allows us to compare and contrast not only among all of the major groups we are studying, but also among the same groups a decade apart. However, while comparing 2000 to 2010, the significant economic recession must be taken into account. When the census was taken in 2010, many Americans were still suffering severely from job loss and low incomes. In addition, the average household size of each racial and ethnic group was unavailable at the time of publication. But we do know that the national average household size held steady at 2.6 occupants, an unexpected finding. The national average household size had been steadily declining in previous decades, so this leveling off could be due to the economic recession or the surge in immigration groups who tend to have larger than average household size, as seen in Asian and Hispanic homes from the 2000 Census data.[54]

Non-Hispanic White

As of 2010, non-Hispanic Whites made up 64.9 percent of the U.S. population, a decrease of just over 4 percent from 2000. White women slightly outnumbered White men, totaling 50.9 and 49.1 percent of their race, respectively. White women were still the most likely of all racial groups differentiated by sex to live past 85 years old; 1.6 percent of white women achieved this longevity of life, while only 0.7 percent of white men did.

Educationally, it is clear that there was an increase among whites who received an advanced graduate degree, from 10 percent of whites in 2000 to 11.6 percent in 2010. While the economic recession complicates the comparison of economic data between 2000 and 2010, we can still examine how the recession impacted each racial and ethnic group. Whites boasted a lower than average rate of unemployment at 8.4 percent for those over the age of 16. This is lower than the national average of 9.9 percent and is the second lowest unemployment rate behind Asian Americans. These numbers are consistent with the higher than average median income for white householders, which came in at $54,671. The national average for all races was $50,221 in 2010. Nearly 73 percent of whites lived in a home owned by someone in the household, while only 27 percent rented from an outside owner. Only 10 percent of white households lived below the national poverty line in 2010, the lowest of all racial and ethnic groups. The proportion of whites living in metropolitan and nonmetropolitan areas didn't change much since 2000. In 2010, they made up 61.8 percent of the metropolitan population and 69.7 percent of the nonmetropolitan population.[55]

Black

Black Americans constituted 12.1 percent of the general population in 2010, a very slight decrease from 12.3 percent in 2000. Black females had a large edge as the majority over men, totaling 52.4 and 47.7 percent, respectively. Only 0.3 percent of black males were over the age of 85, while 0.8 percent of black females were over 85. Educational data are hard to compare between 2000 and 2010, but it is clear that there is a marked increase among blacks who received an advanced graduate degree, increasing from 5 percent in 200 to 6.1 percent in 2010. Blacks suffered greatly during the late-2000s financial crisis, surpassing the 9.9 percent national unemployment rate with an unemployment rate of 16.2 percent. Black households had a median income of just $33,463, the lowest in the nation, and 26 percent of black households lived below the national poverty line. Nearly 45 percent of blacks lived in a home owned by someone in the household, while 55 percent rented from an outside owner. The percentage of blacks in metropolitan and nonmetropolitan areas changed by just a few tenths of percent since 2000; they represented 12.4 percent and 11.6 percent of the populations, respectively.[56]

Asian

Of the U.S. population in 2010, 4.5 percent were Asian, meaning that Asian Americans represented one more out of every 100 people in America in 2010 than in 2000. Among them, 48 percent of Asians were male and 52 percent were female. Of Asian men, 0.4 percent were over the age of 85, and 0.6 percent of Asian females were over 85. Educational data show that Asians were already the most likely in 2000 to receive advanced graduate degrees, but in 2010, one out of every five held an advanced degree, weighing in at 20.2 percent, up from 17 percent 10 years prior. Asians fared the best during the late-2000s recession, with an unemployment rate of 7.7 percent and median income of $68,780 for households with Asian householders, the highest of all racial and ethnic groups. Almost 60 percent of Asian Americans lived in a home owned by someone in the household in 2010, while 40 percent rented from an outside owner. Only 11 percent of Asian households lived below the national poverty line in 2010. Asians represented an increased percentage of the population in both metropolitan and non-metropolitan areas in 2010, when they accounted for 5.0 percent and 3.7 percent, respectively.[57]

Native American or Alaska Native

In 2000, 0.9 percent of the American population was Native American or Alaska Native. But 2010 data showed a steep decline. Only 0.6 percent of the American population was Native American or Alaska Native, a decline of 33 percent in only 10 years. Men made up 49.3 percent of the Native American and Alaska Native population in 2010, and 0.2 percent of them were over the age of 85. Women made up 50.7 percent of the Native American and Alaska Native population in 2010, and 0.4 percent of them were over 85. Educationally, the data are hard to compare between 2000 and 2010, but it is clear that there was a slight increase among Native Americans and Alaska Natives who held an advanced graduate degree, increasing from 4 percent in 2000 to 4.5 percent in 2010. Native Americans and Alaska Natives suffered greatly during the late-2000s recession, surpassing the 9.9 percent national rate of unemployment with an unemployment rate of 15.8 percent. And while the median household income across the entire United States was $50, 221 in 2010, Native American and Alaska Native households had a median income of only $35,381. Nearly 55 percent of Native Americans and Alaska Natives lived in a home owned by someone in the household, while 45 percent rented from an outside owner. In 2010, 27 percent of Native American and Alaska Native households lived below the national poverty line. The percentage of Native Americans in metropolitan and non-metropolitan areas was unchanged from 2000 to 2010.[58]

Hispanic or Latino

Showing an increase from the 2000 number, 15.8 percent of the U.S. population in 2010 identified themselves as Hispanic, making this the largest minority group in the country. Hispanics were the only group with more men than women, at 51.7 percent and 48.3 percent, respectively. Just 0.2 percent of Hispanic men were over the age of 85 in 2010, while twice that percentage of Hispanic women was older than 85. Educationally, the data are hard to compare between 2000 and 2010, but perhaps of great significance, Hispanic Americans showed no increase in the number of advanced degree holders. Both 2000 and 2010 data reflect that 4 percent of Hispanics achieved this level of education. Hispanics also suffered during the late-2000s recession, surpassing the national rate of unemployment with a rate of 11.9 percent. And while the median household income across the entire United States was $50, 221 in 2010, Hispanic households had a median income of only $39,923. Among Hispanics, 48 percent lived in a home owned by someone in the household, while 52 percent rented from an outside owner. And in 2010, 24 percent of Hispanic households lived below the national poverty line.[59]

2000 FINDINGS ON FOREIGN-BORN POPULATION

Racial differences in the United States are changing in part because of immigration. Just exactly how much immigration exists is difficult to measure because it is estimated that many immigrants come to the United States illegally. One way to look at this issue is to review the census data on foreign-born individuals.

Between 1990 and 2000, the foreign-born residents within the United States increased from 19.8 million to 31.1 million. This changed the total percentage of foreign-born individuals within the U.S. population from 8 percent in 1990 to 11 percent in 2000, with a growth rate of about 57 percent. The growth between 1990 and 2000 meant that many more people in the United States were likely to know a foreign-born resident. Even states where the foreign-born population was previously low, such as Georgia, which only boasted a 2.7 foreign-born percentage in 1990, were impacted by this growth; in 2000, 7.1 percent of Georgians were foreign-born. That is an increase of more than 162 percent. However, the three states with the highest percentage of foreign-born residents, California, New York, and Texas, were home to more than half of all foreign-born residents in 2000. Los Angeles County, California, was home to just over one out of every 10, or 3.4 million, foreign-born residents in 2000. Large cities such as Los Angeles, New York, Chicago, and Houston were home to more foreign-born residents than smaller cities.[60]

In 2000, the citizenship status of the foreign-born population did not increase along with the foreign-born population increase. Less than half, or 40 percent, of foreign-born residents had become U.S. citizens by 2000. The top 10 countries of birth for foreign-born residents of the United States in 2000 were, in descending order, Mexico, China, the Philippines, India, Vietnam, Cuba, Korea, Canada, El Salvador, and Germany. More than half, 51.7 percent, were born in Latin America, with Mexican births accounting for 29.5 percent of that number. Behind Latin America, Asia was home to the second most births of immigrants, at 26.4 percent. In addition, foreign-born residents of the United States were at the prime working age; 59 percent of foreign-born residents, compared to 42 percent of native residents, were between the ages of 25 and 54.[61]

2010 FINDINGS ON FOREIGN-BORN POPULATION

In 2010, the foreign-born population in the United States increased to 38.5 million. While this shows a bit of a slow-down when compared to the data from 1990 to 2000, it was still a growth of about 24 percent from 2000. In 2010, of the 307 million residents of the United States, one in eight was foreign-born. More than half of the foreign-born residents lived in four states: California, New York, Texas, and Florida. California had the largest number of foreign-born residents, at 9.9 million, which is more than one-fourth of all foreign-born residents in the United States. New York had less than half as many as California, with 4.2 million. Texas and Florida had 4 million and 3.5 million foreign-born residents, respectively.[62]

Marking a very dramatic increase, 58 percent of foreign-born residents were noncitizens in 2010. This increase is substantial after this statistic remained unchanged between 1990 and 2000.[63] The top 10 countries of birth among foreign-born residents were Mexico (29.8 percent), China (5.2 percent), the Philippines (4.5 percent), India (4.3 percent), El Salvador (3.0 percent), Vietnam (3.0 percent), Korea (2.6 percent), Cuba (2.6 percent), Canada (2.1 percent), and Guatemala (2.1 percent). All Latin American births account for 53.1 percent of foreign-born births among U.S. residents.

STATE-BY-STATE COMPARISON

Just as immigrants tend to live in enclaves upon their arrival in a new land, so too do racial minorities tend to form their own communities within the larger white-dominant American culture. For this reason, the overall racial breakdown in the United States is not equally represented within all 50 states. Upon looking at the non-Hispanic white map, it is clear that whites are represented widely in the entire United States. Some pockets of decreased White population, such as in New Mexico and South Dakota, correspond with Native American reservations. The correspondingly high percentage of Native Americans can also be seen on the corresponding map. There are also fewer whites in South Texas, which corresponds with the large percentage of Mexican immigrants inhabiting those lands. It must be noted that while many view whites as the

State-by-State Racial Population Percentages

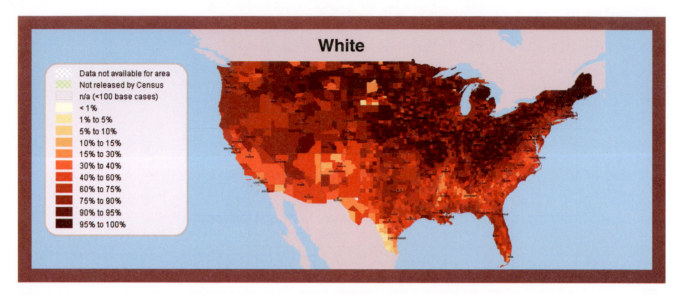

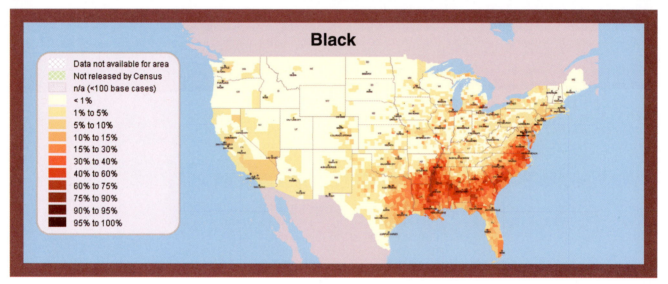

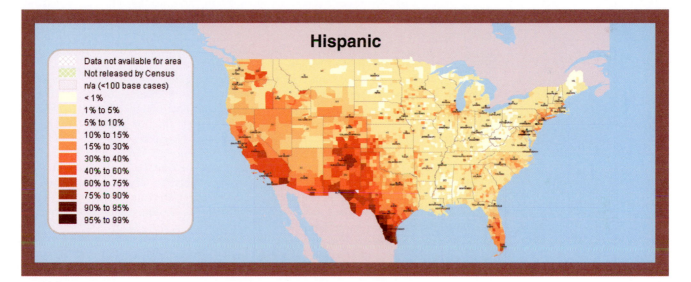

Figure 3.4 Sources: Social Explorer, *"1790 to Present,"* U.S. Decennial Census Files, http://www.socialexplorer.com/pub/home/home.aspx

American default race, both Native Americans and Native Mexicans occupied U.S. soil long before whites. Whites have done the most displacing of peoples throughout American history. This fact is important in the study of geography and racial classes, because the conflict over land is often caused by centuries-old invasions, not simply current disputes. Some racial groups, such as Asians, do not have the same claims to American soil, so their exact placement within the United States has less historical significance. Some states, especially border states with higher than average percentages of immigrants, boast higher numbers of foreign-born immigrants and racial minority groups simply because they are on the border, not because of historical ties to the land.

It is clear from the non-Hispanic black map that blacks in the United States are largely still concentrated in states with historically significant ties to slavery-based economies, such as Mississippi, Alabama, and Georgia. While blacks make up a large percentage of the population in the South, they did not originally choose these locations as their homes; rather, they were forcibly immigrated and placed where it best suited white plantation owners. More recently, however, many black Americans moved away from the South into other regions during the Great Migration of the early 20th century. This migration established many black communities in the West and Midwest, where jobs could be found. However, as stated earlier in this chapter, many blacks are now migrating back to the South in search of work.

As with blacks, the non-Hispanic Native American and Alaska Native map is heavily influenced by the fact that Native Americans were placed in certain geographic reservations by the federal government. Upon removal from their tribal lands in the East, many tribes were forcibly migrated to the current locations for their reservations, which show up well on the map. Although home to many nonnative whites, Alaska remains home to Alaska Natives, hence their heavy representation in their homeland.

Current statistics show both Asian and Hispanic groups concentrated heavily in California. While Asian Americans make up a much smaller percentage of the population than Hispanics in California, their economic and educational presence is heavily felt, as explained when comparing the data among the racial groups from 2000 and 2010. Asians are also notably present in the Mid-Atlantic region, particularly New Jersey, Maryland, and New York, and Houston, Texas, shows a heavy Asian population as well. Hispanics are seen most heavily in South Texas, with some counties nearing 100 percent Hispanic. New Mexico, Southern Arizona, and California show similarly strong populations of Hispanics. While the states of the Southwest are the most natural landing place for Mexican immigrants, Florida is the most natural landing place for Cuban and Puerto Rican immigrants, as reflected by the strong Hispanic showing in Florida.

The data and perspectives represented in this chapter reflect changing cultural attitudes, migration patterns, and lifestyle trends as they relate to race. These demographic shifts are affected by everything from natural disasters like Hurricane Katrina to the economic recession impacting the international community. Factors like these are difficult enough to predict, but the Census Bureau also has a history of changing the way it classifies and collects race data. Although this creates a challenge for comparing data from one census to another, these changes also provide their own historical account of race in the United States.

KEY TERMS

Race is the differentiation of people based on physical traits. *35*

Ethnicity is the grouping of people who share heritage. *35*

Majority group is the subset of the general population holding the most power. *35*

Minority group is a subset of the general population with less power than the majority group. *35*

Mulatto was a term to describe a person of mixed race. *36*

Quadroon was a term to describe an individual with one-fourth black ancestors. *36*

Octoroon was a term to describe a person who had one-eighth black ancestors. *36*

Voluntary immigration is the willing movement of people from one social system, often a nation, to another. *38*

Xenophobia is the fear of foreigners and their customs. *38*

Involuntary immigration is the forced removal of people from one society and bringing them to another society. *39*

Ethnic enclaves are neighborhoods characterized by a particular culture, race, or ethnicity *39*

Refugees are immigrants who leave their country of origin in order to avoid harm. *39*

Asylum is shelter from harm. *39*

Labor immigrants are people who migrate to find work. *39*

Professional immigrants are people who migrate to the United States because they have special skills or experiences that this country desires. *39*

Entrepreneurial immigrants are people who want to start their own business in a new country. *39*

Householder is the term used to indicate the person through whom all other persons on a household's census are identified, often the owner or primary renter of the home. *41*

CHAPTER QUIZ

1. Which of these details cannot be used as a factor in determining race?
   a. Place of birth
   b. Eye color
   c. Skeletal structure
   d. Skin color

2. Which of the following factors does not contribute to a person's ethnicity?
   a. Spoken language
   b. Religion
   c. Nationality
   d. Neighborhood of residence

3. What was the first year all residents of the United States were able to select their own race on the census?
   a. 1850
   b. 1890
   c. 1950
   d. 1960

4. What was the total foreign-born population in 2010?
   a. 19.7 million
   b. 31.1 million
   c. 38.5 million
   d. 41.2 million

5. What racial group was the most likely to attain an advanced graduate degree in both 2000 and 2010?
   a. Whites
   b. Blacks
   c. Native Americans and Alaska Natives
   d. Asians

Answers: 1. a; 2. d; 3. d; 4. c; 5. d

ESSAY QUESTIONS

1. Using President Barack Obama as a case study, compare and contrast his race, ethnicity, and upbringing. How might he have been categorized on the U.S. census in 1850, 1890, 1940, and 2010?

2. What is the distinguishing characteristic that determines a group of people as a minority group? Aside from race, describe what other factors can classify a group as a minority.

3. Discuss why there was such a specific interest in mixed-race individuals on the 1850–1890 censuses. Compare and contrast this racially based gathering of data to similar events in world history.

4. Analyze why immigrant, racial, and ethnic groups settle in enclaves. How might life have been more difficult for those who didn't live in an ethnic neighborhood?

5. Compare and contrast the citizenship statuses of foreign-born immigrants from 1990, 2000, and 2010. How do you think citizenship status might affect educational attainment, ability to own property, and other social factors?

SOURCES FOR FURTHER RESEARCH

2010 Census data:
2010.census.gov/2010census/data/

Quick facts about race:
www.pbs.org/race

Collected articles on race in the United States:
www.nytimes.com/library/national/race/

Collected stories on underreported communities:
edition.cnn.com/SPECIALS/in.america/

Racial distributions based on the American Community Survey:
http://projects.nytimes.com/census/2010/explorer?ref5us

4 Demographic Changes in America—Gender

On average, more men are born than women each year, creating a pronounced difference in gender distribution in the United States. (AZP Worldwide/Shutterstock)

A LARGER POOL OF MEN AND WOMEN

Practically, everyone has felt like it is hard to meet a person to date at one time or another. But population data show that for some single people in their 20s—specifically for non-African-American women looking for a male mate of the same race—the search may be a little easier. Of course, there's more to attraction than just gender and race, but having a sizable pool of potential mates can help people in their hunt to find romantic partners. Competition for the members of that pool may vary, however, depending on the **sex ratio** between men and women—the ratio of men to women in a population—in any given place. Although the sex ratio differs from city to city and state to state, across the nation, the Census Bureau determined recently that for every 100 single, non-Hispanic white women in their 20s, there were 120 single, non-Hispanic white men in the same age group. Among comparable Hispanics, men outnumbered women by a ratio of 153 to 100; among comparable Asian Americans, men also outnumbered women, this time by a ratio of 132 to 100. The exception? African Americans. For every 100 single African American women in their 20s, there were just 92 comparable men. Taken as a whole, these figures produce a nationwide figure of 120 men in their 20s who have never been married, widowed, or divorced for every 100 women in the same age range.[1]

Why this gender gap? Some of the differences are easily attributable to the simple fact that slightly more men than women are born each year, a disparity scientists often attribute to biology's way of adjusting for the increased risk of early death for males in relation to females.[2] In the United States, African American men are somewhat more likely than men of other racial groups to be killed or imprisoned at a young age, accounting for the opposite dynamic among that group.[3]

Studying the split between African Americans and other racial groups reveals the surprising consequences of differences among sex ratios. The median age at which people marry for the first time has been rising for decades, reaching 25.8 for women and 27.4 for men in 2004. Most non-African American women marry by their late 20s and most non-African-American men by their early 30s. Age, as well as economic status, can have a big impact on a person's likelihood of being married. For example, among African American women, the majority of members in every age group are unmarried with the exception of above-average income earners in their mid-30s and 40s. Similarly, among African American men, only above-average income earners aged 50 to 84 are more likely to be married than not.[4]

The percentage of people in the population around you to whom you may be attracted can have a significant influence on your likelihood of marrying or forming other long-term mutual relationships. Believe it or not, few things about you define your life more than whether you were born male or female. This chance distinction can shape how you live, what you do for a living, and how much money you earn. As we consider the issue of gender in this chapter, we will investigate how the census has viewed gender, what population data have shown over time, and what recent differences have emerged between women and men in the United States. The data we'll look at come not just from the decennial censuses, but also from other surveys conducted by the Census Bureau. Many of these surveys are sponsored by other organizations within the U.S. government.

THE CONCEPT OF GENDER

When you sign up for a social networking site or fill out a registration form, you probably have to check a box to indicate your gender. You know that gender can be simply used to indicate one's status as male or female, and you may think the words *gender* and *sex* are synonymous. But **gender** carries more implications than just your biological state of being male or female, which is considered your **sex**. *Gender* also encompasses the personal and social traits associated with the status of being a man or a woman.

If you've ever called a young niece who likes princesses and pink a "girly girl" or referred to your brother's hangout zone as a "man cave," you've tapped into some of the generally acknowledged traits that define gender in American society. These traits may range from dress—women in skirts or high heels, men in three-piece suits or baseball caps—to behavioral patterns, skill sets, and family roles. However, such overly simplistic correlations may do more to support the notion that ideas about gender are based on sex, while in reality, gender has more to do with socialization.[5] The Census Bureau has always asked respondents to select a sex. The roles that person may or may not play have not traditionally been important to the bureau. This may be because of the historical reality of patriarchy.

Patriarchy and the Census

The concept of patriarchy goes back thousands of years. In ancient Roman times, a family's male head of household, or *paterfamilias*, exerted absolute legal authority over the life and death of his wife and children. He could order them to be sold into slavery, cast out of the family home, or even killed for disobeying him.[6] Although this practice eventually died out, both the Latin word for father, *pater*, and the idea of male social superiority live on in the concept of **patriarchy**. Simply put, patriarchy is a system of social organization in which men hold authority over women and children. In a patriarchy, men's power may touch nearly all aspects of society, including politics, business, and religion. If you doubt you live in a patriarchal society, consider from whom you received your last name. It was your husband, your father, or your mother's father. There have been loose accounts and legends about **matriarchal societies**—ones in which women are in control—but no true matriarchal society has ever been documented. The Greeks wrote about a society of women warriors called the Amazons, but even that fabled society is believed to have turned into a patriarchy.[7]

One common result of a patriarchal social system is **sexism**. Sexism occurs when one sex—most commonly the male sex—claims superiority over the other sex—typically the female sex. Although it may seem counterproductive, women have at times bought into sexist social expectations by making themselves subservient to men in professional, educational, and familial roles.

Throughout the history of the United States, the census has always counted the number of free men and women. As you learned in Chapter 1, that number is then used to establish political representation through apportionment, or the determination of proportional number of representatives from each state to the House of Representatives. What is fascinating about this practice is that women were counted for purposes of representation even though they lacked voting rights at the federal level until the passage of the 19th Amendment in 1920. Perhaps this disconnect stems from the differences in gender roles in American society.

Gender Roles

Suppose for a moment that you're a woman living in an episode of the television show *Mad Men*. Your status as a woman—and your status as single, engaged, married, childless, or a mother—will drive your actions and opportunities throughout the course of the episode's events. If you're a young, single character, you will probably be portrayed as working in a low-authority job and flirting with the men around you. If you're married with children, your focus will be on your family life and household responsibilities. Now, fast forward 50 years and suppose that you are one of the female detectives on the *CSI* series or a highly educated female doctor on *Grey's Anatomy*. What social changes have made such drastic shifts in the portrayal of women and their roles possible? Various factors such as war, industrialization, social movements, public policy amendments, and cultural expectation shifts have contributed to modifying the way in which women are perceived in American society. We will discuss the impact of these factors in more detail later in this chapter.

Culture and socialization allow society, peers, and family members to help determine widespread ideas about gender roles. Women may have made significant strides in crossing gender barriers to escape highly restrictive professional and personal spheres, but men and women are still expected to fit into certain **gender roles**—socially expected styles of thought and action. From a young age, children are encouraged to adopt certain gender roles through exposure to culture, entertainment, and even toys. A quick visit to Target's website reveals that the mass retailer divides its toys into sections, including "Girls' Toys" and "Boys' Toys."[8] Within these categories lie distinctly different playthings. The popular Bratz line of dolls exposes preteen girls to a world of miniskirts, makeup, feather boas, and fishnet stockings. Some psychologists have noted that such toys encourage not only identification with traditionally female ideals of beauty and clothing, but also increased **sexualization**, or undue emphasis on sexuality and sexual appeal, of girls at younger and younger ages.[9] Meanwhile, the site directs shoppers for preteen boys to Lego building sets and Hasbro's Nerf toys, perfect for mock wars and other aggressive games.[10]

Of course, society does not expect all women to walk around in fishnet stockings or all men to build and then shoot down Lego spaceships. Gender roles in the United States are constantly changing as the expectations of men and women begin to approach, if not merge with, one another. Women and men may wear exactly the same popular Converse low-top sneakers and sport the same style of Levi's jeans. Men increasingly share home and child-care duties as modern households rely on the incomes of two full-time working parents.

Some sociologists have drawn a distinction between "doing gender" and "having gender." A young boy who "has" the male gender is not inherently required to "do" that gender by acting in a way typically associated with masculinity. While "having" a gender is simply the state of biologically being male or female, "doing" gender would see the young boy playing rough with his friends because he thinks that is just what boys do.[11] A little girl clomping around in her mother's high heels or a little boy grabbing for his father's tools is learning to "do gender." As we investigate the historical trends of gender in the United States, we should ask ourselves what role gender construction has played in the creation of these data. What biases may underlie the seemingly straightforward statistical data collected by the Census Bureau? Do men and women even today continue to make choices for their lives and livelihoods that are related to how they believe they should "do gender"?

SEX RATIOS AND THE CENSUS

You have learned that the census asks each respondent just a few questions to determine basic demographic data. Since 1790, one of these questions has asked respondents to identify their sex. The U.S. Census Bureau explains its reasoning for this data collection simply: "Census data about sex are important because many federal programs must differentiate between males and females for funding, implementing and evaluating their programs. For instance, laws promoting equal employment opportunity for women require census data on sex. Also, sociologists, economists, and other researchers who analyze social and economic trends use the data."[12] However, what appears to be a straightforward question with a straightforward goal can pose a complex problem for some. The census requires that each respondent select one of two choices relating to sex: male or female. Those who are **transgendered**—self-identified as a member of the gender not matching one's biological sex—must select one of these two options despite having personal characteristics of both.

Since 1790, population data show how the relative population of men and women in the United States has shifted subtly over time. One way that demographers may employ such a statistic in their research is to use the sex ratio. The sex ratio can tell us a great deal about a society, and is thus a valuable tool for understanding and applying population data. The sex ratio may be taken at a variety of times in life, from birth to old age, and as such may vary relative to the age of the population it encapsulates. In general, a human population comprises more boys than girls at birth. Over time, however, this ratio shifts bit by bit so that at the end of life, women clearly outnumber men. The normative sex ratio is about 105 boys for every 100 girls. Interestingly, geography seems to hold a noticeable influence over the sex ratio of a given population. For example, the closer a population lives to the equator, the more likely the sex ratio will tilt toward more girls and fewer boys, even at birth—the direct opposite of a typical population. This deviation may be a result of some evolutionary trend that encourages humans to produce more females or some other unknown evolutionary pressure affecting the sex of humans at birth.[13]

Applying the Sex Ratio

Why does it matter if there are a few more men than women in a given segment of the population or the other way around? Keep in mind that the disparities brought about by the difference of just two or three people per 100 become much greater when scaled up to reflect the total U.S. population. That figure of 120 non-Hispanic white single men in their 20s to every 100 non-Hispanic White single women, for example, represents an actual difference of hundreds of thousands of individuals. This numerical difference means that the sex ratio has a significant impact on marital patterns; if men outnumber women, men may find it difficult to marry and thus defer marriage or simply give up on the idea altogether. Alternatively, men may seek partners in a different age range. While American society may snicker slightly at the rise of middle-aged women partnering with much younger men, the sex ratio may dictate that such an arrangement makes sense in a population in which younger single men outnumber their traditionally age-appropriate counterparts while older women face a similar quandary. The sex ratio may also influence other aspects of society, such as education and employment trends.

Despite rapid population growth between 1790 and 1880, the sex ratio stayed remarkably even, tilting further in favor of men for a time before returning to the level established with the first census. Yet the most obvious, and arguably the most significant, shift in the U.S. sex ratio is the flip from male numerical dominance to female numerical dominance in the mid-20th century. Since that time, women have continued to outnumber men by greater or lesser amounts. These changes in the sex ratio may have occurred for a number of reasons. Perhaps they are due to years of war, perhaps medical breakthroughs in women's health, and/or an increased immigration of one sex or the other. Let's explore these differences over time in greater depth.

U.S. Sex Ratio over Time, All Ages

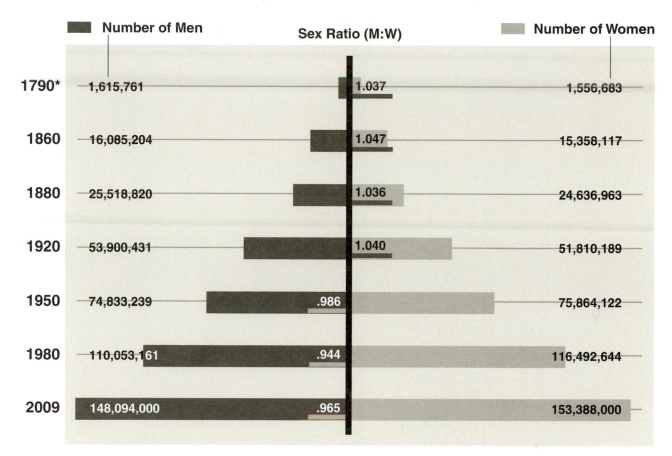

The census did not measure the number of non-white men and women until 1820, so figures reflect whites only.

Figure 4.1 The sex ratio of the U.S. population has shifted subtly over time. What might explain these changes?
Source: Based on Susan B. Carter, Scott Sigmund Gartner, Michael R. Haines, Alan L. Olmstead, Richard Sutch, & Gavin Wright (eds.), *Historical Statistics of the United States: Millennial Edition*, (Cambridge: Cambridge University Press, 2006).

WOMEN IN THE NEW NATION The 1790 Census recorded the sex of only white respondents, meaning that the 757,181 enslaved and free black Americans residing in the young nation are not represented in the sex ratio of 1.037 that results from census records.[14] Despite the obvious statistical bias and problems caused by excluding nearly one-fifth of the population from the calculated ratio, this figure serves as a starting point from which the early United States and its people can be studied. (To refresh your knowledge of how the Census Bureau has dealt with race and ethnicity over time, revisit Chapter 3.) The ratio also provides a helpful point to which later population data can be compared in order to analyze the changing makeup of the U.S. population.

George Washington's familiar powdered wig and form-fitting fashionable trousers, so unlike the short hair and baggy jeans popular with men of the 21st century, are not the only symbols of changing gender roles. Women of the 18th century had markedly fewer legal rights than those of today, and this status may have been partially influenced by the sex ratio of the era. During the earliest colonial times, for example, single women who made their way to North America were sometimes eligible to receive free land. This practice soon ended, however, perhaps because land ownership afforded women a level of independence that discouraged them from marrying in a time when the number of eligible bachelors outstripped available women.[15]

The dominance of men extended throughout society, which was so patriarchal that it encouraged ignorant stereotypes, such as women having smaller brains than men. Although most black women in the United States during this time were enslaved and thus forced to participate in the unpaid labor force, white women's primary duties lay in maintaining the home and bearing children; the average woman gave birth to eight children. Despite high childhood mortality rates, this high birthrate also factors into a sex ratio favoring men. Childbirth was dangerous and could result in the death of the mother, depressing the overall numbers of women within the U.S. population.[16]

THE DEVASTATING IMPACT OF THE CIVIL WAR

The 1860 Census indicates a sex ratio within the U.S. population more firmly tilted toward males than that of 1790 and, interestingly, nearly identical to the normative sex ratio of about 105 male babies born for every 100 female babies. This slight widening of the sex ratio came despite immense overall population growth in the United States between 1790 and 1860, with the total figures for both men and women rising approximately 10 times over.

Women had made some limited gains in the areas of work and education during this period. Colleges had begun educating women, albeit to perform traditional gendered occupations such as teaching and nursing.[17] The 1860 Census gave the first estimates for female workforce participation. Census figures placed white women's participation in the labor force at 13.1 percent, while the system of slavery kept the labor force participation of black women at an astonishing 90 percent.[18] Among all free women, labor force participation was highest during their teens and early 20s, before women were likely to have married. By the time women reached their late 30s, just 8.52 percent of free women worked outside the home, compared to 21.5 percent of 16- to 19-year-olds and 18.55 percent of 20- to 24-year-olds. This rise in working women may also be partially attributed to the First Industrial Revolution. With commercially produced household goods and products ranging from candles and brooms to cloth and furniture replacing those previously made at home, women were freed of some of their home-based duties. Young women sought personal and economic independence by taking jobs in the growing industrial economy, perhaps partially encouraged by the desire to buy some of the fashionable new dresses and household goods freshly on the market.[19]

A grimmer reality also forced women into the labor force: widowhood. The eruption of the Civil War in 1861 brought a period of bloody conflict that directly caused the deaths of an estimated 610,000 Union and Confederate troops through battle or disease. Hundreds of thousands of other young men were nonfatally wounded.[20] The change in the balance of men and women from 1860 to 1870 demonstrates the devastating impact of the war on the male population. The 1860 Census recorded 2,911,558 men aged from 20 to 29, an age group likely to have participated in the Civil War. A decade later, this same group—now aged 30 to 39—numbered only 2,452,999. This decrease of more than 450,000 came at a time when the U.S. population grew by more than 7 million overall. Thus, the war contributed to a dramatic change in the nation's sex ratio from 1.047 favoring males in 1860 to just 1.022 favoring males in 1870.[21]

IMMIGRATION AND INDUSTRIALIZATION

By 1880, the male population of the United States had begun to rebound from the effects of the Civil War, and the sex ratio had again broadened to numerically favor men over women at a ratio of 1.036. Immigration played an important role in this growth. Between 1820 and 1860, two out of every five immigrants to the United States had been women, but by the beginning of the 20th century, this figure had declined to two out of every seven immigrants. This shift in the immigrant sex ratio accompanied a general change in the geographical origin of immigrants from northern Europe—particularly Ireland and Germany—to southern and eastern Europe beginning in the mid-1870s.[22]

Women continued to grow their participation in the labor force, although this trend affected primarily unmarried females. In 1880, 33.7 percent of single, never-married women and 23.5 percent of widowed and divorced women worked outside the home, but only 5.7 percent of married women did so.[23] However, labor force participation increased to a larger or smaller degree in every age group as the trend toward women's work grew. The majority of working women found jobs as domestic servants or factory laborers, a reflection of the gender roles prevalent at the time that saw household chores as women's work and of the general lack of advanced educational opportunities for women. Slightly fewer than 55 percent of white working women held service or laborer positions, as did some 95 percent of non-white working women. Less than 2 percent of the female workforce acted in a clerical or sales capacity.[24]

WOMEN GO WHITE COLLAR

A period of heavy immigration led to a sizable population increase between 1880 and 1920 essentially doubling the U.S. population from 50,155,783 to 105,710,620. During this time, the sex ratio remained relatively stable, however, shifting to a slightly more male ratio of 1.040 from 1.036 according to the 1920 Census. The toll of World War I made the sex ratio among people in affected age groups somewhat different; however, what had been a total population of some 18,120,587 15- to 24-year-olds in 1910 dropped by slightly over 1 million to a figure of 17,157,684 25- to 35-year-olds in 1920, a reflection both of World

War I casualties and of a devastating influenza epidemic that swept the globe in the late 1910s. During this period, the sex ratio for this cohort actually shifted slightly in favor of men but, at about 1.02, remained slightly lower than the sex ratio for the population as a whole.[25]

Because the wording of the 1910 Census is believed to have caused inflated female labor force participation figures, it's difficult to compare these figures to those of 1920 in order to measure the effect of World War I on women's work. However, the participation of men in the U.S. military during the late 1910s certainly caused a great many women to take jobs that men had previously held, and the percentage of women in the labor force increased across the board for every group younger than 50. At the same time, technologies such as the typewriter and new business practices expanded demand for clerical labor, and women increasingly stepped up to fill these positions. Between 1910 and 1920, for example, census figures show that the percentage of working women in clerical and sales jobs roughly doubled, to about 25 percent, even as the share of women working in domestic service or labor declined.[26]

THE EFFECTS OF WORLD WAR II The 1950 Census marked a new demographic trend in the United States that has endured to today: the numerical dominance of women. For the first time, the sex ratio tilted slightly in favor of women, at 0.986 (which equates to approximately 99 men to every 100 women), a sharp decline from 1920 but a more gradual yet still noticeable change from 1940, when the sex ratio had stood at 1.006.[27] So what gives?

The Great Depression hit the U.S. birthrate hard. In the years prior to the Depression, specifically 1905 to 1910, the total fertility rate stood at 3,551 births per 1,000 women. By the time the Census Bureau began measuring the total birthrate in 1933, that figure had plummeted to 2,210 births per 1,000 women. That figure remained relatively stable until the baby boom of the late 1940s sent births skyrocketing.[28] This shift may have benefitted the relative growth of the female population in two ways. Giving birth to fewer children meant fewer chances to die in childbirth, which, if not as risky an undertaking as it had been in colonial days, was still a potential cause of death for otherwise young, healthy women. At the same time, the economic woes of the era deterred potential immigrants—a group that had historically included significantly more men than women—from coming to the United States. World War II, which saw U.S. deaths of about 300,000, also contributed slightly to the sex-ratio shift.[29] In 1940, the population of U.S. men in their 20s numbered 11,143,054; in 1950, the population of men in their 30s stood a bit lower, at 11,142,267, despite overall population gains of approximately 20,000,000. Equally, the number of women living longer lives than men increased, marking a trend that has continued to the present day.[30]

Women went to work in droves during World War II. Many gave up their jobs voluntarily or involuntarily during the economic decline and baby boom of the 1940s, and labor force participation among women in their 20s actually declined slightly between 1940 and 1950 in a rare reversal of the trend toward women's economic participation in U.S. society.[31] Yet the women who did work—both white and non-white—were more likely to fill clerical or professional positions and less likely to work in domestic service or manual labor.

AN AGING POPULATION The 1980 Census confirmed that the face of the United States was becoming more female even as it became older. Decreasing rates of immigration from the mid-20th century onward, particularly by men, contributed to the increasing numerical dominance of women during this time period.[32] So did rising female life expectancies. Between 1950 and 1980, women enjoyed a rise in life expectancy from about 71 years to about 78 years. Although men also saw their life expectancies rise during this time, the rise was both smaller and altogether lower, from about 66 to nearly 70.[33] Women's proportion of the sex ratio thus became even more pronounced in older age cohorts. The 1980 Census recorded that of the 25,549,427 Americans aged 65 and older, 15,244,512 were women; this resulted in a highly unbalanced sex ratio of 0.676, meaning there were approximately 68 men for every 100 women for that segment of the population. Further, women made up greater and greater proportions of the population as age increased. Among the oldest Americans—those 100 or older—women outnumbered men more than 2 to 1.[34] Clearly, if having your 100th birthday announced on the *Today* show is among your life goals, one of the best ways to attain your dream is to have had the good fortune to be born female.

The implications of the graying of the U.S. population, which will be discussed in greater depth in Chapter 5, have been profound. For senior women in 1980, membership in this growing demographic group brought with it possibilities that were barred to them because of their gender at the time of their birth. Women such as Maggie Kuhn, who founded the political activist group the Gray Panthers in 1970 when she was 65, were born during an era when women did not yet have the right to vote. By promoting the rights and concerns of senior citizens, women such as Kuhn helped redefine national opinion on old age.[35]

★TABLE 4.1 U.S. SEX RATIO BY AGE, 2009[36]★

2009 Age	Male	Female	Sex ratio
All ages	148,094,000	153,388,000	0.9655
Under 5 yrs	10,842,000	10,345,000	1.0480
5 to 9 yrs	10,351,000	9,894,000	1.0462
10 to 14 yrs	10,181,000	9,726,000	1.0468
15 to 19 yrs	10,782,000	10,445,000	1.0323
20 to 24 yrs	10,420,000	10,212,000	1.0204
25 to 29 yrs	10,867,000	10,389,000	1.0460
30 to 34 yrs	9,574,000	9,691,000	0.9879
35 to 39 yrs	10,169,000	10,275,000	0.9897
40 to 44 yrs	10,322,000	10,556,000	0.9778
45 to 49 yrs	11,162,000	11,550,000	0.9664
50 to 54 yrs	10,611,000	11,043,000	0.9609
55 to 59 yrs	9,083,000	9,671,000	0.9392
60 to 64 yrs	7,423,000	8,112,000	0.9151
65 to 69 yrs	5,632,000	6,193,000	0.9094
70 to 74 yrs	3,769,000	4,810,000	0.7836
75 to 79 yrs	3,167,000	4,162,000	0.7609
80 to 84 yrs	2,248,000	3,428,000	0.6558
85 yrs +	1,492,000	2,886,000	0.5170

INTO A NEW CENTURY Walking down a city street or people watching at a nearby restaurant, you probably don't pay much attention to the sex ratio of the people around you. Yet studying the sex ratio of the contemporary United States shows some distinct differences in the number of men and women living in the nation today. These splits vary greatly depending on age. Check out the information about the 2009 sex ratio. What might cause these variations?

As is readily visible in the table, the sex ratio changes dramatically between birth and old age. At the beginning of life, the sex ratio is about 1.048 in favor of men—essentially the normative birth ratio of 105 males to every 100 females common in this part of the world. From that point on, however, the sex ratio shifts in favor of women. Beginning in childhood, the sex ratio slips very slightly to about 1.046 before undergoing a more precipitous decline to about 1.032 in the population's late teens and about 1.020 in the population's early 20s. When the overall population reaches its 30th birthday, the transition is complete: Women now outnumber men slightly, with a sex ratio of about 0.988 (about 99 men for every 100 women). From that time on, women steadily gain the upper numerical hand. Among the senior population, the population data show that the sex ratio is particularly exaggerated due to women's longer life expectancies. The population of men begins to fall steeply in the mid-50s, some 10 years before a comparable drop-off begins among the female population. By the time the Census Bureau counts the oldest Americans, the population of women is nearly double that of men, with a sex ratio of about 0.517 (about 52 men for every 100 women).[37]

Although sex-ratio shift in later life is easily attributable to the life expectancy **gender gap**—the divide between men and women—why do the scales begin to tilt toward women so early in life? The leading cause of deaths for all people aged 1 to 35 years is unintentional injury, often related to car crashes. During the later teen years and early 20s, homicide and suicide are also key causes of death, while complications relating to pregnancy and childbirth—a major killer of women in centuries past—rank a distant 10th, tied with HIV and blood poisoning.[38] Perhaps channeling gender role-related expectations of speed and prowess, male drivers are about 77 percent more likely to die in a car crash than women; elderly women may be the most likely to die in a crash, but they are closely followed by male drivers aged 16 to 23 years.[39] In 2005, men were almost four times more likely to be murdered than women.[40] Statistics also show that men were about four times more likely to commit suicide.[41] With men making up the largest number of people who fall victim to the most common causes of death among young people, it's no surprise that women begin to survive men from a relatively early age.

WOMEN IN THE 21ST CENTURY

As the 20th century ebbed into the 21st, "Girl Power!" became a rallying cry espoused by pop-culture figures ranging from the Powerpuff Girls to the Spice Girls. Buffy the Vampire Slayer fought dark forces on network television, and the women of *Sex and the City* pursued careers and personal fulfillment even as they sought the perfect dates. But how do girls and women really stack up against their male counterparts in terms of education, employment, income, and other socioeconomic indicators? Let's look at some data to help provide an important look at American women in the 21st century.

Overall, women's lives show dramatic shifts since those of their ancestors a century or even 50 years before. Women are more likely to wait to marry or start families, leaving them with more time to pursue higher education and lucrative careers.[42] In fact, women now outpace men in educational achievement, although those gains are not mirrored by higher salaries.[43] According to the 2010 Census, among 25- to 29-year-olds, women are more likely to graduate from high school and college at a ratio of 1.05 and 1.20, respectively. Yet the census also reveals that women in the workforce earn roughly two-thirds of men's earnings.[44] More women are participating in the workforce, and at times, their jobs are more secure than those of men, perhaps due to differences in the types of work that each gender tends to perform.[45] While women still make up a minority of political leaders, they are as a group more likely to vote; in the 2008 presidential election, for example, African-American women had the single highest voter turnout, at 68.8 percent, followed closely by white women, at 67.9 percent.[46] Women also continue to have higher life expectancies than men, even as women are more likely to suffer from certain chronic medical conditions, depression, and obesity.[47] Before delving deeper into the situation of women in the 21st century, however, first it is helpful to point out the elephant in the room: gender bias.

The Gender Bias

People sometimes say that numbers don't lie. Yet population statistics may rely on numbers that are not completely accurate and are in some ways misleading. One of these misleading sets of numbers is the measure of labor force participation, which many social scientists have pointed out contains an inherent **gender bias**—the unfair practice of treating men and women differently.

This bias stems from the Census Bureau's method of defining the concept of work exclusively as paid labor. Certainly, "work" includes paid labor. However, work may also include numerous unpaid activities, many of which are much more likely to be performed by women than by men. Supposedly nonworking women may provide child care for friends and family or make items to sell online on Etsy.com, for example. Women who do not perform paid labor may nevertheless spend a great deal of time caring for their homes and families, as well. A 1999–2000 study of married couples with at least one child aged 5–18 found that wives spent an estimated 24.4 hours each week performing tasks such as cooking, cleaning, doing laundry, paying bills, shopping for household needs, and working in the yard. Husbands, however, spent just an estimated 15.3 hours on these same tasks.[48] Yet, the Census Bureau does not record this work because it is unpaid.[49] Federal research on educational attainment does not include nondegree programs that grant certificates or provide other workplace-specific training, meaning that women's true educational levels are likely underrepresented to some extent.[50] Despite these issues, some data are better than no data at all. With this caveat, let's study the official data about the role of women in U.S. economic, social, and political life today.

Changing Roles for Women at Home

Changing gender roles and demographic shifts have affected all areas of American life for both men and women. Increased educational and professional opportunities, in particular, have changed the focus of many women from the home to the professional realm. Although the sex ratio may mean that women have more potential partners from which to choose, for example, women have shown themselves to be in no rush to marry. In 2009, the average age at which women first married was 26, and the average age at which men first married was 28—an increase of some five years since the 1950s. At the same time, the percentage of adult women who were presently married had dropped to 62 percent from 72 percent in 1970, and that of adult men had declined to 66 percent from 84 percent in 1970. This disparity reflects the greater numbers of women in the U.S. population, particularly older, widowed women. Women were also delaying childbirth or choosing not to have children at all. In 2008, 18 percent of all women aged 40 to 44 had never had a child, nearly double the 1976 figure.[51]

Education

Visualize one of your classes. Look around you while you're eating lunch in the student union or studying in the library. What does the ratio of males to females appear to be? Whether you attend a two- or a four-year undergraduate college or an advanced degree program with numerous graduate programs, chances are you're surrounded by more women than men. Yet women are relative newcomers to higher education, with Oberlin College in Ohio enrolling the first coeducational university class in 1837 and women making up fewer than half of undergraduate enrollees well into the 1970s.[52] Since 1972, however, Census Bureau data show that women have made significant strides in education that, by 2010, had made them as a group more likely to enroll in college, more likely to attend college, more likely to complete a bachelor's degree, and even more likely to go to grad school than their male counterparts.[53]

What might explain this shift? Researchers have argued that gender roles play into the educational divide. From a young age, boys are expected to be somewhat rambunctious and many rise to these expectations. Teachers expect that behavior and, in turn, allow behavioral problems to impede learning.[54] College also offers more immediate benefits for women in terms of likely starting wages, meaning that men have less of an economic incentive to complete their degrees or attend graduate school.[55]

Gender roles also play a part in the fields that students choose to pursue. From early ages, young women perform better on reading assessments and young men on math tests.[56] This trend continues into postsecondary education. Women—perhaps constrained by societal expectations that men excel in math and hard science and women in humanities—are markedly less likely than their male counterparts to pursue college study in science and technology. Although women earn the majority of all college degrees, they complete just 20 percent of engineering degrees, for example, and less than half of all degrees in math, physical science, and computer science. At the same time, women earn the vast majority of college degrees in health and education, particularly in teaching. Interestingly, even as male and female gender roles grow seemingly closer together, this educational disparity has increased: between 1998 and 2009, the number of women earning engineering degrees declined, and the number pursuing health and education studies increased.[57]

Employment

Just as women pursue different fields of study than men, a clear gender gap exists in the types of jobs that women and men typically perform. Some of these differences stem from gender roles: the image of the perky female elementary school teacher has endured in part because the wide majority of elementary school teachers are, in fact, female. Altogether, the 10 most common occupations for females accounted for some 30 percent of all working women. Men showed greater occupational diversity, with the 10 most common jobs for males—including such traditionally male fields as truck driver, janitor, and construction worker—employing about 20 percent of all working men.[58]

A strong gender gap breaks male and female employment in some respects along the lines of what might be considered blue- and white-collar work. The largest proportion of women work

★TABLE 4.2 MOST COMMON OCCUPATIONS FOR WOMEN, 2009[59]★

Occupation	Number of Female Workers	Percentage of Occupation Represented by Women
Secretaries and administrative assistants	3,074,000	96.8%
Registered nurses	2,612,000	92%
Elementary and middle school teachers	2,343,000	81.9%
Cashiers	2,273,000	74.4%
Nursing, psychiatric, and home health aides	1,770,000	88.5%
Retail salespersons	1,650,000	51.9%
First-line supervisors/managers of retail sales workers	1,459,000	44.1%
Waiters and waitresses	1,434,000	71.6%
Maids and housekeeping cleaners	1,282,000	89.8%
Customer service representatives	1,263,000	67.9%

in professional occupations—particularly in education, health, and government—with decreasing but significant percentages represented in the service industry; office and administrative support; sales; and managerial, financial, and business fields. In 2009, 5 percent or fewer of working women held jobs in production, transportation, natural resources management, or construction. Yet these fields were among the highest employers of men, with the lowest portion of men working in office and administrative support.[60]

THE "MANCESSION" Sometimes, women may benefit somewhat from their tendency to select different types of occupations than men. During the intense economic recession that rocked the U.S. economy in the late 2000s, men lost jobs more quickly and in greater numbers than women, inspiring the media to dub the downturn a "**mancession**." The divide was so steep that women very nearly overtook men as the majority in the U.S. labor force, reaching 49.96 percent in October of 2009.[61] Although both men and women experienced rising unemployment rates from early 2007 on, men faced an unemployment rate of 10.5 percent in May 2009, while women had an unemployment rate of just 8 percent. Additionally, men consistently had a higher unemployment rate than women during the full course of the official recession, aggravated by the fact that 80 percent of the job losses between mid-2007 and mid-2009 affected men.[62] This divide reversed the trend that had largely prevailed since the government first began calculating unemployment data in 1948. Interestingly, women have tended to do better during economic recessions than men, at least as far as jobs go. Women had lower unemployment rates during economically turbulent times in the early 1980s and early 1990s, and for much of the 2000s.[63]

BUSINESS OWNERSHIP One occupation that women are less likely to choose than men: entrepreneur. In 2007, the Census Bureau found that of more than 26 million businesses in the United States, women owned roughly 7,793,000, men owned a little more than 13,900,000, and male and female partners owned the balance jointly. Businesses owned by men were more than three times as likely to have employees and brought in gross proceeds four times greater than those held by women. Interestingly, the figures for firms jointly owned by men and women more closely resemble those for businesses owned solely by women; such businesses brought in just slightly larger incomes, but were statistically far more likely to have paid employees.[64] Such differences may stem from the types of firms that men and women tend to own. After all, women are more likely to volunteer and more likely to work part time than men, so perhaps the drive for financial compensation is not the primary motivating factor in women's work.[65]

INCOME INEQUALITY Modern women have made a name for themselves in practically every field imaginable. J. K. Rowling and Stephenie Meyer have sold millions of books, and Hillary Clinton and Angela Merkel exercise a great deal of political power in the United States and Germany, respectively. Yet the census shows that American women—despite their greater levels of college enrollment and dominance in the sex ratio—continue to face greater or lesser levels of income inequality. This gender gap holds true for every income level. The Census Bureau reports that among American workers aged 16 years and older, the median annual income in 2009 was $34,645 for men and only $23,628 for women. This difference may be due to the vast disparity between men and women in the highest income brackets. Among male workers, 12.9 percent earn more than $100,000; among women, however, only 5 percent earn more than $100,000.[66] These bald figures, however, do not account for possible differences in education and work experience. Could these factors, and not mere gender, be to blame?[67]

The answer is no. Men and women working in the same occupations earn different incomes, as do men and women with equivalent levels of education. With a few notable exceptions, all of these variations favor men, to the tune of an overall pay gap of about 20 percent in 2010. The only fields in which women outperform men in terms of income are food preparation and serving, bill and account collection, and stock and order filling—none of which are particularly lucrative occupations.[68] Although education increases overall earnings for both men and women, the wage gap persists. In 2009, the median weekly earnings of a woman with a college degree or better were slightly under $1,000, while men with similar levels of education made a median weekly wage of $1,300.

Topping the list of earnings for both men and women? CEO, an occupation held by men a whopping 75.7 percent of the time. Pharmacists rank second as income earners for both men and women, followed by lawyers. Men's fourth most lucrative profession, physician/surgeon, ranks sixth for women, possibly because women are likely to choose specializations that generate less income. Female physicians, on average, earn just 64.2 percent of the incomes of their male counterparts. Even in well-paying jobs, the wage gap is so great that the highest-paying female

★TABLE 4.3 OCCUPATIONS WITH THE HIGHEST MEDIAN EARNINGS FOR MEN AND WOMEN, 2009[70]★

Occupation	Men Median (dollars)	Women Median (dollars)	Women's earnings as % of men's
All year-round full-time workers	$42,588	$34,164	80.2%
Chief executives	$108,368	$80,756	74.5%
Pharmacists	$101,608	$76,700	75.5%
Lawyers	$100,568	$75,348	74.9%
Physicians and surgeons	$99,528	$63,856	64.2%
Computer and information systems managers	$92,976	$73,372	78.9%
Computer software engineers	$80,600	$68,172	84.6%
Human resources manager	$80,496	$55,744	69.3%

positions carry a median salary of $1,553 per week—just $5 more than the 10th highest paying job for men, human resource manager.[69]

This trend is not a new one. According to Daniel H. Weinberg, assistant director, Decennial Census, U.S. Census Bureau, evidence from the 2000 Census revealed that even when adjusting for education and age, men continued to out-earn women in a way that is not explainable by any reason except for gender bias. For example, when comparing the median earnings of male and female physicians and surgeons—the top-earning job field in the 2000 Census—for a group aged 35 to 54 with a bachelor's degree or higher, women earned just 69 percent of what men earned. A similar pattern exists for jobs at the low end of the wage spectrum. Men and women working on one of that census's identified lowest-paying occupations—dishwasher—again in a similar age bracket and in this case with less than a high school education earned salaries with a gender wage gap of 13 percent.[71]

Despite the undeniable reality of the wage gap, emerging data show some promising signs. Among younger workers—those aged 25 to 34—women fared much better in relation to men, garnering about 89 percent of men's average earnings. This figure is well above the national average for all ages, and a sharp increase from a wage gap that saw women in that group earning just 68 percent of men's wages 30 years previously. The wage gap was also narrowed among minority groups. In 2009, Asian-American women earned about 82 percent of Asian-American men's salaries, Hispanic women garnered incomes 90 percent as large as Hispanic men, and African-American women earned 94 percent of black men's salaries.[72]

STATE-BY-STATE COMPARISON

Of course, the United States is a large nation rich with diversity in its geography, economy, and people. As can only be expected, the sex ratio varies from place to place, as does the median income earned by both men and women. For as long as the Census Bureau has been collecting information about the U.S. population, various factors have contributed to the shifting sex ratio. Life expectancy and age, immigration levels, regional economies—all of these and more continue to shape the gender divide today.

The regional variation in the sex ratio is quite striking. The Northeast and South have a markedly higher proportion of women than men, including the nation's most female locations: the District of Columbia (0.893), Rhode Island (0.939), Alabama (0.939), Maryland (0.939), and Mississippi (0.941). The three states closest to the national sex ratio of 0.965 also all lie in the South—Georgia (0.966), Virginia (0.966), and Florida (0.966). As the population moves west, it becomes largely more male, with the nation's most male states mostly lying west of the Rockies. The most heavily male state in the United States is also the state with the nation's westernmost territory, Alaska (108.6). Other states with sex ratios either even or tilting in favor of males include California (100), Arizona (100.4), North Dakota (100.9), Utah (101.2), Colorado (101.4), Hawaii (102.4), Wyoming (103.5), and Nevada (103.7).

Median income as divided by gender does not show such a quickly identifiable pattern. Although men and women both earn the highest median income in the same five locations—the District of Columbia, Connecticut, Maryland, Massachusetts, and New Jersey—only the District of Columbia occupies the same position for both men and women (first). From there, Maryland (second), Connecticut (third), New Jersey (fourth), and Massachusetts (fifth) round

State-by-State Comparison: Sex Ratio and Median Incomes

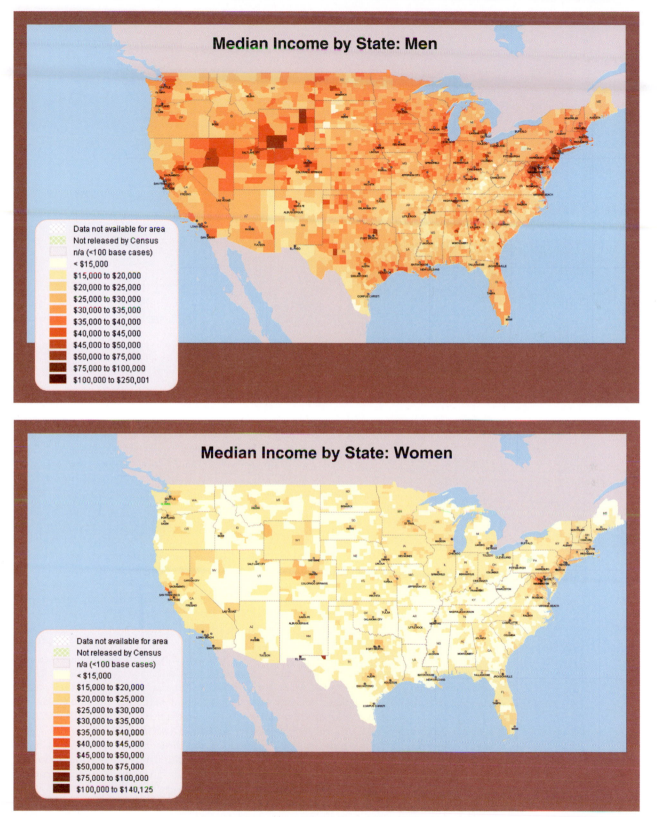

Figure 4.2 The sex ratio and median incomes of men and women vary across the United States. What patterns can you identify?

Sources: Social Explorer, "American Community Survey 2005–2009 Census Tract Data," http://www.socialexplorer.com; U.S. Census Bureau, "GCT-T3-R. Sex Ratio of the Total Population," http://factfinder.census.gov/servlet/GCTTable ?_bm=y&-geo_id=01000US&-_box_head_nbr=GCT-T3-R&-ds_name=PEP_2009_EST&-format=U-40Sb

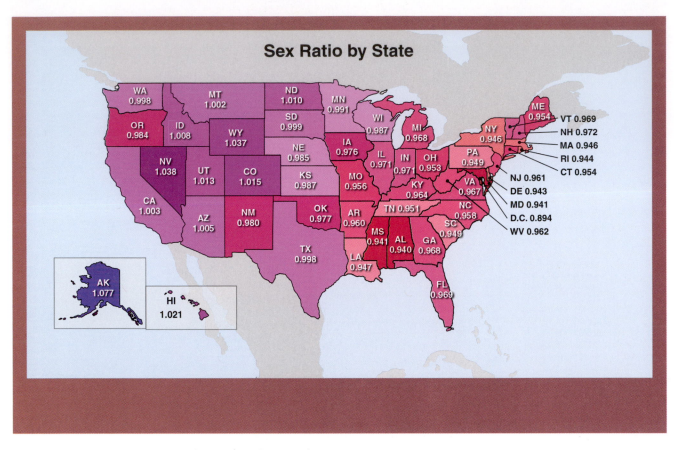

Figure 4.2 (Continued)

Sources: Social Explorer, "American Community Survey 2005–2009 Census Tract Data," http://www.socialexplorer.com; U.S. Census Bureau, "GCT-T3-R. Sex Ratio of the Total Population," http://factfinder.census.gov/servlet/GCTTable ?_bm=y&-geo_id=01000US&-_box_head_nbr=GCT-T3-R&-ds_name=PEP_2009_EST&-format=U-40Sb

out the top earnings spots for women, while men fare best in Connecticut (second), New Jersey (third), Massachusetts (fourth), and Maryland (fifth). With these disparities come varying gender gaps in wages. Although women earn about 89 percent of men's median salaries in the District of Columbia, that figure slips to 76 percent in Connecticut, 77 percent in New Jersey, 78 percent in Massachusetts, and 81 percent in Maryland, showing that high wages do not necessarily mean equitable wages.

However, the wage gap is even more pronounced at lower income levels. Women make the lowest median incomes in West Virginia (51st), Mississippi (50th), Montana (49th), Arkansas (48th), and South Dakota (47th). In West Virginia, this means that women earn just 68 percent of what men earn, in Mississippi 74 percent, in Montana 72 percent, in Arkansas 76 percent, and in South Dakota 76 percent—all below the national median wage gap of 80.2 percent.[73] Only seven states actually exceed that median wage gap, including Hawaii (80.9 percent), Maryland (81 percent), Florida (81.1 percent), New York (81.4 percent), Arizona (82.7 percent), California (83.3 percent), and the District of Columbia (88.3 percent). Interestingly, the two most equitable locations in the United States are not states at all; topping the list of smallest wage gaps after the District of Columbia is the territory of Puerto Rico, a low-earning location in which women earn a median salary that is 99.6 percent of men's salaries.[74]

Examining the population data provides a fascinating look at the relative lives and positions of women and men throughout the nation's history. Although data show that women have made great strides in life expectancy, health, education, and work, frustrating gender gaps remain, particularly that of the wage gap. Gender segregation remains common in the U.S. workplace, with women continuing to fill such traditionally feminine jobs as secretary and teacher even as men dominate the boardroom and the construction site. What lies in the future for these demographic trends?

Equality, one would hope, but income data from the Census Bureau that shows a persistent disparity between male and female wage earners suggests women will continue to get shortchanged into the near future and gender will continue to play a significant role American society.

KEY TERMS

Sex ratio is the ratio of men to women in a population. *52*

Gender encompasses the personal and social traits associated with the status of being a man or a woman. *52*

Sex is the biological state of being male or female. *52*

Patriarchy is a social system in which men dominate nearly all aspects of society, including politics, business, and religion. *53*

Matriarchies are social systems in which women hold authority over men. *53*

Sexism is holding one sex— typically male—superior to the other sex. *53*

Gender roles are socially expected styles of thought and action for members of each gender. *53*

Sexualization is the undue emphasis on a person's sexual appeal and sexuality. *53*

Transgendered is being self-associated with a gender

that doesn't correspond to one's biological sex. *54*

Gender gap is the divide between men and women in various social, economic, and political fields. *58*

Gender bias is the unfair practice of treating men and women differently. *59*

Mancession is the term the media gave the recession of the late 2000s, during which men lost jobs more quickly and in greater numbers than women. *61*

CHAPTER QUIZ

1. Gender roles are determined primarily by
   a. educational attainment.
   b. government decree.
   c. family and peer socialization.
   d. gender bias within the census.
2. The sex ratio measures the
   a. relative return rate of the census among men and women.
   b. proportion of men and women in a population.
   c. income gap between men and women.
   d. differences in gender roles between men and women.
3. The shift from male to female prevalence in the sex ratio can be partially explained by
   a. rising male life expectancies.
   b. lower infant mortality rates.
   c. decreasing immigration after 1950.
   d. improved education for women.

4. One example of gender bias in the census is its
   a. method of defining work as paid labor.
   b. indication that women make up a minority of the labor force.
   c. preference for making men the head of household.
   d. refusal to collect information relating to income inequality.
5. Women outpace men in all of the following, EXCEPT
   a. population.
   b. educational achievement.
   c. life expectancy.
   d. income.

Answers: 1. c; 2. b; 3. c; 4. a; 5. d

ESSAY QUESTIONS

1. Explain how gender roles may have created biases in the collection and interpretation of U.S. population data.
2. Describe how demographers use population data relating to gender to draw conclusions about a population and give at least one example to demonstrate this process.
3. Discuss notable changes in the sex ratio and explain how these changes both reflected and shaped events of their time.
4. Compare and contrast the gender gap present in education and employment.
5. Analyze how gender roles contribute to income inequality between men and women.

SOURCES FOR FURTHER RESEARCH

Census Bureau statistics on women:
http://www.census.gov/population/www/socdemo/women.html

Bureau of Labor Statistics on women workers:
http://www.bls.gov/bls/cpswomendata.htm

Historical Census Browser:
http://mapserver.lib.virginia.edu

Population Reference Bureau:
http://www.prb.org

Women in America: Indicators of Social and Economic Well-Being:
http://www.whitehouse.gov/administration/eop/cwg/data-on-women#Population

5 Demographic Changes in America—Aging

Aging statistics tell a story about generations and their impact on those around them.
(Paul Prescott/Shutterstock)

RISING YOUNG HISPANICS IN TEXAS POISED TO PICK UP AGING TAB

Policy makers in the United States face an unprecedented concern. The demographic of retirees is, in some cases, twice as large as the younger working generation. What does this mean? It means that retirees are placing greater demands on Social Security and Medicare. It means that younger generations are less able to fully fund those programs through payroll taxes. The trend is not reflected in every geographic area. The situation changes from state to state. However, an interesting development in aging demographics is brewing in Texas, one that points to a national trend.

Census Bureau predictions for Texas suggest that the Hispanic demographic grew by 48 percent from 2000 to 2010 and will be the largest ethnic group in the state by 2015.[1] As of 2011, non-Hispanic whites make up about 47 percent of the total population of Texas, while Hispanics are about 37 percent of the total population.[2] The rise of the Hispanic population is a national trend, but the situation in Texas is unique. The 2010 Census demonstrated that 68 percent of non-Hispanic whites in Texas were older than 65 and only 33.8 percent were under the age of 18.[3] This data reveal that a younger generation of mostly Hispanics will be funding Texas programs for an older generation of mostly non-Hispanic whites. This older group will be leaving the workforce and depending on the younger generation for their support. Unfortunately, nearly 43 percent of Hispanics in Texas left high school without graduating in 2008, making forecasts of the future Texas labor pool particularly bleak—and forecasts of future tax revenue even worse.

Like most states, Texas faces deficits. These shortages have led to political battles over the allocation of funds from the shrinking state revenue to particular programs. Older generations are defending state programs that favor the aging, such as long-term care assistance, while the growing, younger Hispanic generations are defending state programs that favor the young, such as education.[4] These conflicting agendas are the result of different self-interests. Most individuals in the older white population do not have school-aged children; therefore, their desire to fund education programs is weak. Similarly, the younger generation is decades from senior citizen status, and so they have little immediate motivation to fund programs that support seniors. Politicians struggle to cope with the developing situation. Older whites are the dominant political demographic, but their control is tenuous. As younger Hispanics become the ethnic majority in Texas, the political landscape is sure to undergo radical changes. Texas is an early indicator of trends that will soon be seen on a national level.[5]

THE IMPACT OF AGING POPULATIONS ON THE NATION

The government and other institutions track the way a population ages for more than just the sake of good record keeping; it helps society plan for the future. An aging population means that a higher percentage of people will reach old age than in years past, and society must prepare for the upcoming needs of this growing group. For example, if a city's officials knew that its elderly population was going to grow by 25 percent in the next 10 years, they would need to increase hospital beds, nursing care services, meal programs for shut-ins, and social activities for the elderly by about 25 percent. Concerns about how the public will react to the increasing percentage of elderly people in society have drawn the attention of psychologists, medical professionals, and sociologists. These individuals examine the process of aging and the particular problems of aging people, a discipline is known as **gerontology**. While this may not seem like the most exciting field of study, it is critically important to the United States' future.[6]

On a structural level, information on age demographics can help businesses and policy makers make informed decisions about the allocation of funds and resources in the future. On a micro level, this information can provide a lens through which we can understand how people's lives interact and change. As our lives change, our relationships to objects also change. When children are in grade school, playground equipment is important. As working adults, however, such equipment carries less value. There is an interaction and interdependence between how aging influences our social processes and how we stratify people by age. The fact that age plays a role in understanding how people interact is obvious. Not so obvious are the trends related to aging. In this chapter, we hope to address this.[7]

HISTORICAL TRENDS: THE GRAYING OF THE UNITED STATES

Through the gathering of personal information, the Census Bureau has been able to document the maturation of the U.S. population. During the first century of census taking, from 1790 to 1890, reports showed a rise in the **median age** from 16 to 22. By 2009, the median age reached 36.8.[8]

Worldwide Aging Trends

Aging is something everyone on Earth has in common. With each year, we all get a bit older. This consistency, however, is not present when aging is examined on a population level rather than an individual level. The median age of the United States has outpaced the median age of the world, which was 29.1 in 2000. However, the world has also seen a steady increase in its median age, which is projected to reach 38.4 by 2050. A closer look at the numbers explains a few reasons behind the aging population. More developed countries such as Japan, France, and Canada had a median age of 39.7 in 2010, while less developed countries and territories such as Ghana, Guatemala, and the Gaza Strip had a median age of only 19.9 in 2010.[9] Because individuals in more developed countries live longer than individuals in less developed countries, it can be inferred that the rise in the median age of the world population is, in part, due to the rise in number of developed and developing nations.

LIFE EXPECTANCY The median age is directly affected by **life expectancy**. Life expectancy worldwide has increased from 46 in 1955 to 66 in 2005.[11] Life expectancy has risen most dramatically in developing countries, which have benefited greatly from increased sanitation and nutrition. Life expectancy in developed countries has steadily increased, with an age of 76 in 2005 and projected age of 82 by 2050.[12] Increased life expectancy has caused major demographic changes throughout the world and can be linked to a number of theories. For example, research suggests that delaying birth has positive effects on extending life for both infants and mothers.[13] Additionally, some theorists suggest that medical treatments for once fatal diseases have increased the overall survival rate, thus increasing life expectancy. Perhaps more importantly, public health measures such as clean water and sewage disposal have further decreased the spread of deadly diseases, thereby increasing the median age around the world.[14]

BIRTHRATE Increased life expectancy is only partially responsible for the increase in median age. A falling **birthrate** around the world has also played a large role. In many cases, increased fertility education and professional opportunities in the industrialized world have led many individuals to delay having children. Factors such as declining female fertility have attributed to the drop in birthrates and the average birth per woman in all nations.[15] Worldwide, the number of births per woman has fallen by nearly half, from 5.0 in 1955 to 2.7 in 2005. This drop has occurred in both industrialized and less developed countries, with a change from 2.8 to 1.6 and 6.2 to 2.9, respectively.[16] This significant drop in births per woman is known as **birth dearth**. This phenomenon eventually leads to the elderly outnumber the young, a fact so alarming that Japan and many European countries offer child-care incentives designed to encourage births, fearing their populations would no longer be self-sustaining.[17]

★ TABLE 5.1 WORLDWIDE POPULATION TRENDS[10] ★

The differences between the population growth in more and less developed regions are key reasons for the discrepancies in median age.

Year	1950	1960	1970	1980	1990	2000	2010	2050
World (billions)	2.5	3.0	3.6	4.4	5.2	6.1	6.9	9.1
Less Developed Regions (billions)	1.7	2.1	2.6	3.3	4.1	4.9	5.6	7.9
More Developed Regions (billions)	0.8	0.9	1	1.1	1.15	1.2	1.23	1.28

Aging in the United States

As an industrialized nation, the United States has followed the trend of increased life expectancy. In fact, since the days of colonization, the average American has continued to live longer than previous generations.[18] Early colonists' ability to survive multiple generations, particularly those who lived in the relatively developed areas of New England, has lead some historians to suggest that grandparents were "invented" in America. While this increased longevity gave many people the joy of watching their children's children grow up, it also introduced issue of elderly care in America.[19]

Traditionally, care for the elderly was offered in the home by relatives. Shortly after the American Revolution, however, an increasing number of citizens became unable or unwilling to provide care for aging relatives and turned to the government for assistance. The almshouse in Philadelphia, in particular, enrolled no more than 50 people annually through 1750. By 1815, it had enrolled over 2,000 for the year, one-third of whom were elderly.[20] Due to the increasing number of elderly poor, research on aging developed toward the end of the 19th century, along with possible solutions to the problem.

In 1875, a major corporation, the American Express Company, instituted a retirement **pension** system for its employees. By 1900, there were 12 known private pension plans in the United States. These plans generally provided pensioners with 20 percent of their former incomes.[21] They had to either live off that money or come up with other means of income. Military veterans were given pensions, but other federal government workers were provided with no retirement. Many legislators and citizens believed providing pensions for workers was a form of socialism, a theft from taxpayers. Bills to provide pensions for federal employees were introduced in nearly every session of Congress, but, due to a lack of political will, nothing passed until 1920.[22]

As the nation debated the morality of granting the elderly assistance, the situation grew worse for the elderly poor. Elderly dependence was estimated at 23 percent in 1910, 33 percent in 1922, and 40 percent in 1930. By 1940, as the nation stumbled under the Great Depression, two-thirds of the elderly population was dependent. As social protest rose over the living conditions of the elderly, representatives in Congress drafted a **Social Security Act**, authorizing a payroll tax on Americans for the purpose of funding their retirement.[23]

After Congress passed the Social Security Act in 1935, the American public gained a greater appreciation of the science of aging. By 1950, a number of major cities had developed facilities and programs for the elderly. Treatment of the elderly began to focus on the mental and physical aspects of aging rather than simply financial needs. Gerontology and geriatric societies formed in the mid-20th century to address the needs of the growing population. The Medicare and Old Americans acts passed in the 1960s, resulting in the public's wider focus on the needs of the elderly. Professional industries rapidly developed to address these needs. Efforts by gerontologists and others attempted to remove the stigma from aging. The term "**ageism**" was coined in 1968 to refer to prejudice against the elderly.[24] The Age Discrimination in Employment Act passed in 1967, forbidding the firing of workers because of their age. To this day, the law continues to uphold the rights of the elderly in the face of challenges.[25]

Figure 5.1 illustrates the rise of the over-50 demographic in the United States between 1930 and 2010. The bars represent the percentage of the total population of the United States, meaning that as the older demographic increases, younger populations decrease. The over-55 population nearly doubled over the 80 years represented, from 12.4 percent in 1930 to 23.4 percent in 2010. The over-65 population more than doubled in that same period, from 5.6 percent in 1930 to 12.4 percent in 2010. While the numbers of the last three censuses seem to indicate a plateau among the 65 and older demographic, the percentages for those over 55 continue to increase. This increase may be attributed to the **baby-boom generation**, those born between 1946 and 1964. This group of Americans who are nearing retirement age represents one of the largest birth **cohorts**—or populations born during specific time periods—in U.S. history, and their aging will affect the country in dramatic ways.[26]

The graph begins in 1940 because prior censuses did not record age brackets consistently. Censuses from 1870 to 1920 placed everyone 45 and older in the same demographic. By today's standards, it seems odd to lump a 45-year-old in the same age demographic as, say, an 80-year-old; however, including these ages in the oldest demographic would have been consistent with life expectancy in the late 1800s, as a 45-year-old would be approaching the final years of his or her life. It is worth noting that in the 1850 Census, when the Census Bureau began counting the age of the entire population, only 8.9 percent of the population was older

Aging in the 20th Century

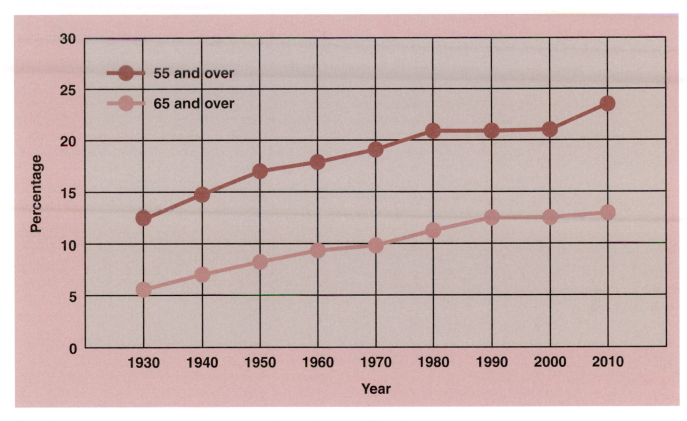

Figure 5.1 Aging populations have changed dramatically over the course of the 20th century.
Source: Social Explorer, "1790 to Present," *U.S. Decennial Census Files,* http://www.socialexplorer.com

than 50.[27] More than 150 years later, the 2005–2009 ACS found that 30.3 percent of the population was older than 50.[28]

Aging and Demographic Change in the United States

Many of the differences in the aging graph are the results of generational fluctuations. Certain age groups share a number of statistical characteristics due to historical circumstances. These age groups can be followed through their statistical development, and statisticians can anticipate their impact on the nation with some degree of success. Different age groups are commonly referred to by a specific generation. Terms like *baby boomers* and **Generation X**, those born between 1965 and 1981, are social markers for different populations as they move through various stages of life. Different cohorts are isolated according to their perceived cultural and social values. Although every individual is different, various cohorts share similar cultural experiences. For example, most people living in 1900 would never hear the actual voice of the president of the United States. Those coming of age in 1940, however, would be well acquainted with the president's voice as he spoke to the country through a radio set in their living room. That same cohort would be well acquainted with war on a global scale, something that an individual born in 1980 could only experience through film and books.

The idea of cohorts with shared cultural experiences gave rise to the use of the term *generation* in the early 20th century. The use of the word is so common now that it is hard to imagine a time when people were not categorized as members of a particular generation. The term, when applied to social demographics, means "a category of people born within a specific historical era or time period." Grouping cohorts into generations is done in an attempt to better understand how various age groups interact. Generations are identified according to historical events or trends that mark them. The generation is then analyzed according to its consumer habits, health, psychology, and a host of other traits.[29]

Today, the Census Bureau even uses common generational terms in its literature. A 2001 Census Bureau brief on age in the 2000 Census referred to the "baby-boom cohort" but did not mention any other generations.[30] A 2006 Census Bureau report on the baby boomers went so far as to say that "understanding the demographic and socioeconomic characteristics of this generation in the present day is essential."[31]

BABY BOOMERS The largest identified cohort in the history of the United States is the baby boomers. As noted earlier, this group covers individuals born between 1946 and 1964. The term comes from the high birthrate during this period, peaking at 3.58 children per woman in 1957. The span of time is a wide one, and many have pointed out differences within the cohort, making the case that the baby boomers are not a homogenous group. So-called **leading-edge boomers**, those born between 1946 and 1954, were in their teens when President John F. Kennedy was assassinated, while the youngest of the boomers were not yet born. The **trailing-edge boomers**, those born between 1955 and 1964, were generally young enough to avoid service in the Vietnam War. These two groups have distinctive lifestyles and behaviors based on their particular life experiences.[32]

The boomers are aging in a way that makes them demographically unique. They are entering old age with a higher level of education, a more diverse racial makeup, and greater life expectancy than any previous generation. Their generation's size will also place a great toll on the rest of the society to meet their medical, financial, and emotional support needs.[33] Presently, however, the baby-boomer generation finds itself tending to the needs of adjacent generations. As the result of increasing life expectancy and delayed childbearing, many baby boomers are challenged with the responsibility of providing care for both dependent children and aging parents at the same time. This phenomenon has given baby boomers the additional label of the **sandwich generation** as they are stuck between two dependent generations.[34] Given the trends in this direction, subsequent generations will most likely be characterized in the same way.

GENERATION X Generation X has been defined by various ranges of birth years, but 1965 to 1981 seems to be referenced most consistently. These children inherited the results of cultural revolutions that their boomer parents enacted. A declining birthrate and shifting family structures made members of Generation X stand out statistically. By 1980, children living with parents married only once decreased to 56 percent.[35] The proportion of children younger than 5 years with working mothers increased from 20 percent to 46 percent from 1960 to 1980. In relation, children under 14 who were left home alone after school doubled in the 1970s.[36]

Generation X is a significantly smaller cohort than the baby boom. It accounted for 20 percent of the U.S. population in 2001, whereas baby boomers accounted for 41 percent.[37] Like most population groups, Generation X has its own unique set of values. Members have been found to prioritize family over careers, in marked contrast to baby boomers, who tend to prioritize careers and self-fulfillment. The trends in gender roles have also continued from those seen in the baby boom. Three-quarters of Generation X women worked in 2000, compared to only half of women of the same age group in 1975.[38] Women were also less likely to be married than their counterparts from the 1970s. Men's roles have consequently changed, with fewer Generation X men seeking jobs with more responsibility and married men taking on more responsibility in the home.[39]

The term Generation X, with its perceived attitudes and social habits, sticks out in the popular imagination. A number of books have been written about coping with the demographic both in the workplace and in advertising. The Census Bureau has also specifically targeted this generation in an attempt to assess its attitudes toward the decennial census. A special survey oriented toward Generation X was carried out in 2000. The survey confirmed the demographic's prioritization of family over career and the wider community. Contrary to popular opinion, participants in the survey were actively involved in their community. Respondents differed from baby boomers in the way they engaged their communities, favoring daily unsanctioned involvement over institutionally based efforts such as a philanthropic club. The Census Bureau has used this type of research to improve the outreach of the decennial census, while stressing the importance of the census toward community life and depicting it as a vehicle for the voices of a disaffected generation.[40]

MILLENNIALS The 2010 Census was the first to document the arrival of the **millennials** into adulthood. The millennial cohort includes individuals born after 1981. Millennials have continued the demographic trend of increasing diversity, with only 61 percent of the population as non-Hispanic whites, as compared with Generation X at 62 percent and the baby boomers at 73 percent.[41] One millennial demographic feature hearkens back to older generations—the high percentage born to an immigrant parent. In 2010, this was 11 percent for millennials, 7 percent for Generation Xers, and 5 percent for baby boomers.[42] The millennial percentage is actually equal to that of the generation whose parents immigrated to the United States from Europe and Asia in the 1800s.

The millennials are the most educated generation for their age group. More than half of the population had some college education in 2010, compared with 49 percent of Generation X at the same age and 36 percent of baby boomers.[43] Family dynamics have continued the trend toward later marriages and delayed childbearing. Millennial children tend to live with family members longer than any other generation at their age, 47 percent, making up for the dearth of married households within the same cohort.[44]

A single defining factor of millennials, distinguishing it from other generations, is a reliance on technology. Baby boomers and Generation Xers have adapted to technology, but they did not come of age when texting and social networking were in full force. Millennials send more texts, are more likely to have a social networking profile, and post more videos of themselves online than any other generation. These behaviors attest to a new generational cohesiveness among millennials and a possible generation gap with other cohorts.[45]

COPING WITH AGING GENERATIONS

The use of generations as a statistical tool helps us forecast statistical trends. For example, the millennials' reliance on technology will make the technological infrastructure a top factor in the generation's ability to work and function effectively. Wireless networks will be forced to keep up with generations that are increasingly dependent on the Internet as a form of media. Per capita income of specific generations helps us make assumptions on future tax revenue. And, as we've seen, one of the most heralded generational impacts on the nation's economy is the approach of the baby-boomer generation toward retirement age.

The prediction of a rapidly aging population increases the changes for what some have termed **structural lag**. This is a concept that refers to the resistance of social institutions to change with the times. When social structures encounter rapid changes in demography, economy, or culture, they often lag behind in adjusting to these rapid changes. For example, at the time that Social Security was invented, the age structure of the United States suggested that the country would have many young people paying into a system to support the small population of the elderly. However, the Social Security system stands to encounter structural lag, resulting from increased life spans.[46] This means that the institution is no longer designed to meet the increased demand without some form of change. At the printing of this text, no serious effort is being made to consider either increasing funds to the system or decreasing benefits.[47] This problem is a persistent one, and statistical demographics play a large role in understanding it.

Health Care

Aging generations have had an enormous impact on the changing role of health care in the United States, accounting, in part, for the increasing amount of money spent on health care. Late 20th century medical advances have caused a shift in the health issues of older Americans. At one time, infectious diseases and acute illnesses such as pneumonia were the major source of death among older Americans. The leading cause of death among older age groups in 2007 was chronic disease and degenerative illnesses such as cancer and diabetes.[48] Because smoking, poor diet, and physical inaction were cited as the causes of these chronic conditions, more funding has gone toward education and behavioral changes. Although some may balk at the prospect of funding public health initiatives aimed at education rather than actual treatment, the cost of treating older individuals for chronic conditions is three to five times higher than treating someone under 65.[49]

The graph in the previous section indicated that the over-65 demographic more than doubled in 80 years. Increased longevity and the size of the soon-to-retire baby boom indicate that the population of older adults will double again—and in a mere 25 years. This demographic boom and the threat of chronic disease make the challenge of providing health care for the elderly a daunting one. In 2007, nearly 80 percent of adults older than 65 had a single chronic condition, and 50 percent had at least two. Chronic conditions drastically diminish quality of life. They also incur tremendous costs; nearly 95 percent of health care expenditures are a result of chronic conditions.[50]

Social Security Funding

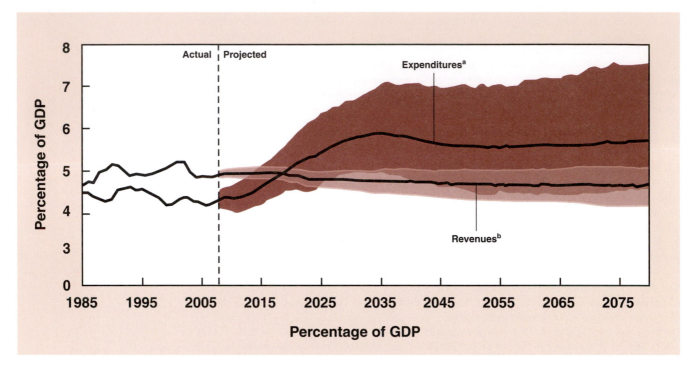

Figure 5.2 The Congressional Budget Office projects that Social Security expenditures will exceed revenues before 2025. The shaded area indicates the 80 percent range of uncertainty around each figure. Source: Congressional Budget Office, *Updated Long-Term Projections for Social Security*, 2008, http://www.cbo.gov/ftpdocs/96xx/doc9649/08-20-SocialSecurityUpdate.pdf

AGING IN THE RECENT CENSUSES

Census reports categorize individuals 65 and over as the older demographic. The data show how this demographic is faring in categories that range from health to education. Recent figures since 2000 can provide an indication of the ways in which this demographic can change in a short number of years.

2000

In 2000, the youngest members of the over-65 population were born in 1935, while the oldest could have been born before 1900. The oldest may have fought in World War I and had children during the Great Depression. The youngest were too young to serve in World War II or even to remember the Depression. These differences make it deceptive to lump these individuals together in one age range, but, as the statistics prove, their contrast with younger generations make their internal differences less obvious.

Just as 15- and 25-year-olds have distinctly different needs, so do 65- and 75-year-olds. For this reason, the elderly can be broken down into two major cohorts: the "young old" and the "old old." The **young-old** cohort consists of people between 65 and 75, while the **old-old** cohort refers to those older than 75. The young old are generally in good health, live alone, and are financially independent. The old old tend to have failing health, live with family or in a retirement home, and rely on others for financial support. The young old are the largest cohort, consisting of about 53 percent of the elderly population, but living past the age of 75 is not uncommon.[51]

The number of women 65 and older greatly outnumbers the men, with 20.6 million women to 14.4 million men. The ratio of men to women is called the **sex ratio**, and it is expressed as the number of males per 100 females. The sex ratio for the entire population in 2000 was 96.1, while the ratio for the 65 and older population was 69.8. The figure drops considerably with the older age groups. These statistics indicate what many already know, namely that women live longer than men.[52]

Statistics on living arrangements for older Americans show that only 5.7 percent lived in group quarters, compared with 2.8 percent of the entire population. Thus, the older a person gets, the more likely he or she is to live with others in some type of a group setting. This may reflect the trend to live in nursing homes and assisted living centers. Nearly 66 percent of the elderly lived with others in a household, compared with 88 percent of the total population. Consequently, older Americans who still live in their own home are more likely to live alone. This is supported by the fact that 28.2 percent of those over 65 lived alone, as compared with only 9.7 percent of the total population. In that figure, the gender difference is striking. In the 65 and over bracket, approximately 7.5 million women, versus only 2.4 million men, lived alone, reinforcing the data on increased longevity for women.[53]

Not all figures show a disparity. Eleven percent of the total population and 10 percent of the 65 and older population was foreign born. While 82.1 percent of the total population spoke only English at home, 87.4 percent of those over 65 spoke only English at home. Thus, older people are more likely to be English speakers.

Considering the percentage of households that speak another language, 59.9 percent of them speak Spanish, while 21.3 percent speak other Indo-European languages such as French or German. The remaining groups speak a variety of other languages. Of the 65 and older population, however, the Indo-European households outnumber the Spanish-speaking households at 43.8 percent and 38 percent, respectively.[54] These statistics indicate that while the proportion of foreign born is nearly the same in the total population and the older demographic, the makeup of that percentage is very different. The higher proportion of Indo-European speakers in the 65 and older group points to older trends of immigration from Europe.[55]

Education provides another interesting look at generational differences. For example, of those who are older, the rate of having less than a high school diploma goes up, moving from 30 percent of those 65–74 up to 47 percent of those older than 85. Essentially, as we move up through the age groups, the educational attainment level goes down. For example, 17 percent of those 65–74 have bachelor's degrees, compared to 12.5 percent of those older than 85.[56]

Beyond the 2000 Census

Looking at the data available in 2010, the youngest of the 65 and older population would have been born in 1945, while the oldest were probably born after 1910. The oldest could have fought in World War II and grown up during the Great Depression, while the youngest would have no personal involvement in the war and only experienced the aftermath of the Depression. Just as it did in the 2000 Census, the 65 and older cohort in 2010 includes individuals from a wide age range. This cohort experienced a great deal change as its members moved through each decade of the 21st century—and that change continued on into the new millennium.

The 65 and older population in the United States rose from 35 million in 2000 to 39 million in 2010, accounting for slightly more than 13 percent of the entire population. Thus, this segment of the population grew by percentage and in total number. The 85 and older segment of this population grew from 4.2 million in 2000 to 5.7 million in 2010, which indicates that people are living even longer.[57] By 2030, the older population is projected to reach nearly 20 percent of the total population, where it will remain steady as the last of the baby boomers enter retirement. The women in the 65 and older group continued to outnumber the men, 22.4 million women versus 16.4 million men, keeping the sex ratio nearly the same in 2010 as it was in 2000. The 85 and older population showed 1.8 million men and nearly double the women at 3.8 million. These statistics indicate that older men's health continues to fare poorly compared to women's.[58]

Projections for the sex ratio suggest that shorter life spans for men than women will be a continuing trend, but they also estimate that the gap between the sexes will decrease as men's health improves. In short, the Census Bureau predicts that men will start living longer with time. These projections are also useful for anticipating the type of health care and other services the older population will need. Gender differences result in contrasting health needs, which are generally carried into older age. For example, men are more likely to suffer from prostate cancer and women are more likely to suffer from ovarian or breast cancer. Because of the larger population of older women, the health care system can use this information to take additional measures to address the conditions and disease that commonly affect this group.[59]

As minority populations continue to grow, the older population is projected to become more ethnically diverse. The 2010 figures put the white segment of the older population at 87 percent. By 2050, this figure is projected to decrease by 10 percent, while every minority group in this age bracket is expected to increase.[60] The smallest minority populations, such as American Indians, Alaska Natives, and Pacific Islanders, are projected to have the greatest increases among minority groups in the 65 and older bracket, seeing as much as a fourfold increase by

2050. Figures from 2010 showed that 7 percent of the 65 and older population was Hispanic. This figure is projected to make a strong increase to 20 percent by 2050.[61]

Education statistics changed for the 65 and over generation in the 2009 figures. (At the time of printing this book, 2010 data were not yet available.) While in 2000, 34.5 percent of the 65 and older population did not finish high school, only 21.7 percent of the same group did not graduate in 2009, much closer to the 19.6 percent rate for the entire population over 25 that was noted in 2000. Of the older population, 20.2 percent had received some college or an associated degree in 2009, compared with only 18.1 percent in 2000. Education numbers demonstrate that the aging population had an increasingly higher level of education than previous generations.[62]

Geographic Age Distribution

Age distribution varies from state to state. In many states, the elderly population falls along the national average numbers of 13 percent of the total population, but some states have anomalous proportions of elderly. In 2009, the states with the highest percentage of individuals aged 65 and older were Florida (17.2 percent), West Virginia (15.8 percent), Maine (16 percent), Pennsylvania (15 percent), Iowa (14.8 percent), North Dakota (14.7 percent), Montana (14.6 percent), Hawaii (14.5 percent), South Dakota (14.5 percent), and Vermont (14.5 percent). States with the lowest percentage of older people in 2009 were Alaska (7.6 percent), Utah (9 percent), Texas (10.3 percent), and Georgia (10.3 percent).[63] In the 2000 Census, Alaska had an even lower rate of older people, at 5.7 percent. States such as Utah (8.5 percent), Georgia (9.6 percent), and Texas (9.9 percent) all had lower rates as well.[64]

Population projections made by the Census Bureau for 2015 show that the elderly population is expected to take on a greater percentage of the population in every state; the state rankings, however, are expected to remain essentially the same. This expectation indicates that people throughout the country will get older but are unlikely to move to other regions. Of those that do relocate, Florida is indicated as the most likely destination, as its elderly population is projected to rise 2 percent to 19.5 percent in 2015. Conversely, Utah is indicated as the least

Figure 5.3 This map shows the percentage of the population over 65 years of age.
Source: Social Explorer, "1790 to Present," *U.S. Decennial Census Files,* http://www.socialexplorer.com

likely destination, as its elderly population is projected to increase approximately 1 percent to 10.1 percent.[65] Longevity plays role in deciphering these numbers. As people live longer, the percentages of the elderly in any state will continue to grow; therefore, if a state's percentage of elderly is expected to increase at a below-average rate, then the state will likely lose numbers from its total population, most likely as the result of out-migration.[66]

The Census Bureau separates the country into four main regions: the Northeast, the South, the Midwest, and the West. The Southern and Western regions have seen the highest growth rate for the 65 and older population. Western states such as Arizona, California, and Nevada are top retirement destinations, causing an older population boom in the West as well. The South has long appealed to older populations who favor warm weather. This may account, in part, for the general trend of increasing numbers of the elderly living in these regions.[67]

Older populations also tend to live more in metropolitan areas. By 2004, the percentage of 65 and older individuals living in metropolitan areas had risen to 77 percent. Nearly two-thirds of this group lived in suburban areas, and the other third lived in cities. Generally, metropolitan growth among older demographics has occurred in the South, Midwest, and the Northeast. Nonmetropolitan percentage increases have occurred in the Midwest. This is due, in part, to the migration of younger populations away from the Midwest. Young people leaving changes the balance, and so the percentage of older people increases merely by an exodus of the young. It sets the percentage of older people higher, even if they are not moving into the area.[68]

These types of shifts in the demographic of an area can have a serious impact on the total population. Using census information to find out where and when these shifts occur is a vital resource to help society prepare for the future. This preparation will be appreciated particularly by the baby-boomer generation and any other "booms" that may come in the future.

KEY TERMS

Gerontology is the study of aging. 68

Median age is the average age of a population. 69

Life expectancy is the average life span for a member of a population. 69

Birthrate is the number of births per 1,000 women for a given population. 69

Birth dearth refers to declining birth rates. 69

Pensions are retirement plans set up for an employee by an employer. 70

Social Security Act was an act passed in 1935 authorizing a payroll tax on Americans for the purpose of funding their retirement. 70

Ageism is discrimination against an individual because of his or her age. 70

Baby-boom generation is the generation born between 1946 and 1964 and is the largest identified cohort in the history of the United States. 70

Cohorts are populations born during specific time periods. 70

Generation X is the generation born between 1965 and 1981. 71

Generation refers to categories of people born within a specific historical era or time period. 71

Leading-edge boomers are individuals born between 1946 and 1954. 72

Trailing-edge boomers are individuals born between 1955 and 1964. 72

Sandwich generation is a generation that cares for both its children and its parents. 72

Millennials is the generation born after 1980. 72

Structural lag is the lag between changes in age structures and changes in lives. 73

Young old is a cohort that consists of people between the ages of 65 and 75. 74

Old old is a cohort that consists of people older than 75. 74

Sex ratio is the number of males per 100 females. 74

CHAPTER QUIZ

1. A rising _____ population will outnumber the older white population in Texas in the coming decades.
   a. young, black
   b. middle-aged, Asian
   c. young, white
   d. young, Hispanic

2. The median age of the United States is _____ the worldwide median age.
   a. greater than
   b. less than
   c. the same as
   d. not comparable to

3. In 1935, the _____ was passed in an effort to cope with the growing problem of elder poverty.
   a. Medicare Act
   b. Discrimination Against Older Americans Act
   c. Volstead Act
   d. Social Security Act

4. The generation born between 1946 and 1964 is called _____.
   a. Generation Y
   b. Generation X
   c. the baby boomers
   d. the millennials

5. A decreasing retirement age and an increase in longevity means that, without policy changes, the _____ will most likely run out of money within the next 80 years.
   a. government
   b. National Trust
   c. Social Security System
   d. AARP

Answers: 1. d; 2. a; 3. d; 4. c; 5. c

ESSAY QUESTIONS

1. Discuss the ways in which immigration will likely affect aging demographics in the United States.

2. Explain the major causes of the trend toward an older population both worldwide and in the United States.

3. Compare and contrast your generation, as identified in the text, with that of your parents. Explain the ways in which the statistics attributed to these generations are, or are not, born out in your lives.

4. Explain the concept of structural lag and its consequences in the areas of retirement, health care, and labor productivity.

5. Discuss the relevance that projections for the 65 and older population have for public policy and society as a whole.

SOURCES FOR FURTHER RESEARCH

Census data on age:
http://www.census.gov/population/www/socdemo/age/

Statistical reports and maps, sorted by age:
http://www.socialexplorer.com/pub/home/home.aspx

Centers for Disease Control and Prevention: Aging issues:
http://www.cdc.gov/aging/

National Institute of Aging, part of the National Institute of Health:
http://www.nia.nih.gov/

Administration on Aging, part of the Department of Health and Human Services:
http://www.aoa.gov/

U.S. Senate Special Committee on Aging:
http://aging.senate.gov/

6 Marriage and Family

The American family has changed from traditional notions of family to include a broader range of living arrangements and lifestyles. (FlemishDreams/Fotolia)

THE NEW AMERICAN FAMILY

The American family is changing. Even in regions of the country that are considered more conservative or traditional, the nature of family is morphing, becoming far broader and including far more types of arrangements than ever before. A recent article explored the growing trend in the South of gay couples feeling freer to be open about their sexuality. By examining results of the Census Bureau's 2009 American Community Survey, demographer Gary Gates discovered there are more gay parents in the Southern United States than any other region of the country. In 2009, 32 percent of gay couples in Jacksonville, Florida, and 34 percent in San Antonio, Texas, were raising children.[1] Gay couples in the South tend to raise children more often than those in other regions, in part due to the diversity of such couples in the South. Notably, black and Latino gay couples are two times as likely to be raising children as white gay couples. They are also more likely to live in poverty.[2]

As more and more gay couples become parents, there is an increase in families whose makeup is different than those typically portrayed as "normal." In the South, where family and religion hold a very high value, many churches have identified that these families are especially in need of their support. The increasing awareness and openness of gay families have resulted in gay-friendly churches offering programs for the children of gay couples, a level of acceptance that has long eluded the gay community, and a record number of lesbian participants in the church.[3]

The inclusion of gay couples in the census questionnaires began in 1990, and only in 2010 were married gay couples counted. There was some controversy regarding their inclusion, as originally the Census Bureau had claimed it could not report gay couples as married because of the 1996 Defense of Marriage Act, as the act bars the federal recognition of same-sex marriages and allow states to do so as well. By 2011, however, New Hampshire, New York, California, Vermont, Iowa, Connecticut, Massachusetts, Rhode Island, Maryland, and the District of Columbia had all passed legislation to recognize gay marriage in some form. States such as Hawaii, Illinois, New Jersey, Oregon, Washington, Wisconsin, and Nevada all allow some form of either civil union or spousal rights to gay unmarried couples.[4] The fact that so many states have begun to consider the rights of gay couples resulted in them being counted for the first time in the 2010 Census.[5] Around the same time, Congress began considering a repeal of the Defense of Marriage Act; the Respect for Marriage law would enable the federal government to recognize same-sex marriages without forcing individual states to do so.[6]

Gathering information about gay families can shed light on difficulties they face that "traditional" families may never even consider. By including same-sex couples, the Census Bureau will be able to provide previously unavailable data to the public. In the future, we may be able to keep track of trends in marriage and coupling patterns in the United States for both gay and straight couples. Such information could be very useful to researchers, policy makers, and the moral entrepreneurs on both sides of this contentious issue.[7]

Despite the increasing percentage of gay parents in the South, the social stigma continues to exist and many questions about marriage and family have yet to find a collective answer. Perhaps most importantly: What is a family? What are the trends of marriage and divorce? How has the family changed over time? Is cohabitation a new form of family? In this chapter, we will investigate these questions and other marriage- and family-related questions. Because the data on same-sex families is new, there will be little we can say at this time about such couples. However, the fundamental question to investigate in this chapter remains: Who have been and who are the "typical" American family?

THE CHANGING AMERICAN FAMILY

What is a family? What behaviors or linkages are required to make two people family members? When you think of a "traditional" family, what comes to mind? Depending on the culture in which we are raised, our conceptions of what makes up a "normal" family may differ. In American culture, the typical notion of a traditional family probably involves a husband, wife, and one or more of their children, a dynamic that is referred to as a **nuclear family**. In other cultures, the average family may include grandparents, aunts and uncles, or cousins. And while these conceptions of normality are reinforced by many sources—television programs, movies, magazines, and so forth—more and more families don't resemble this norm. The Census Bureau has tracked and adapted to the changing makeup of families over time. For example, due to a growing number of married people not living with their spouse due to marital discord, the Census Bureau added the category of "separated" to the census starting in 1950.[8] Looking at these changes, we can consider why they have emerged and to what extent they reflect changing cultural values.

Despite the changes in what makes a family over time and across cultures, defining it has become hotly debated. For this text, we consider a **family** to be a group of two or more people who are related by blood, marriage, or adoption and who reside together and consider themselves as one unit.[9] Therefore, when you move away from home permanently, you are no longer a part of your family of origin, at least according to the way the Census Bureau tracks family data. While many people consider close friends to be family, for the purposes of the census, they are not counted as such. This definition also highlights the problem of gay couples and couples who cohabitate without marriage. Without being linked by marriage, these couples cannot be considered in the family data produced. The debate continues to rage, with many states defining marriage as the union between one man and one woman. In fact, 39 states have laws and/or constitutional amendments defining marriage as so.[10]

If we consider what a family is, we realize the definition has changed a great deal over time. Stephanie Coontz, a researcher in marital history, suggests that the most common definition of marriage and family varies so much throughout history that it almost defies the concept of a definition.[11] We know, for example, many European nations now have a form of family that does not involve actual marriage, but instead is long-term cohabitation in which children are raised and couples stay together, often for longer periods of time than the "American family."[12]

Perhaps a more accurate and inclusive definition of **marriage** is the union of two people that is recognized by their laws and/or cultures. Yet, this is still limiting, as other cultures, even within the United States, recognize polygamous marriages. Thus, it is important to consider that definitions of marriage have within them a social construct; each culture decides what it means to be married and who is allowed to marry. Even within the United States limitations on marriage vary a great deal. For example, in the United States, 19 states allow first cousins to marry under any circumstances, 25 states do not ever allow them to marry, and the rest allow them to marry with exceptions, such as if they cannot have children.[13] Do we have a universal definition of marriage? Clearly not.

In fact, throughout history, most marriages and families were not really what we today call a nuclear family. Frequently, a grandmother or other relative lived with the family.[14] Even today, this may occur, as the elderly woman may move in with her child as she ages or a single mother's sister may join the household to help raise her nieces and nephews. These are examples of an **extended family**—a family structure that includes one or more additional relatives. Yet, even this term does not encompass all the variations that might exist in the same household.

To clarify the data it collects, the Census Bureau uses the term "household" to indicate all of the people who reside together in a housing unit, regardless of their relationships.[15] This is a broader term that could include roommates living together, a couple cohabitating but not married, or someone renting a room in a family's home. In some cases, the census also asks for details about these relationships, such as couples in intimate relationships who are not married, regardless of sexual orientation. Such relationships will be examined in depth in this chapter. Often, members of a household, such as an unmarried gay couple, consider themselves a family while the Census Bureau does not. It is useful to keep in mind the implications of these terms. Do you feel differently when you think of someone as a member of your household as opposed to a member of your family?

These definitions are important and they tell us much about our society, the lifestyles people live, and what choices they make regarding their relationships. The census and other surveys can be used to explore the changing definition of family in the United States and throughout the rest of the world.

Unmarried Adults

One notable change in the American family is the increase of those who aren't in the process of starting one—that is, those who are not married. In 2009, 43 percent of all Americans age 18 or older were unmarried. Among them, 53 percent were women, which means that out of every 100 unmarried Americans, 53 were women and 47 were men. Of these 96.6 million single adults, 61 percent had never been married, 24 percent were divorced, and 15 percent were widowed. Seventeen percent of unmarried people are age 65 or older. In terms of households, 52.5 million, or 45 percent of all American households, are headed by an unmarried man or woman.[16]

These numbers reflect a recent increase in unmarried people in the United States. Notably, in 2005, married couples had become a minority of American households for the first time. More women were unmarried than married; 51 percent were living without a spouse.

These numbers reflect the trend of adults, men and women, marrying later in life, often delaying marriage until after obtaining higher education degrees and establishing careers.[17] Also adding to these numbers are the many couples who choose to **cohabitate**, or live together in an intimate relationship without marrying. This could include gay couples as well. Many choose to cohabitate rather than enter into a second or third marriage following a previous divorce; still others don't value marriage in the traditional sense and are happy to honor their commitment to each other without it for many years.[18] In 2008, 6.2 million households consisted of unmarried couples, 565,000 of which were same-sex couples.[19]

Race and gender play a role in who marries as well. For example, approximately 70 percent of black females are unmarried, while less than 50 percent of white women are in this category. Women are more likely to live longer than men, and this reality seems to increase the unmarried population of women in the United States. Overall, 31.7 million people of both genders were single in 2009, representing 27 percent of all households, a significant increase from 17 percent in 1970.[20]

These trends have important implications for American culture and policy. Politicians often focus their attention and campaigning on attracting families to their policies and crafting legislation to improve the lives of families. If the nature of family has become something far different from the traditional definition—and if large numbers of the voting population are delaying starting families and living the single life instead—such policies may not appeal to most Americans.

UNMARRIED PARENTS The trends in the United States indicate that more and more people are having children without being married. Unmarried parents could include a mother raising children on her own, without the father, or vice versa. In the United States, both the number and percentage of single-parent households increased, from 1980 to 2008, from 19.5 percent of all households with children to 29.5 percent. The majority of these households were headed by single mothers. Children born to single mothers increased from 18.4 percent to 40.8 percent, a tremendous increase in less than 30 years.[21] Of women who gave birth within the 12 months prior to a survey in 2006, 33 percent were widowed, divorced, or never married. Approximately 199,000 were living with a partner to whom they were not married.[22] In total, there were 11.6 million single parents living with their children in 2009, 9.9 million mothers and 1.7 million fathers.[23] Besides single parents, many unmarried parents live together with their children. In fact, 38 percent of unmarried, opposite-sex couples who live together have at least one child who is the biological son or daughter of one or the other partner.[24] Among grandparents raising their grandchildren, 766,000 were unmarried in 2008—three out of every 10 such grandparents.[25] It is likely that many were widowed.

From 1980 to 2008, many countries around the world had an increase in the percentage of single-parent households. In the United States, percentage of all births to single parents climbed from 18 percent in 1980 to 40 percent in 2008, but we were not alone in the growth of unmarried births in that time period. In France, for example, the percentage increased from 11.4 percent to 52.6 percent; and in Spain, the percentage increased from 3.9 percent to 31.7 percent. Actually, the percentages of births to single women grew in most wealthy nations.[26]

These commonalities suggest these changes are not due to something unique about the American family, but rather a change that pervades many Western cultures. This could occur for a number of reasons, including increases in the rate at which unmarried women have children; decreases in the rate at which married women have children, in turn, making the percentage of single parents seem greater; and/or decreases in the total proportion of married women and increases in the proportion of unmarried women. As previously stated, there appears to be a retreat from marriage today, and so it is possible that the percentages of single parents grew, partially because the rate of marriage declined.

In contrast to the global trend, however, the frequency of unmarried mothers remains extremely low in Japan, increasing only slightly from 0.8 percent to 2.1 percent from 1980 to 2006. In Japanese culture, the frequency of teenage sex is low, and abortions are readily available for those who want them. Most crucially, there is a strong stigma against single motherhood. Japanese single mothers are humiliated and denigrated by their fellow Japanese, even suffering tax penalties for being single that are not issued to widowed mothers. Even their children suffer lifelong consequences, such as rejection by their families and discrimination in education and careers.[27]

Age at First Marriage

As mentioned previously, advanced education and other factors have led many people—both men and women—to delay the age at which they marry. At the start of the 20th century, the median age for marriage was 25.9 years for men and 21.9 years for women.[28] In the 1950s, the median ages lowered to 22.8 years for men and 20.3 years for women.[29] Since then, the median age rose again, to 27.5 for men and 25.6 for women in 2007, the year of the most recent data.[30] To answer the question why the delay of marriage is continuing, it seems obvious that the next generation is less interested in marriage than their grandparents. Perhaps it is the increased acceptance of cohabitation, or an increased interest in personal and/or career goals. Regardless, the trend indicates that the age of first marriage is likely to continue to get older.

Divorce

"'Til death do us part" may be the vow many couples take upon getting married, but many don't make it that far. The divorce rate has increased considerably over time. In the 1950s, 85 percent of marriages lasted at least 10 years, but in 2001, only about 70 percent did.[31] There are many reasons why a couple may decide to divorce. Spouses may grow apart or develop irreconcilable differences. Under more unfortunate circumstances, spouses may become unfaithful, abusive, or neglectful. Regardless of the reason, the stigma of getting divorced has lessened, and on the whole, society today is more tolerant of divorce.

Certain factors seem to predict whether a marriage will end in divorce. Marrying at an early age tends to lead to increased likelihood of divorce, so delaying marriage may be beneficial if avoiding divorce is the goal. Cohabiting before marriage, however, may not be beneficial. Research suggests that those who live together before marriage are more likely to get divorced, perhaps because of a lower premium being placed on the marriage commitment.[32]

There are several lifestyle factors that increase the likelihood of keeping a marriage intact. Religion is once such factor: Catholics are 11 percent less likely to get divorced than others. Additionally, having similarities in education level (e.g., both spouses have a college education rather than only one), getting married in your mid-20s or older, waiting until marriage to have children, and not having a family history of divorce all decrease your odds of divorce. [33]

Comparing the United States to other nations, America has both the highest rate of marriage and the highest rate of divorce when measuring these by the rate of married/divorced people per every 1,000 citizens. Both these rates decreased from 1980 to 2008, from 15.9 marriages to 10.6 marriages per 1,000. Divorce also dropped from 7.9 people out of a 1,000 reporting they are divorced to 5.2 per 1,000. The United States is not alone. All Western nations seemed to exhibit a similar decrease in the rate of marriage, but not all showed a corresponding decrease in the divorce rate.[34]

2000–2001 FINDINGS IN THE FAMILY

The decennial census has asked questions about marital status since 1880; the separated category was added in 1950. With this data, a student of marriage can gain vital information about the history of marriage in the United States, which can help build a framework for the understanding of marriage in the social construction of the country. In 2000, the long form of the decennial census provided detailed information on the state of marriage in the United States. Of the 221.1 million people age 15 years or older, 54.4 percent declared that they were married, 9.7 percent stated they were divorced, 2.2 percent stated they were separated, 6.6 percent stated they were widowed, and 27.1 percent stated they had never married.[35]

Unsurprisingly, the rate of widowhood increases with an increase in age, and 35 percent of those 85 years or older said they were widowed. Divorce rates peak for both men and women during middle age, roughly 35 to 55 years. The never-married rate drastically declines with a decrease in age; about 95 percent of both men and women aged 15 to 19 say they have never been married.[36]

Regions also play a role in these rates. For example, the Midwest and the South report the highest percentage of those reporting to be married: 55.2 percent and 55.1 percent, respectively. The Northeast and West report the lowest percentage at 52.7 percent and 53.8, percent, respectively. Later in this chapter, we'll look more closely at the effects of geography on marriage and family.

To increase the data on the U.S. population, the Census Bureau instituted the Survey of Income and Program Participation (SIPP). While its main objective is to collect information about the income and program participation of U.S. households, its data also provides a unique look at marriage and divorce trends over time.[37] The survey examined trends based on **birth cohort**, a group of people born at the same time, often within the same five-year period, or based on **marriage cohort**, a group of people who married during the same set of years. Birth cohort can examine the effect of generation on trends—whether people born at a certain time in history share certain behaviors. Marriage cohort can compare the effect of beginning a relationship at a certain point in time and how that might affect factors such as marriage length.[38] For instance, one might imagine that someone born in 1920 would be raised to think of divorce as a more dishonorable behavior than someone born in 1980—that would be an effect of birth cohort. By contrast, if one had been married for 20 years in 1940, perhaps one would have a different tendency to embrace the possibility of divorce than someone who had been married for 20 years in 1980—this would be an effect of marriage cohort.[39]

Marriage and Divorce

First, we will examine the historical data provided by this survey. The SIPP data strongly support that younger people are delaying marriage longer. Indeed, of those born in the late 1930s, a full two-thirds of men and more than 80 percent of women were married by age 25. By contrast, of those born in the early 1970s, only 39.4 percent of men and 53.4 percent of women were married by the same age. The pattern stabilized starting with those born in the mid-1960s, as their rate of marriage by age 25 was not significantly different from those born in the 1970s.[40] It still remains to be seen whether these cohorts are still delaying marriage or if they may remain unmarried. As the generation born in the 1970s ages, the census and other surveys will show if we will see an increase in the percentage of people marrying for the first time in their 30s and 40s as compared to earlier generations.

The proportion of people divorced at any point in time is a complex measure due to the fact that it is a function of how many people have ever been married. In this way, it is a completely separate set of information from the marriage data above, as only those who have been married are included. For women, the rate of divorce, or the percentage of married people who have ever been divorced, did increase over time until the late 1970s, when those born in the late 1950s and early 1960s began to marry. At this point, the divorce rate leveled off, and even decreased slightly. Correspondingly, marital longevity (the length of marriages) decreased between the marriage cohorts of 1955 to 1959 and 1975 to 1979, but has since leveled off and may even be increasing slightly. A similar pattern exists for men.[41]

For both men and women, the rate of remarriage—marrying again after being divorced or widowed—increased for those born from 1945 to 1950, which would make this cohort a part of the baby-boom generation. Since the baby boom resulted in more people, with no decrease in the marriage rate, more total marriages of all types seem likely. So, as fewer people marry and the number of divorces remains relatively steady, what might one expect to happen to the rate of remarriage? Predictably, it decreased for men, from 22 percent to 17 percent of men between the birth cohorts of 1945 to 1949 and 1955 to 1959.[42] Interestingly, women did not experience this decrease. The possible reasons are unclear; however, this may indicate an increased number of remarriages for one person. For example, there are many people who are on their third and/or fourth marriages. Such individuals muddy the waters of these data, making a clear understanding of the data difficult to ascertain.

Notably, and contrary to common belief, fewer Americans than one might assume had ever been divorced in the year 2000. While the percentage of couples divorced tends to increase based on the length of that marriage, on average, only 20 percent of people—not the 50 percent as often cited—had ever divorced. Disparities in the rate of divorce are also due to the couple's cohort as well as age. For instance, 40.8 percent of men and 38.9 percent of women aged 50 to 59 years had ever been divorced, whereas only 18.6 percent of men and 17.7 percent of women 70 years of age or older had ever been divorced.[43] The lower divorce rate among these oldest couples may be influenced by the social norms of past decades that disapproved of divorce or mortality because they have the highest likelihood of being widowed.

The rate of divorce also tends to increase for second and later marriages. Of those married in the late 1970s, 55.8 percent of men and 54.1 percent of women made it to their 20th wedding anniversary if it was their first marriage, while only 49 percent of men and 47.2 percent of women had second marriages that lasted as long. Indeed, among those who had ever been divorced, only between 35.9 percent and 58.4 percent of men and between 35.5 percent and 49 percent of women were in second or subsequent marriages as of the SIPP survey.[45] These repeat divorces tend to inflate the apparent rate of divorce in the country, thus leading some to suggest that divorce is more rampant than it actually is. In fact, for those on their first marriages, divorce becomes increasingly unlikely the longer they stay together. These figures are limited to spouses who survived until that data point, so these percentages are not affected by

★ TABLE 6.1 MARITAL HISTORY FOR PEOPLE AGES 15 OR OLDER, 2001[44] ★

Overall, the divorce rate in the United States is not as high as many people think it is.

	15 to 19 years	20 to 24 years	25 to 29 years	30 to 34 years	35 to 39 years	40 to 49 years	50 to 59 years	60 to 69 years	70 years and over
Men Never Married	99.1	83.9	50.8	29.5	21.5	14.2	6.3	4.3	3.3
Men Ever Divorced	0.1	1.0	7.5	15.4	22.9	29.5	40.8	30.9	18.6
Women Never Married	96.3	72.4	37.3	21.7	15.6	10.5	6.4	4.1	3.3
Women Ever Divorced	0.2	2.6	11.9	18.6	28.1	35.4	38.9	28.4	17.7

All numbers in percent.

mortality rate. Thus, the often-claimed "50 percent" divorce rate is not supported at all by these data.[46]

Divorce is not the only way marriages end, of course—they often end with the death of one spouse. Of married men 15 years or older, 3.6 percent have been widowed, and of same-age women, 11.6 percent have been widowed. This difference is likely due to the tendency of women to outlive men. Indeed, the difference in percentages becomes more pronounced as we look at older age groups. The gender difference remains within one percent until 40 to 49 years of age but becomes much larger in the subsequent decades of life. Among those 70 or older, 23.1 percent of men have been widowed, while 56.3 percent of women have been. In short, more than twice as many women than men in this age group had suffered the death of their spouse; differences in longevity between men and women are the obvious cause of this difference.[47]

In addition to all these marriages, divorces, and remarriages, still 30.9 percent of men and 24.6 percent of women 15 years of age or older had never been married. The percentage of women who had never been married was lower than the percentage of men for early life, and this difference was most pronounced among people in their late 20s; among them, 50.8 percent of men but only 37.3 percent of women had never been married. Marital rates for men catch up to those for women by their 50s, becoming and remaining nearly identical to women.[48]

Marriage and Race

Race also played a role. In the 2000 Census, Asians had the highest marriage rates and the lowest divorce rates of any group, with about 60 percent married for both men and women—with men reporting only 4 percent divorced, while that rate was 7 percent for women. Blacks had the lowest percentages of married—with 42 percent of men reporting they were married but only 31 percent of women reporting as such.[49] This difference is the largest of any racial category and may indicate an increase in interracial marriage in the United States, as black men are more likely than black women to be involved in an interracial marriage. For example, 10 percent of black men had a spouse of a different race or origin, compared to only 5 percent of black women. Forty percent of black men and women had never been married, which was also the highest proportion of any racial group.[50] Additionally, American Indians and Alaska Natives reported the highest divorce rates, with 11 percent of men and 14 percent of women saying they were divorced.[51]

When we look at the population divided by race, there are some notable trends related to marriage in the SIPP data as well. White men and women tend to enter into their first marriages at slightly earlier median ages—23.8 for men and 21.6 for women—than blacks, whose first marriages are a median age of 25 for men and 22.3 for women, and Asians/Pacific Islanders, whose first marriages are a median age of 27.1 for men and 24.8 for women. This trend is consistent for second marriages as well; whites remarry at a median age of 35 for men and 32.4 for women; Asians/Pacific Islanders remarry at a median age of 35.3 for men and 35.8 for women; black women remarry at a median age of 34.3. The Census Bureau does not calculate a median statistic for black men who remarry due to a small and insufficient sample size. These differences among the races suggest that the delay in marriage seen over time may be driven more strongly by non-white races than by whites. This may be due to cultural, religious, and other social differences that vary the importance of marriage by race.[52]

★ TABLE 6.2 MEDIAN DURATION OF MARRIAGES ENDING IN DIVORCE, 2001[53] ★

There is a fair amount of consistency in the number of years marriages that end in divorce tend to have lasted across race. There are some slight differences, however. What might account for these disparities?

(Duration in years)

Subject	Total	White Total	White Non-Hispanic	Black	Asian and Pacific Islander	Hispanic (of any race)
Duration of first marriage for those whose first marriage ended in divorce						
Men	8.2	8.1	8.2	8.9	8.3	7.8
Women	7.9	7.8	7.8	8.4	9.0	8.1
Duration between first marriage and first separation for those who separated						
Men	6.9	6.8	6.8	7.3	6.8	6.3
Women	6.7	6.7	6.6	6.6	7.7	6.8
Duration between first separation and first divorce for those who divorced						
Men	0.9	0.8	0.8	1.1	0.9	0.8
Women	0.8	0.8	0.8	1.2	0.7	0.8
Duration between first divorce and remarriage for those whose first marriages ended in divorce and who had remarried						
Men	3.3	3.3	3.3	3.8	3.1	3.2
Women	3.5	3.3	3.3	4.3	3.7	3.6
Duration of second marriage for those whose second marriage ended in divorce						
Men	9.2	9.2	9.3	8.7	(B)	6.4
Women	8.1	8.0	8.0	8.4	(B)	9.1

B Base less than 200,000. Median duration not shown.
Source: U.S. Census Bureau, Survey of Income and Program Participation (SIPP), 2001 Panel, Wave 2 Topical Module.

For those couples that divorce, the duration of the ended marriage was remarkably consistent. Nationally, of marriages that end in divorce the median number of years is 8.2 for men and 7.9 for women. This statistic shows little change when examined by race. For example, white men who divorce have a median marriage length of 8.1 years, and blacks and Asian/Pacific Islanders show similar numbers, with 8.9 years and 8.3 years, respectively. These numbers do show a bit of greater difference for women. For example, white women tend to divorce more quickly (after a median length of 7.8 years of marriage) than do black women (8.4 years) and Asian/Pacific Islander women (9.0 years).[54]

Lengths of time from marriage to separation and from separation to divorce were similar across race and gender. Once divorced, blacks tended to wait a bit longer to remarry (3.8 years for men, 4.3 years for women) than the national median of all races, which show 3.3 years for men and 3.5 years for women. Once remarried, for those whose second marriages ultimately ended in divorce, the second marriage was of similar length, about 9.2 years for men and 8.1 years for women. White men tended to stay in their second marriages the longest, with a total number of 9.3 years, while white women were the shortest, with a median of 8 years.[55]

Regarding the length of marriages for women who were married at the time of the survey, black and Asian/Pacific Islander women tended to progress through each five-year interval in lesser proportions than white women. For example, 83 percent of white women will reach their fifth anniversary, but only 81 percent of all women reach that milestone. Minority women appear to divorce more quickly, with about 72 percent of blacks, 74.5 percent of Hispanics, and 77.8 percent of Asians/Pacific Islanders reaching this marker.[56] Similarly, minority women are less likely to reach their semicentennial. Of white women, 6.2 percent of those currently married reached their 50th wedding anniversary, while only 3.4 percent of both black and Asian/Pacific Islander women and only 2 percent of Hispanic women do the same. Higher rates of divorce for blacks, in particular, and younger ages of marriage for blacks and Hispanics may contribute to this difference.[57]

When examining the issue of number of marriages, the misconceptions about the frequency of divorce creates a tendency to think that remarriage is more common than it is. The fact is that it is relatively uncommon: 69.8 percent of all current marriages were first marriages for both spouses. However, for those in their first year of marriage, the rate lowers to 62 percent. Only about 7 percent of all married couples involved a wife who was in her second marriage with a husband in his first, while 8 percent of married couples had a husband who was in his second marriage and a wife in her first. Another 8 percent of those married involved a couple in which both partners are in their second marriage.[58] After this point, the statistics become exceptionally low. For example, only 1 percent of all married couples involved a couple in which both the husband and the wife had each been married three or more times.[59] These data also contradict the claim of those who suggest that divorce rates are greater than 50 percent. These claims fail to recognize that rates may be driven up by a massive number of people involved in multiple remarriages.

Characteristics of the Married Population

Those who had experienced a marital event in 2001, including marriage, separation, divorce, or widowhood, can be tracked by race, employment, and other characteristics. Not surprisingly, far more whites experienced each of these events, as non-white races exist in fewer numbers in the U.S. population. Compared to the other statistics, however, it seems as though a disproportionate percentage of black men became separated and a disproportionate percentage of black women became widows. Hispanics and Asian/Pacific Islanders enjoyed a disproportionately high percentage of the total marriages in the country for both men and women, while blacks and whites were low.[61]

Age also plays a role. Those married in 2001 tended to be in their 20s or 30s, accounting for approximately 68 percent of the marriages and creating a median age of 30 for marriage. Perhaps not surprisingly, the older one gets past 35, the less likely he or she is to marry. Individuals working full time (though more women were unemployed after marriage than men) and living at more than 200 percent above the poverty level were among those in the category of people who experienced the most marriages.[62] Apparently, having a job and not being poor encourage marriage. Educational attainment was relatively balanced, with those having less than a high school diploma being the least likely to marry that year. These two issues may be related as poverty and job status are closely correlated with educational attainment. Most marriages do not involve children. For example, approximately 73 percent of marriages in 2001 did not involve a child living in the home of the married couple. Of those marriages that did involve children, only 9.1 percent of marriages involved children younger than age 9. Thus, it appears the majority of marriages are not involving the blended family.[63]

Those separating or divorcing showed the similar patterns except for age. These events are more likely for those in their mid 20s to their mid 50s. The median age for this event was 39 years, and from what we've already pointed to about the length of a marriage in the United States, it seems clear why. Once a couple gets past the age of 54, the ranges drop drastically. It would be interesting to study whether this is a cohort effect or merely a pattern that will continue in every generation. Because earlier data from the Census Bureau is not available, we'll have to wait and see what future studies show.[64]

Men and women who were widowed recently tended to be, predictably, older than those who experienced other marital events—aged 74 for men and 71 for women. Those who were widowed also tended to have lower educational attainment, with those with a bachelor's degree having the lowest percentages. This is most likely a reflection of generational trends and not some health benefit of education. Generally, older generations did not receive the same level of education as many do today. Likewise, most of those who were widowed in the past year were unemployed, likely because they are senior citizens and retired. They also tend to own their own homes, in contrast with those who experienced other marital events.[65]

As discussed earlier, parenthood can have an effect on marital status. Similarly, marriage can have an effect on parental status, namely the number of children one might have. Survey data examining those older than 45 years (under the presumption that any childbearing would likely be complete by that point) revealed that those who divorced and did not remarry were the most likely to not have children: 21.8 percent of men and 16.7 percent of women, as compared with percentages equal to or less than 10 percent for those in their first marriage or

★ TABLE 6.3 CHARACTERISTICS OF THOSE EXPERIENCING MARITAL EVENTS, 2001[60] ★

What might contribute to differing rates of marriages, divorce, or separation?

(Data include first and higher order events)

Characteristic at time of interview	Men				Women			
	Marriage	Separation	Divorce	Widowhood	Marriage	Separation	Divorce	Widowhood
Total (in thousands)	2,476	1,031	1,038	484	2,442	1,201	1,181	1,222
PERCENT	100.0	100.0	100.0	100.0	100.0	100.0	100.0	100.0
Race and Ethnicity								
White	82.7	79.7	84.6	79.5	81.2	83.2	85.2	80.2
Non-Hispanic	63.8	70.3	75.9	76.5	63.9	68.4	75.5	73.3
Black	9.6	16.6	10.7	13.8	9.8	11.1	11.1	16.0
Asian and Pacific Islander	6.1	1.4	4.0	6.7	7.7	3.9	2.2	3.4
Hispanic (of any race)	20.7	10.7	9.2	4.7	19.2	16.4	11.1	7.3
Age								
15 to 24 years	23.2	8.6	4.0	0.7	32.8	19.4	8.9	1.5
25 to 34 years	45.3	31.7	27.6	0.8	41.6	29.4	35.4	1.5
35 to 44 years	17.7	35.9	40.2	2.8	13.8	32.0	36.3	3.7
45 to 54 years	7.2	16.8	20.3	8.0	9.0	12.7	13.5	11.8
55 to 64 years	4.2	4.6	5.9	14.0	1.6	5.8	5.2	19.7
65 years and over	2.4	2.5	1.9	73.7	1.0	0.7	0.8	61.8
Median age (in years)	30.0	37.4	39.2	73.7	28.3	35.6	36.7	70.5
Educational Attainment								
Less than high school	16.2	16.6	13.2	39.9	17.0	18.3	12.3	32.3
High school graduate	30.9	35.5	30.0	28.0	25.2	34.3	29.4	31.8
Some college	28.4	30.1	36.6	13.6	30.0	32.0	35.3	22.8
Bachelor's degree or more	24.5	17.8	20.2	18.5	27.8	15.3	23.1	13.1
Employment Status[1]								
Worked full time last month	82.4	72.9	82.8	11.6	55.3	56.7	65.9	20.4
Worked part time last month	8.0	7.8	3.7	8.8	11.8	14.8	13.3	7.6
Did not work last month	9.6	19.2	13.6	79.5	32.9	28.5	20.7	72.0
Poverty Level								
Below poverty level	11.9	12.7 7.6	13.9	10.7	23.1	23.0	17.3	
100–199 percent of poverty level	17.2	20.7	16.6	27.6	17.4	22.0	21.0	30.8
200+ percent of poverty level	70.6	64.0	73.0	57.9	71.0	50.9	52.2	50.9
Income not reported	0.2	2.6	2.8	0.6	1.0	4.0	3.8	1.0
Household Receives								
Public Assistance								
Cash assistance	4.0	5.2	3.2	10.5	4.8	9.4	8.0	9.4
Noncash assistance[2]	26.7	19.1	15.3	21.6	26.9	39.7	33.5	26.0
Tenure								
Owns home	51.6	52.0	57.1	83.4	52.2	45.2	50.1	73.0
Rents home	47.0	44.2	39.9	14.4	46.3	52.0	46.6	24.7
Occupies without cash payment	1.4	3.8	3.0	2.1	1.6	2.8	3.3	2.4
Family Status[3]								
Not living with own children under 18	73.3	86.1	83.2	95.2	61.4	41.2	43.1	95.3
Currently living with own children under 18	26.7	13.9	16.8	4.8	38.6	8.8	56.9	4.7
Currently living with own children 1–17	20.8	13.3	15.1	4.8	33.0	57.1	55.8	4.7
Currently living with own children under 1	9.1	0.6	2.2	–	9.6	3.9	3.1	0.2

– Represents or rounds to zero.

[1]Full time includes those who usually work 35 or more hours per week; part time includes those who usually work 1–34 hours per week; those who did not work last month include individuals who were unemployed or were not in the labor force.

[2]Noncash benefits include food stamps, WIC, Medicaid, rent for public housing, lower rent due to government subsidy, energy assistance, and free or reduced price lunches or breakfasts.

[3]For the purposes of this table only, own children refers to biological or adopted children. The table excludes stepchildren.

Source: U.S. Census Bureau, Survey of Income and Program Participation (SIPP), 2001 Panel, Wave 2 Topical Module.

remarried. Regardless of marital status or gender, the most common number of children is two. For the divorced and remarried, the frequencies of having one or three children are roughly equal, but for those who are in their first marriage, both genders are almost twice as likely to have three children as they are to have one. This suggests that stability in marriage may lead to having more children.[66]

Cohabitation

In 2000, there were more married couples than unmarried ones. The census measures cohabitating couples, who live together in intimate relationships but are not married, including heterosexual and homosexual couples. About 600,000 cohabitating couples, or one in nine, were of the same sex. Same-sex unmarried couples have a slightly higher rate of living in metropolitan (urban or suburban) areas than opposite-sex unmarried couples or married couples, 85.3 percent versus 80.9 percent and 78.5 percent, respectively. This difference is even more pronounced for urban centers, where 41.6 percent of same-sex unmarried couples live, while only 35 percent of opposite-sex unmarried couples and 24.3 percent of married couples live in urban centers. The exact opposite pattern exists for suburban and rural areas, with a higher proportion of married couples residing there than unmarried couples, and opposite-sex unmarried couples residing there more often than same-sex unmarried couples. This is likely due to regional differences in the acceptance of homosexual couples and families and, to a lesser extent, of unmarried opposite-sex couples.[67]

Likewise, when we examine state and regional differences in residence of these couples, we can see that same-sex couples are, perhaps unsurprisingly, least likely to live in the Midwest as compared with the Northeast, South, and West, and are present in a lower proportion as compared with other types of couples there. By contrast, opposite-sex unmarried couples represent the lowest proportions in the South. On the whole, unmarried couples tend to live in higher proportions in the Northeast and in the West. The District of Columbia has the highest percentage of same-sex couples but also the highest percentage of opposite-sex unmarried couples. It seems as though many unmarried couples have chosen to live in this area, more so than in any state: 20.8 percent of all coupled households are unmarried in the District of Columbia as compared to 12.6 percent or less in every other state.[68]

Consistent with these figures, the top 10 feature box gives the top 10 cities of residence for married, opposite-sex unmarried, and same-sex unmarried couples based on percentage of that type of couple out of all households. Notice that the cities for same-sex couples are mostly on the East and West coasts, four of them in California alone. The majority of top cities for unmarried opposite-sex couples are in the Northeast or Southwest. Married couples were a bit more spread out, residing in high percentages in the West, Midwest, and South.[70]

UNMARRIED COUPLES AND RACE If we look at unmarried couples by race, there are some immediately apparent facts. Of coupled households, whites and Asians had the smallest percentages of cohabitating unmarried couples, at 8.2 percent and 4.7 percent respectively, and blacks and American Indians/Alaska Natives had the largest percentages, at 16.9 percent and 17.4 percent, respectively. Whites and Asians had the lowest percentages of same-sex couples, at 0.9 percent and 0.7 percent, respectively.[71]

The 2000 Census data also provide a glimpse into the households of interracial couples. Like same-sex couples, they have expanded the traditional definition of family to incorporate more diverse groupings of people. While interracial couples are increasingly accepted in many areas of the United States, they remain a small percentage of the married population of the country, at 5.7 percent of all married partner households. The West tends to have the greatest percentage of interracial couples, including interracial married couples, and the Midwest has the least. Roughly 10.6 percent of married couples in the West were of different races, while only 3.5 percent of married couples in the Midwest were of different races. This pattern holds for couples with one Hispanic and one non-Hispanic partner—6.1 percent in the West and 1.7 percent in the Midwest—and in fact holds true across married, opposite-sex unmarried, and same-sex unmarried couples as well. By state, the greatest percentage of interracial couples was in Hawaii, where 34.7 percent of all married couples, 55.6 percent of all opposite-sex cohabiting couples, and roughly 42 percent of all same-sex cohabiting couples were made up of individuals of different races. The greatest percentage of couples of mixed origin (Hispanic versus non-Hispanic) was in New Mexico, where they represented 11.2 percent of all married couples, 18.4 percent of all opposite-sex cohabiting couples, and roughly 15 percent of all same-sex cohabiting couples.[72]

★TABLE 6.4 TOP 10 U.S. CITIES FOR MARRIED COUPLE, OPPOSITE-SEX UNMARRIED, AND SAME-SEX UNMARRIED HOUSEHOLDS, 2000[69]★

Different types of couples tend to reside in different cities. Why might couples of a certain type prefer one city over another?

MARRIED-COUPLE HOUSEHOLD	Percentage of all households
Gilbert, AZ	69.5
Naperville, IL	69.2
Plano, TX	64.3
Simi Valley, CA	63.9
Corona, CA	63.8
Livonia, MI	62.8
Fremont, CA	62.7
Fontana, CA	62.5
Thousand Oaks, CA	62.4
Laredo, TX	62.0

UNMARRIED-PARTNER HOUSEHOLD

Opposite-sex partners

Paterson, NJ.	8.1
Manchester, NH	7.9
Rochester, NY	7.7
Sunrise Manor, NV	7.6
Allentown, PA	7.5
San Bernardino, CA	7.4
Spring Valley, NV	7.4
Hartford, CT	7.4
Lansing, MI	7.3
Green Bay, WI	7.3

Same-sex partners

San Francisco, CA	2.7
Fort Lauderdale, FL	2.1
Seattle, WA	1.9
Oakland, CA	1.8
Berkeley, CA	1.8
Atlanta, GA	1.7
Minneapolis, MN	1.6
Washington, DC	1.5
Long Beach, CA	1.4
Portland, OR	1.3

2005–2009 AMERICAN COMMUNITY SURVEY (ACS)

Since 2001, the Census Bureau has administered more surveys to keep tabs on the changing populace. These estimates reflect data collected between January 1, 2005, and December 31, 2009. They are the most current data available and, as such, provide insight into the patterns that exist in the United States today. The American Community Survey (ACS) shows that a little over half of men and half of women were married and about a quarter of both genders had never been married.[73]

Individuals who fell into the 25–29 age group between the years of 2005 and 2009 were born in the late 1970s and early 1980s. As compared with the earlier samples, this group continued the pattern of delaying marriage. Only 39.8 percent of men had married by age 25 to 29, which is consistent with the group born in the early 1970s. Women's marriage rates declined even further; only 51.6 percent had married by age 25 to 29, a slight decrease in frequency from

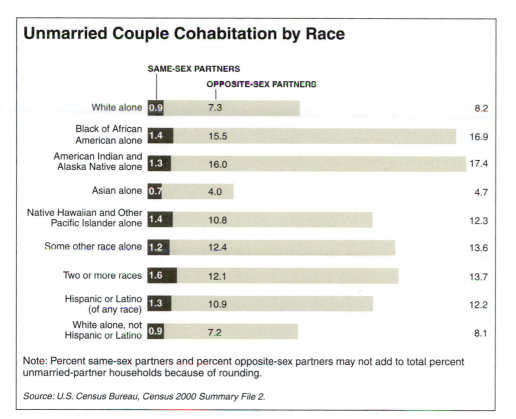

Figure 6.1 The frequency of same-sex versus opposite-sex couple households varies by race, perhaps due to cultural differences in the acceptance of homosexual couples.

Source: Tavia Simmons and Martin O'Connell, "Married-Couple and Unmarried-Partner Households: 2000," *U.S. Census Bureau*, Feb. 2003, http://www.census.gov/prod/2003pubs/censr-5.pdf

the group born in the early 1970s.[74] While it is too soon to tell if this is a true decline or simply the first signs of a plateau, it suggests people are in no hurry to marry and that this trend is likely to continue in the coming years.

The ACS data do not allow measurement of the percentage of people who had ever been divorced, as the 2001 SIPP data did, but they do permit us to look at the ages of those currently divorced. The Census Bureau is limited, however, in its ability to keep current divorce timing questions, as these are always in flux. Consistent with the SIPP data, most male divorcees tended to be between 35 and 60, and they made up 13.9 percent of men, or about 7.2 million men. There was a similar drop-off in rate of those men currently divorced after 60. Women also had relatively high numbers of divorcees at these ages, but did not show a drop-off until 75; about 20 percent of women aged 35 to 75 were currently divorced.[75] Why women continue to divorce in higher numbers as they age is unclear, but it may suggest an increase in women's independence at older ages. It is also unclear if these figures reflect a continuation of the decrease in divorce rates, as the groups being compared are not identical in characteristics, but it is possible that the rates of divorces for both genders are decreasing.

There was also a considerable increase in the rate of widowhood after 65, though again the estimates of those widowed only include those currently widowed, not those who may have been widowed in the past but have since remarried. There is information in the SIPP data that more closely matches the ACS data. These earlier SIPP samples did count those currently widowed (instead of those ever having been widowed), though they looked at widowhood among those 70 or older. The ACS data group those aged 65 to 75 together, so the best comparison looks at those 65 or older 2005 to 2009. Likely due, in part, to the addition of these five years of life (65 to 70), the percentages of widowhood for both genders were lower for the ACS sample than the SIPP samples, but they reveal a consistent pattern. In the SIPP data, for those over 65, 16.8 percent of men and 52.6 percent of women were currently widowed. In the more recent ACS sample, only 16 percent of men 65 years older were widowed, and 43.4 percent of same-aged women were widowed. This may reflect a difference in life span for the genders, though it may also reflect a greater tendency of men to remarry and thus be classified as such. Indeed, looking back at the SIPP data, 23.1 percent of men age 65 or older were ever widowed, but only 16.8 percent of those men were still widowed at the time of the survey. By contrast, 56.3 percent of women age 65 or older had been widowed, while 52.6 percent of those women still were at the time of the ACS.[76] The ratio of those who had remarried (and so were no longer classified as widowed) to those who remained widowed was much greater among men than it was among women in this age group.

In addition, the rate of people who never married continued to increase. While in the SIPP data 30.9 percent of men and 24.6 percent of women aged 15 or older had never married, in the ACS data, those rates increased to 34 percent of men and 27.7 percent of women [77] However, both of these numbers are a considerable increase even over the percentages of those who had never married at the age of 25 in the SIPP data: 50.8 percent for men and 37.3 percent for women. These numbers suggest an increase in those choosing not to marry, both in early life and over the entirety of life.

Is marriage becoming increasingly unnecessary in modern life? Are we creating a new form of family that includes not just same-sex couples but cohabitants and singles? Consider for a moment the impact that has on our society? In what ways do you think it is helpful? In what ways do you think it is harmful?

Race and Marital Status

The data showing how people are delaying marriage, when divided by race, are even more revealing. Comparing the ACS data to the SIPP data shows that in just five to 10 years, people were delaying marriage even longer. In 2000, the median ages of first marriage for whites were 23.8 for men and 21.6 for women. From 2005 to 2009, they were 27.5 years for men and 25.9 years for women. In 2000, the median ages of first marriage for blacks were 25 for men and 22.3 for women. From 2005 to 2009, they had increased a whopping five to seven years, with 30 years for men and 29.7 years for women. In 2000, the median ages of first marriage for Asians/Pacific Islanders were 27.1 for men and 24.8 for women. The ACS presents these data separately for Asians and Pacific Islanders but shows a similar pattern of increase. For Asians, the median age of first marriage was 29.6 for men and 26.6 for women; and for Pacific Islanders, it was 28.4 for men and 26.4 for women. Every racial group measured and both genders for each increased in their median age of first marriage. This is a telling pattern, suggesting it crosses ethnic boundaries and is pervasive throughout the United States.[78]

What do these numbers suggest? On the whole, more men appear to be married than women. Blacks/African Americans tended to be married less often than whites or Asians/Pacific Islanders and were more likely to have never been married or to be separated. Women tended to be widowed more often than men regardless of race. Asians/Pacific Islanders were the least likely to be divorced, with whites and blacks being similar in that regard. You can see the numbers here, but their interpretation is open to debate. Are there cultural differences between groups that affect their rate of divorce? Could economics influence these rates, with racial groups known to be poorer falling into categories that are more likely to avoid marriage? Is it possible that attitudes toward marriage continue to change, making it less and less important in the lives of Americans? Only further study can help us understand the complexities behind these data.

★TABLE 6.5 DIFFERENCES BY RACE AFTER FIRST MARRIAGE, 2001[79]★

Overall, Asians/Pacific Islanders are the racial group that is most likely to be married and least likely to be divorced or separated.

	Married	Never married	Separated	Widowed	Divorced
White men	55.3	30.9	1.5	2.7	9.6
White women	51.8	24	1.9	10.5	11.8
African-American men	34.7	49	3.9	2.7	9.7
African-American women	27	45.3	5.3	9.4	13.1
Asian/Pacific Islander men	59.4	34.3	1.1	1.4	3.8
Asian/Pacific Islander women	58.8	26.3	1.5	7.4	6

Parenting

While the SIPP data allowed a more detailed analysis of in what types of relationships people tend to live in with their own children, and in what frequencies, the ACS data allow us only to compare married couples to all other types of families led by a male householder and all other types of families led by a female householder. From 2005 to 2009, 43 percent of married couples lived with their own children. By contrast, 49.3 percent of unmarried male householders and 59 percent of unmarried female householders lived with their own children. While these statistics are not divided by type of unmarried household—cohabiting partnership, single householder, roommates, and so forth—they are consistent with the SIPP data suggesting that children were more likely to live with unmarried mothers than unmarried fathers.[80]

Earlier, we discussed the separation of marriage and childbirth in the United States. Consistent with this, a full 33.4 percent of women who gave birth in the 12 months prior to the survey were unmarried, including those who never married, were widowed, or were divorced. In addition, 92.3 percent of women of childbearing age who were married did not give birth in the prior year.[81] Thus, as we've already discussed, the increased percentages of children born to unmarried women may be highly correlated to the reality that the vast majority of married women do not give birth in a given year and are perhaps working to control their fertility.

Cohabitating Couples

In the ACS table data, there is limited data on unmarried, cohabitating couples, as often married couples are contrasted with "other households," which is too broad a term to make any comparisons such as we did with the SIPP data. What we do know is that the percentage of same-sex couples decreased to about one in 10 cohabitating, unmarried couples, down from one in nine. The number of male–male households is nearly equivalent to the number of female–female households: 356,719 and 333,316, respectively. Consistent with earlier data, unmarried opposite-sex couples were equally as likely to have a male householder (the partner who fills out the form for the home) as a female householder, suggesting that those who cohabitate, regardless of sexual orientation, tend to experience some amount of gender equality relative to more traditionally married couples.[82]

State-by-State Differences in Marital and Cohabitation Patterns

Comparing ACS data on marital statistics by state shows that those never married seem to be concentrated in Southern and Central California, the border of Arizona and New Mexico, Massachusetts, and the New York City metropolitan area. In addition, never-married people tend to be concentrated in urban areas. Married people, by contrast, seem to be congregated in higher proportions in the Midwest. The lowest concentration of separated people are also in the Midwest, though there are also very few in northern Maine. The highest rates of widowhood seem to occur in the longitude containing North Dakota, South Dakota, Nebraska, and Kansas, and the lowest rates are just to the west of those states, in Utah, Colorado, Wyoming, and Idaho. The rates of divorce do not seem to vary very widely across the country, but are slightly higher in New England and the Northwest.[83]

Unmarried households are most heavily concentrated in the West, Northeast, Florida, and the states bordering the Great Lakes. When we look at only same-sex couples, we see again a higher concentration in the West and Northeast, with more female–female couples than male–male overall. Opposite-sex unmarried couples seem to follow the same pattern as all unmarried couples taken together. The rate of male and female householders is roughly equivalent.[84]

By comparing across all these data, we can see the dramatic changes that have occurred in married life over the decades. The reasons for these changes are, as we have discussed, not always clear and subject to interpretation. However, it is likely that these changes have profound effects on the fabric of American society—how we live, what we expect of ourselves, and what we consider "normal." Of course, what is considered normal may not be typical. It is becoming increasingly typical for people to postpone marriage and/or cohabitate. Data gathered by the Census Bureau allow us to appreciate the frequencies of these different family forms, and help us understand where we stand and where we may be going.

Marriage and Family: State-by-State Comparison

Figure 6.2 Source: Social Explorer, "1790 to Present," *U.S. Decennial Census Files*, http://www.socialexplorer.com

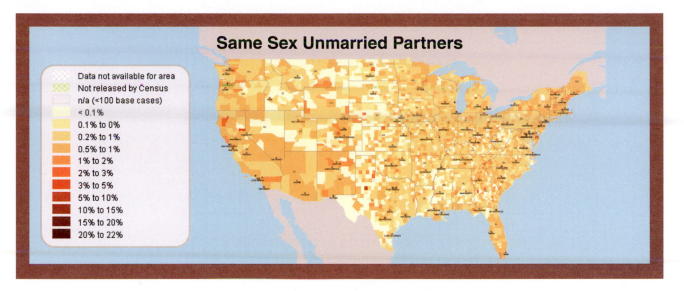

Figure 6.2 (continued) Source: Social Explorer, "1790 to Present," *U.S. Decennial Census Files*, http://www.socialexplorer.com

KEY TERMS

Nuclear family is one with a husband, wife, and one or more children. *80*

Family is two or more people who are related by blood, marriage, or adoption. *81*

Marriage is the union of two people that is recognized by their laws and/or cultures. *81*

Extended family is one with parents, children, and one or more additional family members. *81*

Cohabitate is to live with an intimate partner without being married. *82*

Birth cohort is the group of people born at the same time—either a single year or group of years. *83*

Marriage cohort is the group of people who married at the same time—either in the same year or the same group of years. *84*

CHAPTER QUIZ

1. Which statement is true about gay couples in the South?
   a. There are fewer gay parents in the South than anywhere else in the United States.
   b. There are more gay parents in Florida than in Texas.
   c. Black and Latino gay couples are twice as likely to be raising children as white gay couples.
   d. Latino gay couples have less poverty in the South than in the North.
2. Which of these descriptions defines a family?
   a. Two or more people related by blood, marriage, or adoption who live to together
   b. A wife, husband, and children
   c. A union of two people recognized by law
   d. People who live together

3. As of 2005, _____ couples became a minority of U.S. households for the first time.
   a. same-sex
   b. married
   c. unmarried
   d. parent
4. The frequency of unmarried mothers is increasing to more than 30 percent in many countries, but not in
   a. the United States.
   b. Germany.
   c. France.
   d. Japan.
5. Of the races examined, which tends to enter into second marriages earliest?
   a. Whites
   b. Blacks
   c. Asians/Pacific Islanders
   d. They all enter into second marriages at roughly the same time.

Answers: 1. c; 2. a; 3. b; 4. d; 5. a

ESSAY QUESTIONS

1. Analyze why certain factors, including cohabitation and religious belief, tend to increase the likelihood of divorce.
2. Explore the personal, psychological, and cultural reasons that might contribute to the drop-off in separation and divorce after the ages of 55 to 60 years.
3. Discuss the pros and cons for parents, children, and society for the increasing dissociation between marriage and childbearing/rearing—both that people are having children outside of marriage at increasing numbers and that people are not necessarily having more children when they are in a marriage.
4. Discuss the factors related to the emerging trend of delaying first marriage until later in life and compare and contrast its effects on men and women.
5. Analyze the cultural and biological reasons that may contribute to why biracial and multiracial women have the lowest rate of widowhood?

SOURCES FOR FURTHER RESEARCH

Census Bureau data on marriage and divorce:
http://www.census.gov/hhes/socdemo/marriage/

Census Bureau data on families and living arrangements:
http://www.census.gov/population/www/socdemo/hh-fam.html

Data and attitudes about marriage and family:
http://pewsocialtrends.org/2010/11/18/marriage-and-family-data-and-attitudes

Child and family statistics:
http://www.childstats.gov

CDC data on marriage and divorce:
http://www.cdc.gov/nchs/fastats/divorce.htm

7   Using Census Data

The American people are the discovery of the U.S. censuses. How much more can you know about your neighbors by using census statistics as a resource? (Henrik Winther Andersen/Shutterstock)

A FRESH WAY TO EXPLORE THE CENSUS

Throughout this book, you have been bombarded with data, all of which is either related to the decennial census, or were gathered by the U.S. Census Bureau. Clearly, the data gathered from 1790 to the present day could fill many volumes much bigger than this book. However, the data remain available to all people in the world, providing us a window into our past, our present, and predictions of our future.

Because the Census Bureau recognizes that its data is worthless without individual participation, it significantly changed the 2010 Census in an attempt to increase overall participation. As you read in Chapter 1, the 2010 Census was only 10 questions long, much shorter than many previous censuses. In addition, the Census Bureau launched a nationwide advertisement and media campaign to encourage participation, especially among those who were unfamiliar with or intimidated by the census. And to show the American people how important and useful its data is, the Census Bureau revamped its website and the American FactFinder system. As Internet-based information becomes more popular, the Census Bureau wants to make data accessible online to all. The hope is that the American people will fully understand the importance of participation in the census and be able to benefit from the information themselves.[1]

American FactFinder has been visually redesigned to appear fresh and modern. It also offers easy access to new tools to access the overwhelming amount of demographic data. In fact, once fully updated with the 2010 Census statistics, the FactFinder will hold more than 40,000 tables and 250 billion data cells. That huge sum of data includes information on the more than 9 million blocks and 74,000 census tracts that make up America's "from sea to shining sea." With this overwhelming amount of data, the American FactFinder has been revamped to help users sort, understand, and make use of whatever statistics they might be looking for.

The new FactFinder includes a more powerful search engine that accurately sorts data based on topics and specific statistics. Users can narrow searches within categories such as race, geography, or gender so as to easily find the information they are seeking. The FactFinder also carries the capability to search an exact street address to find data available in that area. Enhanced features allow users to manipulate tables to their liking. Tables can be visually edited to hide, sort, and rearrange rows and columns. In addition, the American FactFinder has advanced mapping capabilities. The new maps generated allow users to see patterns on a geographic level. Users can manipulate the maps to change the colors, zoom in or out, change the boundaries displayed, or add points of interest or text to the map. Hopefully, as a result of the revision of the American FactFinder, as with the other strategies to increase census participation, the 2020 Census will be seen as valuable by all Americans, and they will eagerly participate.[2]

The U.S. Census Bureau provides a doorway to a surprising array of facts and figures about our country, as well as other nations throughout the world. From its modest start in 1790 to the current day, it has sought to provide information about the country's population to policy makers. In this chapter, we look at ways in which ordinary citizens can use census data. We will discover different ways of retrieving census data, from the Census Bureau's Web site to the online research tool Social Explorer. These data can be used to help you write papers, reports, and articles both in and out of the classroom. It can also help you see trends and understand the current state of the country in which you live and understand our country's past.

THE U.S. CENSUS: YOUR SOURCE FOR DATA

The Census Bureau is charged with conducting the decennial census and has more recently expanded its role in conducting other research on a variety of subjects. As we've already discussed, the main purpose of the decennial census is to count the number of people in the United States. However, it also gathers limited additional information about residents' race, age, gender, and other characteristics. You have probably noticed reports in this book that highlight other facets of American life. Some of this data was collected by the U.S. Census Bureau. The most recent survey, the American Community Survey (ACS), discussed in Chapter 1, gathers data on quality-of-life topics such as income, health insurance, education, veteran's status, and disabilities.

The Census Bureau also collects employment data in the Current Population Survey (CPS). In a monthly survey of about 50,000 households, the bureau investigates characteristics of the U.S. labor force, such as employment status, field of employment, earnings, work hours, race, educational attainment, and many other topics. The CPS reports on job losses and gains in specific fields. To keep its fingers on the pulse on the U.S. economy, lawmakers, media analysts, financial planners, and others frequently refer to the CPS. You may have heard the CPS referenced many times since 2008, when the recent economic crisis began so heavily impacting the U.S. labor force.

The Census Bureau also conducts the American Housing Survey (AHS) on behalf of the U.S. Department of Housing and Urban Development (HUD). You can access the reports from either www.hud.gov or www.census.gov. The AHS collects data in odd-numbered years and investigates housing characteristics such as apartments, single-family homes, mobile homes, and so forth. In addition, the survey measures neighborhood quality, housing costs, and other housing issues. The data collected about housing is of national importance to lawmakers, real estate agents, home buyers, and even Wall Street mortgage investment firms. You can imagine how important the topic of housing was, specifically as it related to mortgage-backed securities, after the 2008 housing-market crash that affected every part of the U.S. economy.

Crime control is an important aspect of society for everyone, but especially for policy makers and researchers. Individuals look up crime statistics when deciding where to buy or rent homes. Lawmakers need crime statistics when deciding where to focus crime-fighting resources. And researchers look for trends in crime statistics that can be indicative of large social problems. The **National Crime Victimization Survey (NCVS)** is another survey collected by the Census Bureau on behalf of the U.S. Justice Department. It measures the amount and types of crimes that people in a household encounter. It provides in-depth information about people who have been victims of crimes such as burglary, motor vehicle theft, robbery, assault, and rape, among many others. The Census Bureau collects the pertinent statistics, which are then used by criminologists and policy makers to determine crime-prevention programs as well as other criminal justice issues.

These are just some of the surveys conducted by the U.S. Census Bureau. These important surveys provide a wealth of information to researchers, the public, and policy makers regarding the status of various features of American life. As you can see, the Census Bureau does a lot more than count people every 10 years, and its data is readily available to both curious browsers and serious scholars alike.

American FactFinder

The American FactFinder websites are tools that can help anyone find data about the United States, including territories such as Puerto Rico and Guam. When you go to www.census.gov, you'll notice a link to the "American FactFinder." This link gives you access to some of the most recent data provided by the Census Bureau. It supports the Economic Census, the American Community Survey, the 1990 and 2000 censuses, and the latest population estimates. When you log on to American FactFinder, you can choose the older American FactFinder or American Factfinder2, available at http://factfinder2.census.gov, which provides the newer options previously discussed in this chapter. There are tutorials to help you find your way around the data source, as well as a Quick Start link for you to simply search by topic.

You can search for data a number of different ways. The easiest method is to simply enter search items into the Quick Start option. Filters with appropriate terms become available, and you can select those from a drop-down menu. Once you search something, you can view the data in table form. You can download the data to your computer for your own use, or you can bookmark the results so that you can easily return later. Downloaded data can be printed out or dropped directly into spreadsheet software.

When you have collected the data, you can display them in a variety of ways. First, you can create and modify tables to show only items that are of interest to you. You can view these data geographically by state, or sometimes even by smaller areas such as counties, cities, streets, or census blocks. The website also lets you create maps with customized colors to illustrate the data for reports and easily understood comparisons. Just imagine how this information could help your next paper or report.

At first glance, American FactFinder can seem intimidating. However, spending a short time following the help screen instructions and viewing the tutorials can make you a data-search pro.

EXERCISE 1

Go to http://factfinder2.census.gov/faces/nav/jsf/pages/index.xhtml. In Quick Start, under Topic, type in the word "race." Results in the form of links for a variety of data will appear. Select "Race and Hispanic or Latino: 2010—State—Place Race." Select a state of your choice. Find the total population of that state. Then find the number of people within a select racial/ethnic group, for example, Native Americans and Alaska Natives. What is the total population of this racial group in the state you chose? Is there a city in this state with no Native Americans? Now select the tutorial and create a thematic map of your discovered state data.

Figure 7.1 The American FactFinder website makes it easy to find specific data about demographic variables like race.

2000 AND 2010 DATA   At the time of publication of this book, the U.S. Census Bureau had not yet released all data generated from the taking of the 2010 Census and the 2010 American Community Survey. However, you will soon have access to many important reports and studies generated from the data gathered in these surveys.

Let's start with the 2010 data. When you log into the census website, you'll see the 2010 data link. The current population of the United States is listed at more than 300 million residents. Clicking on that link will take you to the 2010 Census data, which are in the process of being released. Here, you'll find a link called "Apportionment Data." Recall that the apportionment of the congressional representation for the House of Representatives is the constitutional reason we take the census in the first place.

When you click on "Apportionment Data," you'll find how the population of the United States has changed over the past 110 years, as well as view maps indicating which states have gained and lost political representation through apportionment. Thus, when the apportionment from the 2010 Census is put in place, a state like Texas will gain political power while its neighbor Louisiana will lose political power. Based on the discussion in Chapter 3, could Hurricane Katrina be part of the cause for this population shift? Because the number of seats in the House of Representatives determines the number of votes each state has in the Electoral College of the presidential election every four years, how do you think the 2012 election will differ from the 2008 election, in terms of the Electoral College? Do you think the new distribution of political power will greatly favor one political party?

Aside from studying the change from 2000 to 2010 nationwide, spend some time looking at single states and their entire history of apportionment. Which states have previously enjoyed much more political power? Which states have never been so populated and are subsequently enjoying more political power than ever before? Look specifically at New York. While it is still one of the largest states in the country, yielding more representatives and Electoral College votes than most, its status is now significantly less important than it was decades ago. How has your home state measured after the apportionment of each decennial census?

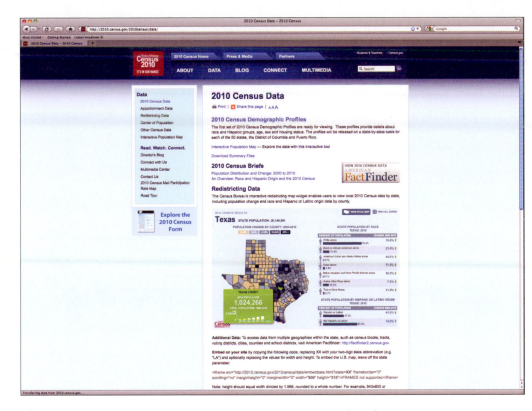

Figure 7.2 States County by County. The U.S. Census Bureau's website features easy-to-navigate interactive infographics that display demographic data at the national, state, and county levels.

From the 2010 page, http://2010.census.gov/2010census/, if you click on the Data link, the first thing to appear will be a map of the United States showing all states that have compiled their data for state redistricting political representation. Within any state, political representation is also linked to population. Redistricting can create changes in local, state, and national politics. In addition, federal funding and funding from nongovernmental organizations is tied to population and gets dispersed differently according to redistricting data. To learn more about a specific state or region, complete the following exercise.

EXERCISE 2

Once at www.census.gov, select "Learn More about Your State" from just below the population counter. On the map, select a state whose data has been released. Click on that state on the map. You will see a quick summary of that state's population based on the 2010 Census. The map is color coded to show where the population grew and shrank compared to any previous decennial census since 1960. Move your mouse over the map to view summaries by county. Compare an urban county to a rural one. How has the population changed in those counties over time? Are people migrating to cities? As you review the state's population, how has it changed since the 2000 Census? Most likely, the total populations you are observing have grown. But have certain racial or ethnic groups grown faster than others? By scrolling over the map, can you find the county in your state with the fastest growth rate? What additional services might planners in that county need to consider because of this new growth? Now consider the counties that show declining populations. How might a declining population in the state you have selected affect everything from services needed to employment shifts to political power?

Return to the www.census.gov main page and find a link to the 2000 Census data. The data available at this link are extensive. You can see what we can expect to receive once the 2010 data are fully compiled. Don't forget, though, that the 2000 Census was the last to use the "long form," meaning that detailed data were gathered from sampled U.S. households in 2000. As we've already discussed in Chapter 1, the long form has been replaced by the American Community Survey, meaning that some of the data available on the 2000 Census Web page, as with previous years as well, will not be found on the 2010 Census Web page. Instead, you will need to search the American FactFinder, and it will link you to American Community Survey information.

HISTORICAL DATA The U.S. Census Bureau makes a vast array of historical data available to you. Trying to sort through the entirety of the material can be overwhelming and confusing. Instead, try searching by specific things such as year, place, gender, and so forth. This will help the information more manageable and understandable. At the Census Bureau website, you can even find results from the 1790 count. Just go to www.census.gov and type what you are looking for into the search box.

EXERCISE 3

In the search box on the Census Bureau home page, type "1790 Census." You will be given a number of choices relating to documents that mention the 1790 Census. Select the "History: 1790 Overview" link, and it will take you to a page where you can see data from the 1790 Census. Click on the link "Publications and population statistics from the 1790 Census." It will take you to a page with links to the first American states and the data collected by each of those states during that very first census. Select a state, and then select to download the data in either PDF or ZIP format. You can then find the data on that state organized by county. Here, you can find the data associated with specific towns. If you live or have lived in one of these states, can you find your town's population in the original Census? How has it grown over the past 220 years? If you have never lived in one of these states, select the year following your state's admission to the union. (You might have to look up the year.) Then do the same thing for your state, county, and hometown. How have they changed over the years?

INTERNATIONAL PROGRAMS As mentioned earlier, the U.S. Census Bureau is a repository of international population data as well. The international programs data are some of my favorite data available from the Census Bureau. This program conducts studies and counts for nations all around the world, while at the same time offering technical assistance and training to governments and international organizations relating to the collection and use of these data. This cooperative side of the Census Bureau is run through its International Assistance arm. U.S. Census Bureau workers often lend expert advice to other countries about how to best collect and maintain high-quality data for future use.

While this information is not helpful to the Census Bureau's main goal of congressional reapportionment within the United States, the information gathered during these endeavors by the bureau and other international governmental agencies and nongovernmental organizations is very valuable. Using the recent military involvement in Libya as an example, it is very useful to have population data to determine possible deaths from attacks, as well as understanding the ages of potential soldiers for both sides. With accurate population estimates, the appropriate amount of supplies can be provided to victims. International data may also serve a purpose in times of natural disasters. Following the 2011 earthquake in Japan, the entire Pacific Rim was threatened by tsunamis. Population estimates and geographic mapping were very important to tsunami warning systems and clean-up efforts. Without the data, governmental agencies and nongovernmental organizations might have wasted valuable time, money, and effort simply identifying where help was needed most. But because population information is available, precious time is saved.

There are two main parts of the Census Bureau's international program data. First, the demographic and socioeconomic research services provide data relating to demographic, socioeconomic, and health issues. For example, you can find population projections and trends for all countries in the world. For instance, you can find out the estimates for the current populations of India, Australia, Egypt, or any other country. You can also see how population experts believe national and international populations will change over the next 50 years. The United States is also included in this list, so you can find out the projected population changes for our country over the next 50 years.

In addition to the population counts and projections, the bureau's international program tracks a number of important world issues. You can discover the rate of HIV/AIDS through the world, as well as the projections for future demographic issues that may arise as a result of the disease. This link, www.census.gov/ipc/www/aboutintl.html, connects you to data on the economic and social ramifications of the projected changes, particularly as they apply to the role and status of women and other globally important issues.

The international database (IDB) provided by the U.S. Census Bureau and its partner agencies around the world is a demographer's gold mine. You can access the IDB at www.census.gov/ipc/www/idb/index.php, or search "IDB" on the main page. The main page includes a series of links. The country rankings provide estimated population sizes of all the countries of the world. You can select a top 10 country, population-wise, or any other country. You can also select any year in recent history and see if the 10 largest countries have changed since that time.

Future estimates, or **population projections**, involve the demographer making guesses about future population patterns. Demographers use projected fertility rates, life expectancies, mortality rates, and migration to predict future populations for each country. After all, a projected population is dependent upon these variables, because if you could know these numbers exactly, you could predict the future.

However, it is impossible to perfectly predict the future. Population projections are no different because it is difficult to guess about complications that may affect future populations. Unforeseen events, such as a disease, war, natural disaster, or famine, could wreak havoc on the world population or the populations of certain countries. Social behaviors such as an increased or decreased use or access to birth control also greatly affect future birth and death rates. This discrepancy between projections and reality will be seen in the near future of Japan, as the earthquake and tsunami of March 11, 2011, killed tens of thousands of people and was completely unforeseeable.

But just because a scientific guess is not perfectly accurate does not mean that these population projections have no value for us today. Demographic projections give policy makers a view toward a likely future, allowing them to plan for the potential needs of the United States and other countries around the world. For example, if population projections estimate rapid growth due to longer lives, resources such as medical care for the elderly will need to expand. At the same time, stable birthrates would allow schools and other services for young people to remain constant.

Population predictions foretell political stability as well. Countries with rapid population growth and weak economies may face civil unrest if a growing population sees its declining standard of living related to an undesirable government. This example likely played a role in the recent political turmoil of North Africa and the Middle East. Young, educated, unemployed citizens have largely fueled uprisings against monarchs and dictators who've held power for decades. In part, the unrest could be the result of leadership that failed to plan for its new generations of citizens.

In the center of the IDB page, there is a link called "Data Access." Here, you will find data for every country. You will see current population data as well as historical population data and projections for future growth. Under Data Access, you can review data based on country, region, or age group. The access point is easy to navigate and provides a wealth of research material for students of international population.

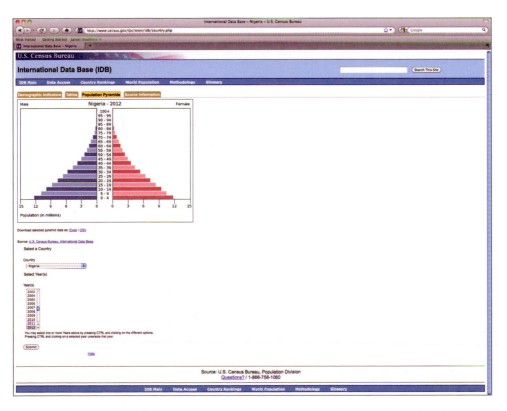

Figure 7.3 International demographic data can also be explored on the Census Bureau's website.

One of my favorite uses for this website is to select a country and a year, and then pull up the data. Then I select the population pyramid to see a graphic representation of that country's data. Population pyramids provide a graphic illustration of certain types of data for countries, and they are useful in understanding the information. In this population pyramid, men are depicted on one side of the graph, while women are on the other side of the graph. Age structure is in the middle of the graph. From here, you can select a year in the future to find what the projected population is for any given year until 2050 and compare it to a graph from the current year or the recent past.

EXERCISE 4

Go to the IDB home page at www.census.gov/ipc/www/idb/index.php. Select the "Data Access" link, which will lead you to a list of countries. Select a nation you know little about and look at the data shown. By 2025, what is the expected growth rate for this country? How does that differ from the growth rate it is experiencing today? Is this country expecting positive or negative migration in the coming years? What are the infant mortality rate and the life expectancy for residents? How are these statistics predicted to change over time? Click on the link for population pyramids. What does this graph look like for the country you are learning about?

   Now return to the country selection page and select a country undergoing turmoil today, like Japan or Libya. By 2025, what is the expected growth rate for the country? How does it differ from the growth rate of today? Are demographers expecting positive or negative migration in the future? What are the infant mortality rate and the life expectancy? How are these things predicted to change over time? Click on the link for population pyramids. What does this look like for the country you chose?

   How would you compare the future of, for example, Japan or Libya to the country you selected in the beginning of the exercise? If you were a policy maker in one of these countries, what services and needs might you be concerned about for your people?

Social Explorer: Simple Access to Census Data

Census data are available to the public in a variety of forms. One such place is the website Social Explorer, found at www.socialexplorer.com. Social Explorer provides both free and paid access to public data in an intuitive and easy-to-use website. A student edition of Social Explorer is available from Pearson via MySocLab and other Pearson products. So, even if you don't have MySocLab, you may have access to Social Explorer through one of your textbooks. If you don't, there is still free access available to everyone.

   Social Explorer provides an easy way to link data to maps. This feature is its strength, and many of the maps in this book came from Social Explorer. It provides these maps with a more precise measure of demographic data than even the U.S. Census Bureau website. For example, you can easily map a change in your neighborhood and compare your own home to larger geographic areas, such as your city, county, or state. Maps can be created from data all the way back to the first U.S. census in 1790. Try referencing the early data in your next history paper and see how well received the source is by your peers and professors. A simple tutorial at Social Explorer can provide you with the means to use the website easily for future assignments for school or work.

   Social Explorer was designed in 1999 by sociologist Andrew A. Beveridge, who wanted to build an easy-to-use demographic website. By 2003, Social Explorer was up and running. It is now the most used demographic site on the Internet. News organizations, teachers, scholars, and scientists regularly use the data available through Social Explorer to find and use the most up-to-date data sets.

   Social Explorer is easy to use and hosts a wide array of data from a variety of sources, including not only the U.S. censuses from 1790 through 2010 but also national data generated from other sources. As of this publication, results from 2010 have not been completely released. Social Explorer also includes all annual updates from the American Community Survey and original tract-level estimates for 2006 and 2007. Social Explorer also provides data on Religious Congregations and Membership Studies from 1980 through 2009. The information from the 2010 edition of this study should be available shortly. Maps and reports can be printed and/or cut and pasted into research papers and reports easily. As a student, you could spend hours at Social Explorer looking at a variety of maps and data that can help you write papers and find interesting information.

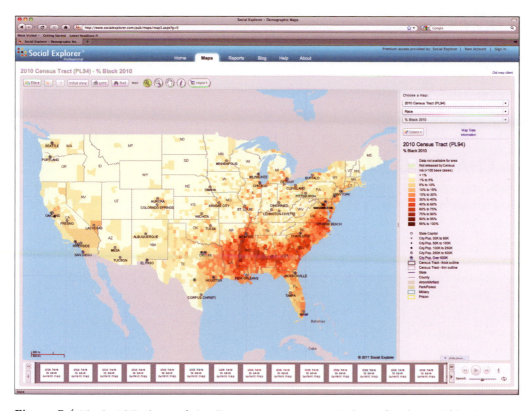

Figure 7.4 The Social Explorer website allows you to create customized maps based on variables that you select, such as this map of black population from the 2010 Census.

EXERCISE 5

Access Social Explorer for free at www.socialexplorer.com. Click on "maps." Click on "U.S. Demographic Maps: 1790–2009." From the menu on the right side of the screen, you can create a map based on three categories: the source of the data, the characteristic you wish you examine (such as population, income, race, etc.), and the specific information you seek related to that topic.

For this exercise, leave the first category as "Census 2000" tract and select "Population" for the second menu. Then, select "Percentage of Urban Population" from the last drop-down menu. Look at the map that has been generated and answer the following questions based on the information found in the map: Which states appear to be the most rural? Which are the most urban?

Make the Most of It

As you have read in this chapter, there are many ways to access and use the information supplied by the U.S. Census Bureau. While lawmakers, educators, scientists, and even bankers have known the value of demographic information for centuries, the hope is that every American will also see the value of the census data. Luckily, we can all access this data without significant inconvenience. Now, as soon as data collected by the Census Bureau are released, you can access it from your home, school, library, or even smartphone as you sit on a park bench or in a coffeehouse.

Throughout this text, you have learned about the history of the U.S. Census Bureau and the data it generates. It is my hope that this helps you appreciate the efforts of those who collect, compile, and distribute these data to all of us. In a world full of information, it is often difficult to discern good data from poor quality data. However, be assured that the data provided by the Census Bureau is of high quality, provided in an unbiased manner. By completing the exercises found in this chapter, you should be well on your way to accessing information about the United States and the world.

KEY TERMS

The National Crime Victimization Survey (NCVS) is a survey collected by the Census Bureau on behalf of the Justice Department, which measures the amount and types of crimes that people in a household encounter. *99*

Population projections are created when a demographer makes guesses about future population patterns. *103*

CHAPTER QUIZ

1. The new American FactFinder offers access to more than _____ data cells.
   a. 74 million
   b. 640 million
   c. 3 billion
   d. 250 billion
2. How many representatives in the House of Representatives did Ohio have in 1950? (Go to http://2010.census.gov/2010census/data/ in order to find this answer.)
   a. 24
   b. 23
   c. 22
   d. 21
3. On what day was the 1790 Census taken? (Easily found during Exercise 3.)
   a. January 1, 1790
   b. April 1, 1790
   c. August 2, 1790
   d. December 31, 1790

4. What was the seventh-largest country by population in 1980? (Go to www.census.gov/ipc/www/idb/index.php to find this answer.)
   a. Japan
   b. Bangladesh
   c. Indonesia
   d. Germany
5. From 2000 to 2010, one county in Nevada had a population decrease of more than 15 percent. Name this county. (Use Social Explorer and the 2010 Census Map to find the name.)
   a. Esmeralda County
   b. Mineral County
   c. Nye County
   d. Lincoln County

Answers: 1. d; 2. b; 3. c; 4. b; 5. a

ESSAY QUESTIONS

1. How can the U.S. Census Bureau encourage full participation in the 2020 Census? What might prevent people from filling out and returning the Census?
2. What is the Current Population Survey? Briefly explain how often it is taken, the sample size, and the material it covers when surveying Americans.
3. Explain the importance of apportionment to the U.S. political system. How does it affect local, state, national, and presidential elections? Do you believe apportionment adequately ensures that all Americans are equally represented in our government?
4. Population projections are an important aspect of U.S. Census Bureau work. Explain the value of population projections as well as the limitations. Use examples from current events.
5. Have you ever researched your family history? How might census records be useful in researching family histories? Where and how might you begin searching for information on your ancestors?

SOURCES FOR FURTHER RESEARCH

2010 Census data:
http://2010.census.gov/news/releases/operations/ad-campaign-release.html

Quick facts about the census:
http://www.pbs.org/opb/historydetectives/diy/gen_census.html

A Census Bureau Video:
http://www.youtube.com/user/uscensusbureau

Appendix I: Selected Population Data by State

Population Change, 2000–2010

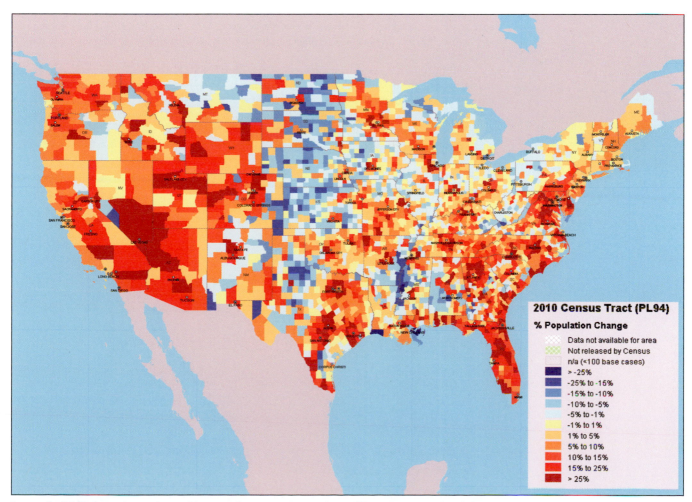

2010 Census Tract (PL94)

% Population Change

- Data not available for area
- Not released by Census
- n/a (<100 base cases)
- > -25%
- -25% to -15%
- -15% to -10%
- -10% to -5%
- -5% to -1%
- -1% to 1%
- 1% to 5%
- 5% to 10%
- 10% to 15%
- 15% to 25%
- > 25%

Source: Social Explorer, "2010 Census Tract PL94—% Population Change," http://www.socialexplorer.com.

Population data for the entire United States provide a big-picture depiction of the nation and how it has changed over the decades. Breaking down these data for individual states allows for the consideration of this issue from another perspective. This appendix contains select population data for the entire United States as well as for each individual state, making it useful for considering the varied stories that can be told by the same data when it is considered from different perspectives.

The population section of these tables contains data for the total population, how much it has changed since 2000, any changes in political representation, the most populated city in each state, the percentage of the population living in urban areas, and the population density. From these numbers, you can see that the total country's increased population doesn't tell the whole story for everyone; Michigan's population dropped by almost 55,000 individuals. Can any of the other data in these tables shed light on this anomaly?

The economy section might be a place to start. The data here show the median household income, poverty rate, and Gini coefficient for each state. Although we must take caution to avoid making simple conclusions about these numbers, they do illustrate the relative positions and economic standing of states in comparison to others. For example, when considering Michigan's population decrease, one might conclude that it has to do with the state's median household income being lower than that of the entire country. It also may be related to the fact that Michigan's poverty rate is above the national average.

If you consider education attainment, these data can illustrate differences in states as well. Data in this section show the percentage of each state's population that has not completed high school, has attained a bachelor's degree, and has attained an advanced degree. While Louisiana and California are separated by many miles and may seem like very different states, it is interesting that the same percentage of the population in both states did not complete high school.

Also worth noting is that different statistics about the same factor, population for example, have slightly different implications. For example, California has the highest state population, at 37,253,956, but Washington, D.C., has the highest population density, at 9,856.49 people per square mile, almost nine times that of the second most dense state. How might the experiences of people living in these states differ as a result? Notice that California's high population affords it 53 representatives, while Washington, D.C., not technically a state, doesn't get any representation. Meanwhile, population density may give us a hint as to how people live in these various states and areas.

Additional data in these tables include racial makeup, Hispanic origin, gender, age, and marital status. With these data, we can consider not just how people in different states experience population but also how life in the United States varies for these different groups. While we may draw conclusions about what life is like in the United States based on data for the overall country, it's important to remember that the nation is not a homogenous place.

★ UNITED STATES ★

POPULATION	2010	2000
Total Population	308,745,538	281,421,906
Population Change 2000–2010	+27,323,632 (+9.7%)	
House of Representatives Seats 2000–2010	435 total seats	
Largest City	New York	New York
Percentage of Population in Urban Areas	79%	79%
Population Density (people per square mile)	87.42	79.6

ECONOMY	2009	2000
Median Household Income	$51,425	$41,994
Poverty Rate (Individual)	13.5%	11.3%
Gini Coefficient (Perfect equality=0, Perfect inequality=1)	.469	.408

EDUCATIONAL ATTAINMENT (25 YEARS AND OVER)	2009	2000
Less Than High School	15.7%	19.6%
Bachelor's Degree	17.4%	15.5%
Master's, Professional School, or Doctorate Degree	10.0%	8.9%

RACE	2010	2000
White alone	72.4%	75.1%
Black or African American alone	12.6%	12.3%
American Indian or Alaska Native alone	0.9%	0.9%
Asian alone	4.8%	3.6%
Native Hawaiian and other Pacific Islander alone	0.2%	0.1%
Some other race alone	6.2%	5.5%
Two or more races	2.9%	2.4%

HISPANIC ORIGIN	2010	2000
Hispanic or Latino	16.3%	12.6%

NATIVITY	2009	2000
Foreign born	12.4%	11.1%

GENDER	2009	2000
Sex Ratio (number of males per female)	0.974	0.963

AGE	2010	2000
Percent Under 18 Years	24.6%	25.7%
Percent Over 65 Years	12.6%	12.4%

MARRIAGE	2009	2000
Percent Married	50.2%	54.4%
Percent Divorced	10.5%	9.8%
Cohabitation	5.5%	5.2%

Source: See end of appendix.

★ ALABAMA ★

POPULATION

Total Population 2000	4,779,736
Population Change 2000–2010	+332,636 (+3.2%)
House of Representatives Seats 2000–2010	7–7
Largest City 2008	Birmingham
Percentage of Population in Urban Areas 2000	55.4%
Population Density (people/square mile) 2010	94.38

ECONOMY – 2009

Median Household Income	$41,216
Poverty Rate (Individual)	16.8%
Gini Coefficient (Perfect equality=0, Perfect inequality=1)	.471

EDUCATIONAL ATTAINMENT (25 YEARS AND OVER) – 2009

Less Than High School	19.2%
Bachelor's Degree	13.7%
Master's, Professional School, or Doctorate Degree	7.8%

RACE – 2010

White alone	68.5%
Black or African American alone	26.2%
American Indian or Alaska Native alone	0.6%
Asian alone	1.1%
Native Hawaiian and other Pacific Islander alone	0.1%
Some other race alone	2.0%
Two or more races	1.5%

HISPANIC ORIGIN – 2010

Hispanic or Latino	3.9%

NATIVITY – 2009

Foreign born	2.9%

GENDER – 2009

Sex ratio	0.940

AGE – 2010

Percentage of Children	24.3%
Percentage Over 65	13.5%

MARRIAGE – 2009

Percent Married	51.0%
Percent Divorced	11.7%
Cohabitation	3.5%

Source: See end of appendix.

★ ALASKA ★

POPULATION

Total Population 2010	710,231
Population Change 2000–2010	+83,299 (+13.3%)
House of Representatives Seats 2000–2010	1–1
Largest City 2008	Anchorage
Percentage of Population in Urban Areas 2000	65.6%
Population Density (people/square mile) 2010	1.24

ECONOMY – 2009

Median Household Income	$64,635
Poverty Rate (Individual)	9.6%
Gini Coefficient (Perfect equality=0, Perfect inequality=1)	.402

EDUCATIONAL ATTAINMENT (25 YEARS AND OVER) – 2009

Less Than High School	9.3%
Bachelor's Degree	17.1%
Master's, Professional School, or Doctorate Degree	9.5%

RACE – 2010

White alone	66.7%
Black or African American alone	3.3%
American Indian or Alaska Native alone	14.8%
Asian alone	5.4%
Native Hawaiian and other Pacific Islander alone	1.0%
Some other race alone	1.6%
Two or more races	7.3%

HISPANIC ORIGIN – 2010

Hispanic or Latino	5.5%

NATIVITY – 2009

Foreign born	6.6%

GENDER – 2009

Sex ratio	1.077

AGE – 2010

Percentage of Children	26.8%
Percentage Over 65	7.0%

MARRIAGE – 2009

Percent Married	49.5%
Percent Divorced	11.8%
Cohabitation	8.0%

Source: See end of appendix.

★ ARIZONA ★

POPULATION

Total Population 2010	6,392,017
Population Change 2000–2010	+1,261,385 (+24.6%)
House of Representatives Seats 2000–2010	8–9
Largest City 2008	Phoenix
Percentage of Population in Urban Areas 2009	88.2%
Population Density (people/square mile) 2010	56.27

ECONOMY – 2009

Median Household Income	$50,296
Poverty Rate (Individual)	14.7%
Gini Coefficient (Perfect equality=0, Perfect inequality=1)	.451

EDUCATIONAL ATTAINMENT (25 YEARS AND OVER) – 2009

Less Than High School	16.1%
Bachelor's Degree	16.4%
Master's, Professional School, or Doctorate Degree	9.4%

RACE – 2010

White alone	73.0%
Black or African American alone	4.1%
American Indian or Alaska Native alone	4.6%
Asian alone	2.8%
Native Hawaiian and other Pacific Islander alone	0.2%
Some other race alone	11.9%
Two or more races	3.4%

HISPANIC ORIGIN – 2010

Hispanic or Latino	29.6%

NATIVITY – 2009

Foreign born	14.7%

GENDER – 2009

Sex ratio	1.005

AGE – 2010

Percentage of Children	26.5%
Percentage Over 65	12.9%

MARRIAGE – 2009

Percent Married	49.7%
Percent Divorced	12.1%
Cohabitation	6.4%

Source: See end of appendix.

★ ARKANSAS ★

POPULATION

Total Population 2010	2,915,918
Population Change 2000–2010	+242,518 (+9.1%)
House of Representatives Seats 2000–2010	4–4
Largest City 2008	Little Rock
Percentage of Population in Urban Areas 2000	52.5%
Population Density (people/square mile) 2010	56.04

ECONOMY – 2009

Median Household Income	$38,542
Poverty Rate (Individual)	17.7%
Gini Coefficient (Perfect equality=0, Perfect inequality=1)	.461

EDUCATIONAL ATTAINMENT (25 YEARS AND OVER) – 2009

Less Than High School	18.7%
Bachelor's Degree	12.6%
Master's, Professional School, or Doctorate Degree	6.3%

RACE – 2010

White alone	77.0%
Black or African American alone	15.4%
American Indian or Alaska Native alone	0.8%
Asian alone	1.2%
Native Hawaiian and other Pacific Islander alone	0.2%
Some other race alone	3.4%
Two or more races	2.0%

HISPANIC ORIGIN – 2010

Hispanic or Latino	6.4%

NATIVITY – 2009

Foreign born	4.0%

GENDER – 2009

Sex ratio	0.960

AGE – 2010

Percentage of Children	24.7%
Percentage Over 65	14.0%

MARRIAGE – 2009

Percent Married	52.8%
Percent Divorced	12.3%
Cohabitation	4.3%

Source: See end of appendix.

★ CALIFORNIA ★

POPULATION

Total Population 2010	37,253,956
Population Change 2000–2010	+3,382,308 (+10.0%)
House of Representatives Seats 2000–2010	53–53
Largest City 2008	Los Angeles
Percentage of Population in Urban Areas 2000	94.4%
Population Density (people/square mile) 2010	239.15

ECONOMY – 2009

Median Household Income	$60,392
Poverty Rate (Individual)	13.2%
Gini Coefficient (Perfect equality=0, Perfect inequality=1)	.467

EDUCATIONAL ATTAINMENT (25 YEARS AND OVER) – 2009

Less Than High School	19.5%
Bachelor's Degree	19.1%
Master's, Professional School, or Doctorate Degree	10.7%

RACE – 2010

White alone	57.6%
Black or African American alone	6.2%
American Indian or Alaska Native alone	1.0%
Asian alone	13.0%
Native Hawaiian and other Pacific Islander alone	0.4%
Some other race alone	17.0%
Two or more races	4.9%

HISPANIC ORIGIN – 2010

Hispanic or Latino	37.6%

NATIVITY – 2009

Foreign born	26.8%

GENDER – 2009

Sex ratio	1.003

AGE – 2010

Percentage of Children	26.0%
Percentage Over 65	10.9%

MARRIAGE – 2009

Percent Married	48.5%
Percent Divorced	9.5%
Cohabitation	6.1%

Source: See end of appendix.

★ COLORADO ★

POPULATION

Total Population 2010	5,029,196
Population Change 2000–2010	+727,935 (+16.9%)
House of Representatives Seats 2000–2010	7–7
Largest City 2008	Denver
Percentage of Population in Urban Areas 2000	84.5%
Population Density (people/square mile) 2010	48.52

ECONOMY – 2009

Median Household Income	$56,222
Poverty Rate (Individual)	11.9%
Gini Coefficient (Perfect equality=0, Perfect inequality=1)	.453

EDUCATIONAL ATTAINMENT (25 YEARS AND OVER) – 2009

Less Than High School	11.1%
Bachelor's Degree	22.9%
Master's, Professional School, or Doctorate Degree	12.6%

RACE – 2010

White alone	81.3%
Black or African American alone	4.0%
American Indian or Alaska Native alone	1.1%
Asian alone	2.8%
Native Hawaiian and other Pacific Islander alone	0.1%
Some other race alone	7.2%
Two or more races	3.4%

HISPANIC ORIGIN – 2010

Hispanic or Latino	20.7%

NATIVITY – 2009

Foreign born	9.8%

GENDER – 2009

Sex ratio	1.015

AGE – 2010

Percentage of Children	24.7%
Percentage Over 65	10.3%

MARRIAGE – 2019

Percent Married	52.6%
Percent Divorced	11.4%
Cohabitation	5.5%

Source: See end of appendix.

★ CONNECTICUT ★

POPULATION

Total Population 2010	3,574,097
Population Change 2000–2010	+168,532 (+4.9%)
House of Representatives Seats 2000–2010	5–5
Largest City 2008	Bridgeport
Percentage of Population in Urban Areas 2000	87.7%
Population Density (people/square mile) 2010	738.09

ECONOMY – 2009

Median Household Income	$67,721
Poverty Rate (Individual)	8.7%
Gini Coefficient (Perfect equality=0, Perfect inequality=1)	.480

EDUCATIONAL ATTAINMENT (25 YEARS AND OVER) – 2009

Less Than High School	11.8%
Bachelor's Degree	19.9%
Master's, Professional School, or Doctorate Degree	15.2%

RACE – 2010

White alone	77.6%
Black or African American alone	10.1%
American Indian or Alaska Native alone	0.3%
Asian alone	3.8%
Native Hawaiian and other Pacific Islander alone	–
Some other race alone	5.6%
Two or more races	2.6%

HISPANIC ORIGIN – 2010

Hispanic or Latino	13.4%

NATIVITY – 2009

Foreign born	12.8%

GENDER – 2009

Sex ratio	0.954

AGE – 2010

Percentage of Children	23.5%
Percentage Over 65	13.6%

MARRIAGE – 2009

Percent Married	51.0%
Percent Divorced	9.8%
Cohabitation	5.6%

Source: See end of appendix.

★ DELAWARE ★

POPULATION

Total Population 2010	897,934
Population Change 2000–2010	+114,334 (+14.6%)
House of Representatives Seats 2000–2010	1–1
Largest City 2008	Wilmington
Percentage of Population in Urban Areas 2000	80.1%
Population Density (people/square mile) 2010	460.82

ECONOMY – 2009

Median Household Income	$57,618
Poverty Rate (Individual)	10.5%
Gini Coefficient (Perfect equality=0, Perfect inequality=1)	.434

EDUCATIONAL ATTAINMENT (25 YEARS AND OVER) – 2009

Less Than High School	13.5%
Bachelor's Degree	16.6%
Master's, Professional School, or Doctorate Degree	11.0%

RACE – 2010

White alone	68.9%
Black or African American alone	21.4%
American Indian or Alaska Native alone	0.5%
Asian alone	3.2%
Native Hawaiian and other Pacific Islander alone	–
Some other race alone	3.4%
Two or more races	2.7%

HISPANIC ORIGIN – 2010

Hispanic or Latino	8.2%

NATIVITY – 2009

Foreign born	7.8%

GENDER – 2009

Sex ratio	0.943

AGE – 2010

Percentage of Children	23.8%
Percentage Over 65	13.8%

MARRIAGE – 2009

Percent Married	49.9%
Percent Divorced	10.5%
Cohabitation	6.2%

Source: See end of appendix.

★DISTRICT OF COLUMBIA★

POPULATION

Total Population 2010	601,723
Population Change 2000–2010	+29,664 (+5.2%)
House of Representatives Seats 2000–2010	0–0
Largest City 2008	Washington
Percentage of Population in Urban Areas 2000	100%
Population Density (people/square mile) 2010	9,856.49

ECONOMY – 2009

Median Household Income	$56,519
Poverty Rate (Individual)	18.3%
Gini Coefficient (Perfect equality=0, Perfect inequality=1)	.532

EDUCATIONAL ATTAINMENT (25 YEARS AND OVER) – 2009

Less Than High School	14.5%
Bachelor's Degree	20.8%
Master's, Professional School, or Doctorate Degree	26.3%

RACE – 2010

White alone	38.5%
Black or African American alone	50.7%
American Indian or Alaska Native alone	0.3%
Asian alone	3.5%
Native Hawaiian and other Pacific Islander alone	0.1%
Some other race alone	4.1%
Two or more races	2.9%

HISPANIC ORIGIN – 2010

Hispanic or Latino	9.1%

NATIVITY – 2009

Foreign born	12.5%

GENDER – 2009

Sex ratio	0.894

AGE – 2010

Percentage of Children	19.4%
Percentage Over 65	11.8%

MARRIAGE – 2009

Percent Married	26.5%
Percent Divorced	9.8%
Cohabitation	5.5%

Source: See end of appendix.

★FLORIDA★

POPULATION

Total Population 2010	18,801,310
Population Change 2000–2010	+2,818,932 (+17.6%)
House of Representatives Seats 2000–2010	25–27
Largest City 2008	Jacksonville
Percentage of Population in Urban Areas 2000	89.3%
Population Density (people/square mile) 2010	350.61

ECONOMY – 2009

Median Household Income	$47,450
Poverty Rate (Individual)	13.2%
Gini Coefficient (Perfect equality=0, Perfect inequality=1)	.469

EDUCATIONAL ATTAINMENT (25 YEARS AND OVER) – 2009

Less Than High School	15.1%
Bachelor's Degree	16.6%
Master's, Professional School, or Doctorate Degree	9.0%

RACE – 2010

White alone	75.0%
Black or African American alone	16.0%
American Indian or Alaska Native alone	0.4%
Asian alone	2.4%
Native Hawaiian and other Pacific Islander alone	0.1%
Some other race alone	3.6%
Two or more races	2.5%

HISPANIC ORIGIN – 2010

Hispanic or Latino	22.5%

NATIVITY – 2009

Foreign born	18.7%

GENDER – 2009

Sex ratio	0.969

AGE – 2010

Percentage of Children	22.3%
Percentage Over 65	16.9%

MARRIAGE – 2009

Percent Married	49.9%
Percent Divorced	12.1%
Cohabitation	6.1%

Source: See end of appendix.

★ GEORGIA ★

POPULATION

Total Population 2010	9,687,653
Population Change 2000–2010	+1,501,200 (+18.3%)
House of Representatives Seats 2000–2010	13–14
Largest City 2008	Atlanta
Percentage of Population in Urban Areas 2000	71.6%
Population Density (people/square mile) 2010	168.44

ECONOMY – 2009

Median Household Income	$49,466
Poverty Rate (Individual)	15.0%
Gini Coefficient (Perfect equality=0, Perfect inequality=1)	.469

EDUCATIONAL ATTAINMENT (25 YEARS AND OVER) – 2009

Less Than High School	17.1%
Bachelor's Degree	17.5%
Master's, Professional School, or Doctorate Degree	9.6%

RACE – 2010

White alone	59.7%
Black or African American alone	30.5%
American Indian or Alaska Native alone	0.3%
Asian alone	3.2%
Native Hawaiian and other Pacific Islander alone	0.1%
Some other race alone	4.0%
Two or more races	2.1%

HISPANIC ORIGIN – 2010

Hispanic or Latino	8.8%

NATIVITY – 2009

Foreign born	9.1%

GENDER – 2009

Sex ratio	0.968

AGE – 2010

Percentage of Children	26.5%
Percentage Over 65	10.0%

MARRIAGE – 2009

Percent Married	48.9%
Percent Divorced	11.2%
Cohabitation	4.7%

Source: See end of appendix.

★ HAWAII ★

POPULATION

Total Population 2010	1,360,301
Population Change 2000–2010	+148,764 (+12.3%)
House of Representatives Seats 2000–2010	2–2
Largest City 2008	Honolulu
Percentage of Population in Urban Areas 2000	91.5%
Population Density (people/square mile) 2010	211.80

ECONOMY – 2009

Median Household Income	$64,661
Poverty Rate (Individual)	9.4%
Gini Coefficient (Perfect equality=0, Perfect inequality=1)	.425

EDUCATIONAL ATTAINMENT (25 YEARS AND OVER) – 2009

Less Than High School	10.5%
Bachelor's Degree	19.5%
Master's, Professional School, or Doctorate Degree	9.8%

RACE – 2010

White alone	24.7%
Black or African American alone	1.6%
American Indian or Alaska Native alone	0.3%
Asian alone	38.6%
Native Hawaiian and other Pacific Islander alone	10.0%
Some other race alone	1.2%
Two or more races	23.6%

HISPANIC ORIGIN – 2010

Hispanic or Latino	8.9%

NATIVITY – 2009

Foreign born	16.8%

GENDER – 2009

Sex ratio	1.021

AGE – 2010

Percentage of Children	22.6%
Percentage Over 65	14.1%

MARRIAGE – 2009

Percent Married	51.7%
Percent Divorced	9.2%
Cohabitation	6.0%

Source: See end of appendix.

★ IDAHO ★

POPULATION

Total Population 2010	1,567,582
Population Change 2000–2010	+273,629 (+21.1%)
House of Representatives Seats 2000–2010	2–2
Largest City 2008	Boise
Percentage of Population in Urban Areas 2000	66.4%
Population Density (people/square mile) 2010	18.97

ECONOMY – 2009

Median Household Income	$46,183
Poverty Rate (Individual)	13.5%
Gini Coefficient (Perfect equality=0, Perfect inequality=1)	.421

EDUCATIONAL ATTAINMENT (25 YEARS AND OVER) – 2009

Less Than High School	12.3%
Bachelor's Degree	16.4%
Master's, Professional School, or Doctorate Degree	7.4%

RACE – 2010

White alone	89.1%
Black or African American alone	0.6%
American Indian or Alaska Native alone	1.4%
Asian alone	1.2%
Native Hawaiian and other Pacific Islander alone	0.1%
Some other race alone	5.1%
Two or more races	2.5%

HISPANIC ORIGIN – 2010

Hispanic or Latino	11.2%

NATIVITY – 2009

Foreign born	5.8%

GENDER – 2009

Sex ratio	1.008

AGE – 2010

Percentage of Children	27.2%
Percentage Over 65	11.8%

MARRIAGE – 2009

Percent Married	57.3%
Percent Divorced	11.5%
Cohabitation	5.5%

Source: See end of appendix.

★ ILLINOIS ★

POPULATION

Total Population 2010	12,830,632
Population Change 2000–2010	+411,339 (+3.3%)
House of Representatives Seats 2000–2010	19–18
Largest City 2008	Chicago
Percentage of Population in Urban Areas 2000	87.8%
Population Density (people/square mile) 2010	231.10

ECONOMY – 2009

Median Household Income	$55,222
Poverty Rate (Individual)	12.4%
Gini Coefficient (Perfect equality=0, Perfect inequality=1)	.469

EDUCATIONAL ATTAINMENT (25 YEARS AND OVER) – 2009

Less Than High School	14.3%
Bachelor's Degree	18.6%
Master's, Professional School, or Doctorate Degree	11.2%

RACE – 2010

White alone	71.5%
Black or African American alone	14.5%
American Indian or Alaska Native alone	0.3%
Asian alone	4.6%
Native Hawaiian and other Pacific Islander alone	–
Some other race alone	6.7%
Two or more races	2.3%

HISPANIC ORIGIN – 2010

Hispanic or Latino	15.8%

NATIVITY – 2009

Foreign born	13.4%

GENDER – 2009

Sex ratio	0.971

AGE – 2010

Percentage of Children	25.0%
Percentage Over 65	12.1%

MARRIAGE – 2009

Percent Married	49.5%
Percent Divorced	9.4%
Cohabitation	5.3%

Source: See end of appendix.

★ INDIANA ★

POPULATION

Total Population 2010	6,483,802
Population Change 2000–2010	+403,317 (+6.6%)
House of Representatives Seats 2000–2010	9–9
Largest City 2008	Indianapolis
Percentage of Population in Urban Areas 2000	70.8%
Population Density (people/square mile) 2010	180.98

ECONOMY – 2009

Median Household Income	$47,465
Poverty Rate (Individual)	13.2%
Gini Coefficient (Perfect equality=0, Perfect inequality=1)	.434

EDUCATIONAL ATTAINMENT (25 YEARS AND OVER) – 2009

Less Than High School	14.3%
Bachelor's Degree	14.0%
Master's, Professional School, or Doctorate Degree	8.0%

RACE – 2010

White alone	84.3%
Black or African American alone	9.1%
American Indian or Alaska Native alone	0.3%
Asian alone	1.6%
Native Hawaiian and other Pacific Islander alone	–
Some other race alone	2.7%
Two or more races	2.0%

HISPANIC ORIGIN – 2010

Hispanic or Latino	6.0%

NATIVITY – 2009

Foreign born	4.1%

GENDER – 2009

Sex ratio	0.971

AGE – 2010

Percentage of Children	25.0%
Percentage Over 65	12.6%

MARRIAGE – 2009

Percent Married	52.3%
Percent Divorced	11.9%
Cohabitation	5.9%

Source: See end of appendix.

★ IOWA ★

POPULATION

Total Population 2010	3,046,355
Population Change 2000–2010	+120,031 (+4.1%)
House of Representatives Seats 2000–2010	5–4
Largest City 2008	Des Moines
Percentage of Population in Urban Areas 2000	61.1%
Population Density (people/square mile) 2010	54.54

ECONOMY – 2009

Median Household Income	$48,052
Poverty Rate (Individual)	11.4%
Gini Coefficient (Perfect equality=0, Perfect inequality=1)	.431

EDUCATIONAL ATTAINMENT (25 YEARS AND OVER) – 2009

Less Than High School	10.4%
Bachelor's Degree	16.8%
Master's, Professional School, or Doctorate Degree	7.4%

RACE – 2010

White alone	91.3%
Black or African American alone	2.9%
American Indian or Alaska Native alone	0.4%
Asian alone	1.7%
Native Hawaiian and other Pacific Islander alone	0.1%
Some other race alone	1.8%
Two or more races	1.8%

HISPANIC ORIGIN – 2010

Hispanic or Latino	5.0%

NATIVITY – 2009

Foreign born	3.8%

GENDER – 2009

Sex ratio	0.976

AGE – 2010

Percentage of Children	23.8%
Percentage Over 65	14.7%

MARRIAGE – 2009

Percent Married	55.2%
Percent Divorced	9.9%
Cohabitation	6.0%

Source: See end of appendix.

★ KANSAS ★

POPULATION

Total Population 2010	2,853,118
Population Change 2000–2010	+164,700 (+6.1%)
House of Representatives Seats 2000–2010	4–4
Largest City 2008	Wichita
Percentage of Population in Urban Areas 2000	71.4%
Population Density (people/square mile) 2010	34.90

ECONOMY – 2009

Median Household Income	$48,394
Poverty Rate (Individual)	12.2%
Gini Coefficient (Perfect equality=0, Perfect inequality=1)	.444

EDUCATIONAL ATTAINMENT (25 YEARS AND OVER) – 2009

Less Than High School	11.0%
Bachelor's Degree	30.7%
Master's, Professional School, or Doctorate Degree	9.8%

RACE – 2010

White alone	83.8%
Black or African American alone	5.9%
American Indian or Alaska Native alone	1.0%
Asian alone	2.4%
Native Hawaiian and other Pacific Islander alone	0.1%
Some other race alone	3.9%
Two or more races	3.0%

HISPANIC ORIGIN – 2010

Hispanic or Latino	10.5%

NATIVITY – 2009

Foreign born	6.0%

GENDER – 2009

Sex ratio	0.987

AGE – 2010

Percentage of Children	25.1%
Percentage Over 65	13.0%

MARRIAGE – 2009

Percent Married	54.4%
Percent Divorced	10.9%
Cohabitation	5.0%

Source: See end of appendix.

★ KENTUCKY ★

POPULATION

Total Population 2010	4,339,367
Population Change 2000–2010	+297,598 (+7.4%)
House of Representatives Seats 2000–2010	6–6
Largest City 2008	Louisville
Percentage of Population in Urban Areas 2000	55.8%
Population Density (people/square mile) 2010	109.90

ECONOMY – 2009

Median Household Income	$41,197
Poverty Rate (Individual)	17.4%
Gini Coefficient (Perfect equality=0, Perfect inequality=1)	.464

EDUCATIONAL ATTAINMENT (25 YEARS AND OVER) – 2009

Less Than High School	19.7%
Bachelor's Degree	11.9%
Master's, Professional School, or Doctorate Degree	8.2%

RACE – 2010

White alone	87.8%
Black or African American alone	7.8%
American Indian or Alaska Native alone	0.2%
Asian alone	1.1%
Native Hawaiian and other Pacific Islander alone	0.1%
Some other race alone	1.3%
Two or more races	1.7%

HISPANIC ORIGIN – 2010

Hispanic or Latino	3.1%

NATIVITY – 2009

Foreign born	2.8%

GENDER – 2009

Sex ratio	0.964

AGE – 2010

Percentage of Children	23.8%
Percentage Over 65	12.9%

MARRIAGE – 2009

Percent Married	52.6%
Percent Divorced	12.1%
Cohabitation	5.0%

Source: See end of appendix.

★ LOUISIANA ★

POPULATION

Total Population 2010	4,533,372
Population Change 2000–2010	+64,396 (+1.4%)
House of Representatives Seats 2000–2010	7–6
Largest City 2008	New Orleans
Percentage of Population in Urban Areas 2000	72.6%
Population Density (people/square mile) 2010	104.93

ECONOMY – 2009

Median Household Income	$42,167
Poverty Rate (individual)	18.4%
Gini Coefficient (Perfect equality=0, Perfect inequality=1)	.473

EDUCATIONAL ATTAINMENT (25 YEARS AND OVER) – 2009

Less Than High School	19.5%
Bachelor's Degree	13.8%
Master's, Professional School, or Doctorate Degree	6.8%

RACE – 2010

White alone	62.6%
Black or African American alone	32.0%
American Indian or Alaska Native alone	0.7%
Asian alone	1.5%
Native Hawaiian and other Pacific Islander alone	–
Some other race alone	1.5%
Two or more races	1.6%

HISPANIC ORIGIN – 2010

Hispanic or Latino	4.2%

NATIVITY – 2009

Foreign born	3.1%

GENDER – 2009

Sex ratio	0.947

AGE – 2010

Percentage of Children	25.3%
Percentage Over 65	12.1%

MARRIAGE – 2009

Percent Married	47.0%
Percent Divorced	11.1%
Cohabitation	5.1%

Source: See end of appendix.

★ MAINE ★

POPULATION

Total Population 2010	1,328,361
Population Change 2000–2010	+53,438 (+4.2%)
House of Representatives Seats 2000–2010	2–2
Largest City 2008	Portland
Percentage of Population in Urban Areas 2000	40.2%
Population Density (people/square mile) 2010	43.07

ECONOMY – 2009

Median Household Income	$46,541
Poverty Rate (Individual)	12.6%
Gini Coefficient (Perfect equality=0, Perfect inequality=1)	.432

EDUCATIONAL ATTAINMENT (25 YEARS AND OVER) – 2009

Less Than High School	10.6%
Bachelor's Degree	17.1%
Master's, Professional School, or Doctorate Degree	9.1%

RACE – 2010

White alone	95.2%
Black or African American alone	1.2%
American Indian or Alaska Native alone	0.6%
Asian alone	1.0%
Native Hawaiian and other Pacific Islander alone	–
Some other race alone	0.3%
Two or more races	1.6%

HISPANIC ORIGIN – 2010

Hispanic or Latino	1.3%

NATIVITY – 2009

Foreign born	3.3%

GENDER – 2009

Sex ratio	0.954

AGE – 2010

Percentage of Children	21.3%
Percentage Over 65	15.0%

MARRIAGE – 2009

Percent Married	52.6%
Percent Divorced	12.6%
Cohabitation	8.0%

Source: See end of appendix.

★ MARYLAND ★

POPULATION

Total Population 2010	5,773,552
Population Change 2000–2010	+477,066 (+9.0%)
House of Representatives Seats 2000–2010	8–8
Largest City 2008	Baltimore
Percentage of Population in Urban Areas 2000	86.1%
Population Density (people/square mile) 2010	594.77

ECONOMY – 2009

Median Household Income	$69,475
Poverty Rate (Individual)	8.2%
Gini Coefficient (Perfect equality=0, Perfect inequality=1)	.448

EDUCATIONAL ATTAINMENT (25 YEARS AND OVER) – 2009

Less Than High School	12.5%
Bachelor's Degree	19.6%
Master's, Professional School, or Doctorate Degree	15.6%

RACE – 2010

White alone	58.2%
Black or African American alone	29.4%
American Indian or Alaska Native alone	0.4%
Asian alone	5.5%
Native Hawaiian and other Pacific Islander alone	0.1%
Some other race alone	3.6%
Two or more races	2.9%

HISPANIC ORIGIN – 2010

Hispanic or Latino	8.2%

NATIVITY – 2009

Foreign born	12.3%

GENDER – 2009

Sex ratio	0.941

AGE – 2010

Percentage of Children	24.2%
Percentage Over 65	11.8%

MARRIAGE – 2009

Percent Married	48.8%
Percent Divorced	9.5%
Cohabitation	5.4%

Source: See end of appendix.

★ MASSACHUSETTS ★

POPULATION

Total Population 2010	6,547,629
Population Change 2000–2010	+198,532 (+3.1%)
House of Representatives Seats 2000–2010	10–9
Largest City 2008	Boston
Percentage of Population in Urban Areas 2000	91.4%
Population Density (people/square mile) 2010	839.43

ECONOMY – 2009

Median Household Income	$64,496
Poverty Rate (Individual)	10.1%
Gini Coefficient (Perfect equality=0, Perfect inequality=1)	.468

EDUCATIONAL ATTAINMENT (25 YEARS AND OVER) – 2009

Less Than High School	11.7%
Bachelor's Degree	21.7%
Master's, Professional School, or Doctorate Degree	16.1%

RACE – 2010

White alone	80.4%
Black or African American alone	6.6%
American Indian or Alaska Native alone	0.3%
Asian alone	5.3%
Native Hawaiian and other Pacific Islander alone	–
Some other race alone	4.7%
Two or more races	2.6%

HISPANIC ORIGIN – 2010

Hispanic or Latino	9.6%

NATIVITY – 2009

Foreign born	14.1%

GENDER – 2009

Sex ratio	0.946

AGE – 2010

Percentage of Children	22.3%
Percentage Over 65	13.4%

MARRIAGE – 2009

Percent Married	47.8%
Percent Divorced	9.1%
Cohabitation	5.8%

Source: See end of appendix.

★ MICHIGAN ★

POPULATION

Total Population 2010	9,883,640
Population Change 2000–2010	−54,804 (−0.6%)
House of Representatives Seats 2000–2010	15–14
Largest City 2008	Detroit
Percentage of Population in Urban Areas 2000	74.7%
Population Density (people/square mile) 2010	174.81

ECONOMY – 2009

Median Household Income	$48,700
Poverty Rate (Individual)	14.5%
Gini Coefficient (Perfect equality=0, Perfect inequality=1)	.453

EDUCATIONAL ATTAINMENT (25 YEARS AND OVER) – 2009

Less Than High School	12.7%
Bachelor's Degree	15.2%
Master's, Professional School, or Doctorate Degree	9.4%

RACE – 2010

White alone	78.9%
Black or African American alone	14.2%
American Indian or Alaska Native alone	0.6%
Asian alone	2.4%
Native Hawaiian and other Pacific Islander alone	–
Some other race alone	1.5%
Two or more races	2.3%

HISPANIC ORIGIN – 2010

Hispanic or Latino	4.4%

NATIVITY – 2009

Foreign born	6.0%

GENDER – 2009

Sex ratio	0.968

AGE – 2010

Percentage of Children	24.3%
Percentage Over 65	12.9%

MARRIAGE – 2009

Percent Married	50.4%
Percent Divorced	10.9%
Cohabitation	5.3%

Source: See end of appendix.

★ MINNESOTA ★

POPULATION

Total Population 2010	5,303,925
Population Change 2000–2010	+384,446 (+7.8%)
House of Representatives Seats 2000–2010	8–8
Largest City 2008	Minneapolis
Percentage of Population in Urban Areas 2000	70.9%
Population Density (people per square mile) 2010	66.61

ECONOMY – 2009

Median Household Income	$57,007
Poverty Rate	10.0%
Gini Coefficient (Perfect equality=0, Perfect inequality=1)	.439

EDUCATIONAL ATTAINMENT (25 YEARS AND OVER) – 2009

Less Than High School	8.9%
Bachelor's Degree	21.2%
Master's, Professional School, or Doctorate Degree	10.0%

RACE – 2010

White alone	85.3%
Black or African American alone	5.2%
American Indian or Alaska Native alone	1.1%
Asian alone	4.0%
Native Hawaiian and other Pacific Islander alone	–
Some other race alone	1.9%
Two or more races	2.4%

HISPANIC ORIGIN – 2010

Hispanic or Latino	4.7%

NATIVITY – 2009

Foreign born	6.5%

GENDER – 2009

Sex ratio	0.991

AGE – 2010

Percentage of Children	24.3%
Percentage Over 65	12.4%

MARRIAGE – 2009

Percent Married	53.8%
Percent Divorced	9.3%
Cohabitation	6.2%

Source: See end of appendix.

★ MISSISSIPPI ★

POPULATION

Total Population 2010	2,967,297
Population Change 2000–2010	+122,639 (+4.3%)
House of Representatives Seats 2000–2010	4–4
Largest City 2008	Jackson
Percentage of Population in Urban Areas 2000	48.8%
Population Density (people/square mile) 2010	63.24

ECONOMY – 2009

Median Household Income	$36,796
Poverty Rate (Individual)	21.4%
Gini Coefficient (Perfect equality=0, Perfect inequality=1)	.470

EDUCATIONAL ATTAINMENT (25 YEARS AND OVER) – 2009

Less Than High School	21.1%
Bachelor's Degree	12.4%
Master's, Professional School, or Doctorate Degree	6.7%

RACE – 2010

White alone	59.1%
Black or African American alone	37.0%
American Indian or Alaska Native alone	0.5%
Asian alone	0.9%
Native Hawaiian and other Pacific Islander alone	—
Some other race alone	1.3%
Two or more races	1.1%

HISPANIC ORIGIN – 2010

Hispanic or Latino	2.7%

NATIVITY – 2009

Foreign born	2.0%

GENDER – 2009

Sex ratio	0.941

AGE – 2010

Percentage of Children	26.2%
Percentage Over 65	12.5%

MARRIAGE – 2009

Percent Married	47.2%
Percent Divorced	10.9%
Cohabitation	4.4%

Source: See end of appendix.

★ MISSOURI ★

POPULATION

Total Population 2010	5,988,927
Population Change 2000–2010	+393,716 (+7.0%)
House of Representatives Seats 2000–2010	9–8
Largest City 2008	Kansas City
Percentage of Population in Urban Areas 2000	69.4%
Population Density (people/square mile) 2010	87.12

ECONOMY – 2009

Median Household Income	$46,005
Poverty Rate (Individual)	13.7%
Gini Coefficient (Perfect equality=0, Perfect inequality=1)	.450

EDUCATIONAL ATTAINMENT (25 YEARS AND OVER) – 2009

Less Than High School	14.4%
Bachelor's Degree	15.6%
Master's, Professional School, or Doctorate Degree	8.9%

RACE – 2010

White alone	82.8%
Black or African American alone	11.6%
American Indian or Alaska Native alone	0.5%
Asian alone	1.6%
Native Hawaiian and other Pacific Islander alone	0.1%
Some other race alone	1.3%
Two or more races	2.1%

HISPANIC ORIGIN – 2010

Hispanic or Latino	3.5%

NATIVITY – 2009

Foreign born	3.5%

GENDER – 2009

Sex ratio	0.956

AGE – 2010

Percentage of Children	24.2%
Percentage Over 65	13.5%

MARRIAGE – 2009

Percent Married	51.6%
Percent Divorced	11.5%
Cohabitation	5.6%

Source: See end of appendix.

★ MONTANA ★

POPULATION

Total Population 2010	989,415
Population Change 2000–2010	+87,220 (+9.7%)
House of Representatives Seats 2000–2010	1–1
Largest City 2008	Billings
Percentage of Population in Urban Areas 2000	54.1%
Population Density (people/square mile) 2010	6.80

ECONOMY – 2009

Median Household Income	$43,089
Poverty Rate (Individual)	14.7%
Gini Coefficient (Perfect equality=0, Perfect inequality=1)	.431

EDUCATIONAL ATTAINMENT (25 YEARS AND OVER) – 2009

Less Than High School	9.6%
Bachelor's Degree	18.7%
Master's, Professional School, or Doctorate Degree	8.3%

RACE – 2010

White alone	89.4%
Black or African American alone	0.4%
American Indian or Alaska Native alone	6.3%
Asian alone	0.6%
Native Hawaiian and other Pacific Islander alone	0.1%
Some other race alone	0.6%
Two or more races	2.5%

HISPANIC ORIGIN – 2010

Hispanic or Latino	2.9%

NATIVITY – 2009

Foreign born	1.9%

GENDER – 2009

Sex ratio	1.002

AGE – 2010

Percentage of Children	23.0%
Percentage Over 65	14.1%

MARRIAGE – 2009

Percent Married	52.1%
Percent Divorced	12.2%
Cohabitation	5.8%

Source: See end of appendix.

★ NEBRASKA ★

POPULATION

Total Population 2010	1,826,341
Population Change 2000–2010	+115,078 (+6.7%)
House of Representatives Seats 2000–2010	3–3
Largest City 2008	Omaha
Percentage of Population in Urban Areas 2000	69.8%
Population Density (people/square mile) 2010	23.77

ECONOMY – 2009

Median Household Income	$47,995
Poverty Rate (Individual)	11.8%
Gini Coefficient (Perfect equality–0, Perfect inequality=1)	.440

EDUCATIONAL ATTAINMENT (25 YEARS AND OVER) – 2009

Less Than High School	10.3%
Bachelor's Degree	18.5%
Master's, Professional School, or Doctorate Degree	8.5%

RACE – 2010

White alone	86.1%
Black or African American alone	4.5%
American Indian or Alaska Native alone	1.0%
Asian alone	1.8%
Native Hawaiian and other Pacific Islander alone	0.1%
Some other race alone	4.3%
Two or more races	2.2%

HISPANIC ORIGIN – 2010

Hispanic or Latino	9.2%

NATIVITY – 2009

Foreign born	5.6%

GENDER – 2009

Sex ratio	0.985

AGE – 2010

Percentage of Children	25.2%
Percentage Over 65	13.3%

MARRIAGE – 2009

Percent Married	54.1%
Percent Divorced	9.7%
Cohabitation	5.3%

Source: See end of appendix.

★ NEVADA ★

POPULATION

Total Population 2010	2,700,551
Population Change 2000–2010	+702,294 (35.1%)
House of Representatives Seats 2000–2010	3–4
Largest City 2008	Las Vegas
Percentage of Population in Urban Areas 2000	91.5%
Population Density (people/square mile) 2010	24.60

ECONOMY – 2009

Median Household Income	$55,585
Poverty Rate (Individual)	11.1%
Gini Coefficient (Perfect equality=0, Perfect inequality=1)	.433

EDUCATIONAL ATTAINMENT (25 YEARS AND OVER) – 2009

Less Than High School	16.3%
Bachelor's Degree	14.3%
Master's, Professional School, or Doctorate Degree	7.2%

RACE – 2010

White alone	66.2%
Black or African American alone	8.1%
American Indian or Alaska Native alone	1.2%
Asian alone	7.2%
Native Hawaiian and other Pacific Islander alone	0.6%
Some other race alone	12.0%
Two or more races	4.7%

HISPANIC ORIGIN – 2010

Hispanic or Latino	26.5%

NATIVITY – 2009

Foreign born	18.7%

GENDER – 2009

Sex ratio	1.038

AGE – 2010

Percentage of Children	25.9%
Percentage Over 65	11.3%

MARRIAGE – 2009

Percent Married	49.7%
Percent Divorced	13.5%
Cohabitation	7.2%

Source: See end of appendix.

★ NEW HAMPSHIRE ★

POPULATION

Total Population 2010	1,316,470
Population Change 2000–2010	+80,684 (+6.5%)
House of Representatives Seats 2000–2010	2–2
Largest City 2008	Manchester
Percentage of Population in Urban Areas 2000	59.3%
Population Density (people/square mile) 2010	147.05

ECONOMY – 2009

Median Household Income	$63,033
Poverty Rate (Individual)	7.7%
Gini Coefficient (Perfect equality=0, Perfect inequality=1)	.431

EDUCATIONAL ATTAINMENT (25 YEARS AND OVER) – 2009

Less Than High School	9.5%
Bachelor's Degree	20.9%
Master's, Professional School, or Doctorate Degree	11.6%

RACE – 2010

White alone	93.9%
Black or African American alone	1.1%
American Indian or Alaska Native alone	0.2%
Asian alone	2.2%
Native Hawaiian and other Pacific Islander alone	–
Some other race alone	0.9%
Two or more races	1.6%

HISPANIC ORIGIN – 2010

Hispanic or Latino	2.8%

NATIVITY – 2009

Foreign born	5.2%

GENDER – 2009

Sex ratio	0.972

AGE – 2010

Percentage of Children	22.7%
Percentage Over 65	12.8%

MARRIAGE – 2009

Percent Married	53.5%
Percent Divorced	11.3%
Cohabitation	7.4%

Source: See end of appendix.

★ NEW JERSEY ★

POPULATION

Total Population 2010	8,791,894
Population Change 2000–2010	+377,544 (+4.5%)
House of Representatives Seats 2000–2010	13–12
Largest City 2008	Newark
Percentage of Population in Urban Areas 2000	94.4%
Population Density (people/square mile) 2010	1,195.49

ECONOMY – 2009

Median Household Income	$68,981
Poverty Rate (Individual)	8.8%
Gini Coefficient (Perfect equality=0, Perfect inequality=1)	.465

EDUCATIONAL ATTAINMENT (25 YEARS AND OVER) – 2009

Less Than High School	13.2%
Bachelor's Degree	21.5%
Master's, Professional School, or Doctorate Degree	12.7%

RACE – 2010

White alone	68.6%
Black or African American alone	13.7%
American Indian or Alaska Native alone	0.3%
Asian alone	8.3%
Native Hawaiian and other Pacific Islander alone	–
Some other race alone	6.4%
Two or more races	2.7%

HISPANIC ORIGIN – 2010

Hispanic or Latino	17.7%

NATIVITY – 2009

Foreign born	19.7%

GENDER – 2009

Sex ratio	0.961

AGE – 2010

Percentage of Children	24.0%
Percentage Over 65	13.2%

MARRIAGE – 2009

Percent Married	51.1%
Percent Divorced	8.1%
Cohabitation	4.9%

Source: See end of appendix.

★ NEW MEXICO ★

POPULATION

Total Population 2010	2,059,179
Population Change 2000–2010	+240,133 (+13.2%)
House of Representatives Seats 2000–2010	3–3
Largest City 2008	Albuquerque
Percentage of Population in Urban Areas 2000	75.0%
Population Density (people/square mile) 2010	16.98

ECONOMY – 2009

Median Household Income	$42,742
Poverty Rate (Individual)	18.1%
Gini Coefficient (Perfect equality=0, Perfect inequality=1)	.453

EDUCATIONAL ATTAINMENT (25 YEARS AND OVER) – 2009

Less Than High School	17.9%
Bachelor's Degree	14.5%
Master's, Professional School, or Doctorate Degree	10.6%

RACE – 2010

White alone	68.4%
Black or African American alone	2.1%
American Indian or Alaska Native alone	9.4%
Asian alone	1.4%
Native Hawaiian and other Pacific Islander alone	0.1%
Some other race alone	15.0%
Two or more races	3.7%

HISPANIC ORIGIN – 2010

Hispanic or Latino	46.3%

NATIVITY – 2009

Foreign born	9.5%

GENDER – 2009

Sex ratio	0.980

AGE – 2010

Percentage of Children	25.7%
Percentage Over 65	12.6%

MARRIAGE – 2009

Percent Married	48.4%
Percent Divorced	12.1%
Cohabitation	6.8%

Source: See end of appendix.

★ NEW YORK ★

POPULATION

Total Population 2010	19,378,102
Population Change 2000–2010	+401,645 (+2.1%)
House of Representatives Seats 2000–2010	29–27
Largest City 2008	New York
Percentage of Population in Urban Areas 2000	87.5%
Population Density (people/square mile) 2010	411.19

ECONOMY – 2009

Median Household Income	$55,233
Poverty Rate (Individual)	13.8%
Gini Coefficient (Perfect equality=0, Perfect inequality=1)	.502

EDUCATIONAL ATTAINMENT (25 YEARS AND OVER) – 2009

Less Than High School	15.8%
Bachelor's Degree	18.2%
Master's, Professional School, or Doctorate Degree	13.6%

RACE – 2010

White alone	65.7%
Black or African American alone	15.9%
American Indian or Alaska Native alone	0.6%
Asian alone	7.3%
Native Hawaiian and other Pacific Islander alone	–
Some other race alone	7.4%
Two or more races	3.0%

HISPANIC ORIGIN – 2010

Hispanic or Latino	17.6%

NATIVITY – 2009

Foreign born	21.3%

GENDER – 2009

Sex ratio	0.946

AGE – 2010

Percentage of Children	23.2%
Percentage Over 65	13.2%

MARRIAGE – 2009

Percent Married	46.1%
Percent Divorced	8.4%
Cohabitation	5.5%

Source: See end of appendix.

★ NORTH CAROLINA ★

POPULATION

Total Population 2010	9,535,483
Population Change 2000–2010	+1,486,170 (+18.5%)
House of Representatives Seats 2000–2010	13–13
Largest City 2008	Charlotte
Percentage of Population in Urban Areas 2000	60.2%
Population Density (people/square mile) 2010	196.13

ECONOMY – 2009

Median Household Income	$45,069
Poverty Rate (Individual)	15.1%
Gini Coefficient (Perfect equality=0, Perfect inequality=1)	.464

EDUCATIONAL ATTAINMENT (25 YEARS AND OVER) – 2009

Less Than High School	17.0%
Bachelor's Degree	17.3%
Master's, Professional School, or Doctorate Degree	8.6%

RACE – 2010

White alone	68.5%
Black or African American alone	21.5%
American Indian or Alaska Native alone	1.3%
Asian alone	2.2%
Native Hawaiian and other Pacific Islander alone	0.1%
Some other race alone	4.3%
Two or more races	2.2%

HISPANIC ORIGIN – 2010

Hispanic or Latino	8.4%

NATIVITY – 2009

Foreign born	6.8%

GENDER – 2009

Sex ratio	0.958

AGE – 2010

Percentage of Children	24.4%
Percentage Over 65	12.4%

MARRIAGE – 2009

Percent Married	51.7%
Percent Divorced	10.0%
Cohabitation	4.9%

Source: See end of appendix.

★ NORTH DAKOTA ★

POPULATION

Total Population 2010	672,591
Population Change 2000–2010	+30,391 (+4.7%)
House of Representatives Seats 2000–2010	1–1
Largest City 2008	Fargo
Percentage of Population in Urban Areas 2000	55.9%
Population Density (people/square mile) 2010	9.75

ECONOMY – 2009

Median Household Income	$45,140
Poverty Rate (Individual)	12.3%
Gini Coefficient (Perfect equality=0, Perfect inequality=1)	.450

EDUCATIONAL ATTAINMENT (25 YEARS AND OVER) – 2009

Less Than High School	11.3%
Bachelor's Degree	19.1%
Master's, Professional School, or Doctorate Degree	6.5%

RACE – 2010

White alone	90.0%
Black or African American alone	1.2%
American Indian or Alaska Native alone	5.4%
Asian alone	1.0%
Native Hawaiian and other Pacific Islander alone	–
Some other race alone	0.5%
Two or more races	1.8%

HISPANIC ORIGIN – 2010

Hispanic or Latino	2.0%

NATIVITY – 2009

Foreign born	2.3%

GENDER – 2009

Sex ratio	1.010

AGE – 2010

Percentage of Children	22.4%
Percentage Over 65	14.6%

MARRIAGE – 2009

Percent Married	54.7%
Percent Divorced	8.0%
Cohabitation	5.3%

Source: See end of appendix.

★ OHIO ★

POPULATION

Total Population 2010	11,536,504
Population Change 2000–2010	+183,364 (+1.6%)
House of Representatives Seats 2000–2010	18–16
Largest City 2008	Columbus
Percentage of Population in Urban Areas 2000	77.4%
Population Density (people/square mile) 2010	282.34

ECONOMY – 2009

Median Household Income	$47,144
Poverty Rate (Individual)	13.6%
Gini Coefficient (Perfect equality=0, Perfect inequality=1)	.453

EDUCATIONAL ATTAINMENT (25 YEARS AND OVER) – 2009

Less Than High School	13.2%
Bachelor's Degree	15.0%
Master's, Professional School, or Doctorate Degree	8.6%

RACE – 2010

White alone	82.7%
Black or African American alone	12.2%
American Indian or Alaska Native alone	0.2%
Asian alone	1.7%
Native Hawaiian and other Pacific Islander alone	–
Some other race alone	1.1%
Two or more races	2.1%

HISPANIC ORIGIN – 2010

Hispanic or Latino	3.1%

NATIVITY – 2009

Foreign born	3.6%

GENDER – 2009

Sex ratio	0.953

AGE – 2010

Percentage of Children	24.0%
Percentage Over 65	13.6%

MARRIAGE – 2009

Percent Married	50.3%
Percent Divorced	11.6%
Cohabitation	5.6%

Source: See end of appendix.

★ OKLAHOMA ★

POPULATION

Total Population 2010	3,751,351
Population Change 2000–2010	+300,697 (+8.7%)
House of Representatives Seats 2000–2010	5–5
Largest City 2008	Oklahoma City
Percentage of Population in Urban Areas 2000	65.3%
Population Density (people/square mile) 2010	54.69

ECONOMY – 2009

Median Household Income	$41,861
Poverty Rate (Individual)	16.4%
Gini Coefficient (Perfect equality=0, Perfect inequality=1)	.460

EDUCATIONAL ATTAINMENT (25 YEARS AND OVER) – 2009

Less Than High School	15.2%
Bachelor's Degree	15.1%
Master's, Professional School, or Doctorate Degree	7.3%

RACE – 2010

White alone	72.2%
Black or African American alone	7.4%
American Indian or Alaska Native alone	8.6%
Asian alone	1.7%
Native Hawaiian and other Pacific Islander alone	0.1%
Some other race alone	4.1%
Two or more races	5.9%

HISPANIC ORIGIN – 2010

Hispanic or Latino	8.9%

NATIVITY – 2009

Foreign born	5.0%

GENDER – 2009

Sex ratio	0.977

AGE – 2010

Percentage of Children	25.0%
Percentage Over 65	13.3%

MARRIAGE – 2009

Percent Married	52.6%
Percent Divorced	12.6%
Cohabitation	4.7%

Source: See end of appendix.

★ OREGON ★

POPULATION

Total Population 2010	3,831,074
Population Change 2000–2010	+409,675 (+12.0%)
House of Representatives Seats 2000–2010	5–5
Largest City 2008	Portland
Percentage of Population in Urban Areas 2000	78.7%
Population Density (people/square mile) 2010	39.91

ECONOMY – 2009

Median Household Income	$49,033
Poverty Rate (Individual)	13.6%
Gini Coefficient (Perfect equality=0, Perfect inequality=1)	.443

EDUCATIONAL ATTAINMENT (25 YEARS AND OVER) – 2009

Less Than High School	11.8%
Bachelor's Degree	18.1%
Master's, Professional School, or Doctorate Degree	10.1%

RACE – 2010

White alone	83.6%
Black or African American alone	1.8%
American Indian or Alaska Native alone	1.4%
Asian alone	3.7%
Native Hawaiian and other Pacific Islander alone	0.3%
Some other race alone	5.3%
Two or more races	3.8%

HISPANIC ORIGIN – 2010

Hispanic or Latino	11.7%

NATIVITY – 2009

Foreign born	9.5%

GENDER – 2009

Sex ratio	0.984

AGE – 2010

Percentage of Children	23.2%
Percentage Over 65	13.2%

MARRIAGE – 2009

Percent Married	51.5%
Percent Divorced	12.4%
Cohabitation	7.0%

Source: See end of appendix.

★ PENNSYLVANIA ★

POPULATION

Total Population 2010	12,702,379
Population Change 2000–2010	+421,325 (+3.4%)
House of Representatives Seats 2000–2010	19–18
Largest City 2008	Philadelphia
Percentage of Population in Urban Areas 2000	77.1%
Population Density (people/square mile) 2010	283.90

ECONOMY – 2009

Median Household Income	$49,737
Poverty Rate (Individual)	12.1%
Gini Coefficient (Perfect equality=0, Perfect inequality=1)	.460

EDUCATIONAL ATTAINMENT (25 YEARS AND OVER) – 2009

Less Than High School	13.1%
Bachelor's Degree	16.1%
Master's, Professional School, or Doctorate Degree	9.9%

RACE – 2010

White alone	81.9%
Black or African American alone	10.8%
American Indian or Alaska Native alone	0.2%
Asian alone	2.7%
Native Hawaiian and other Pacific Islander alone	–
Some other race alone	2.4%
Two or more races	1.9%

HISPANIC ORIGIN – 2010

Hispanic or Latino	5.7%

NATIVITY – 2009

Foreign born	5.3%

GENDER – 2009

Sex ratio	0.949

AGE – 2010

Percentage of Children	22.5%
Percentage Over 65	15.3%

MARRIAGE – 2009

Percent Married	50.2%
Percent Divorced	9.0%
Cohabitation	5.5%

Source: See end of appendix.

★ RHODE ISLAND ★

POPULATION

Total Population 2010	1,052,567
Population Change 2000–2010	+4,248 (+0.4%)
House of Representatives Seats 2000–2010	2–2
Largest City 2008	Providence
Percentage of Population in Urban Areas 2000	90.9%
Population Density (people/square mile) 2010	1,018.14

ECONOMY – 2009

Median Household Income	$55,569
Poverty Rate (Individual)	11.6%
Gini Coefficient (Perfect equality=0, Perfect inequality=1)	.457

EDUCATIONAL ATTAINMENT (25 YEARS AND OVER) – 2009

Less Than High School	16.6%
Bachelor's Degree	18.2%
Master's, Professional School, or Doctorate Degree	11.6%

RACE – 2010

White alone	81.4%
Black or African American alone	5.7%
American Indian or Alaska Native alone	0.6%
Asian alone	2.9%
Native Hawaiian and other Pacific Islander alone	0.1%
Some other race alone	6.0%
Two or more races	3.3%

HISPANIC ORIGIN – 2010

Hispanic or Latino	12.4%

NATIVITY – 2009

Foreign born	12.5%

GENDER – 2009

Sex ratio	0.944

AGE – 2010

Percentage of Children	22.1%
Percentage Over 65	14.0%

MARRIAGE – 2009

Percent Married	46.9%
Percent Divorced	10.5%
Cohabitation	5.7%

Source: See end of appendix.

★ SOUTH CAROLINA ★

POPULATION

Total Population 2010	4,625,364
Population Change 2000–2010	+613,352 (+15.3%)
House of Representatives Seats 2000–2010	6–7
Largest City 2008	Charleston
Percentage of Population in Urban Areas 2000	60.5%
Population Density (people/square mile) 2010	153.87

ECONOMY – 2009

Median Household Income	$43,572
Poverty Rate (Individual)	15.8%
Gini Coefficient (Perfect equality=0, Perfect inequality=1)	.462

EDUCATIONAL ATTAINMENT (25 YEARS AND OVER) – 2009

Less Than High School	17.8%
Bachelor's Degree	15.3%
Master's, Professional School, or Doctorate Degree	8.1%

RACE – 2010

White alone	66.2%
Black or African American alone	27.9%
American Indian or Alaska Native alone	0.4%
Asian alone	1.3%
Native Hawaiian and other Pacific Islander alone	0.1%
Some other race alone	2.5%
Two or more races	1.7%

HISPANIC ORIGIN – 2010

Hispanic or Latino	5.1%

NATIVITY – 2009

Foreign born	4.4%

GENDER – 2009

Sex ratio	0.949

AGE – 2010

Percentage of Children	24.0%
Percentage Over 65	13.1%

MARRIAGE – 2009

Percent Married	49.3%
Percent Divorced	9.9%
Cohabitation	4.6%

Source: See end of appendix.

★ SOUTH DAKOTA ★

POPULATION

Total Population 2010	814,180
Population Change 2000–2010	+59,336 (+7.9%)
House of Representatives Seats 2000–2010	1–1
Largest City 2008	Sioux Falls
Percentage of Population in Urban Areas 2000	51.9%
Population Density (people/square mile) 2010	10.74

ECONOMY – 2009

Median Household Income	$44,828
Poverty Rate (Individual)	13.5%
Gini Coefficient (Perfect equality=0, Perfect inequality=1)	.452

EDUCATIONAL ATTAINMENT (25 YEARS AND OVER) – 2009

Less Than High School	11.2%
Bachelor's Degree	17.6%
Master's, Professional School, or Doctorate Degree	7.1%

RACE – 2010

White alone	85.9%
Black or African American alone	1.3%
American Indian or Alaska Native alone	8.8%
Asian alone	0.9%
Native Hawaiian and other Pacific Islander alone	2%
Some other race alone	0.9%
Two or more races	2.1%

HISPANIC ORIGIN – 2010

Hispanic or Latino	2.7%

NATIVITY – 2009

Foreign born	2.3%

GENDER – 2009

Sex ratio	0.999

AGE – 2010

Percentage of Children	24.7%
Percentage Over 65	14.3%

MARRIAGE – 2009

Percent Married	53.5%
Percent Divorced	10.1%
Cohabitation	5.4%

Source: See end of appendix.

★ TENNESSEE ★

POPULATION

Total Population 2010	6,346,105
Population Change 2000–2010	+656,822 (+11.5%)
House of Representatives Seats 2000–2010	9–9
Largest City 2008	Memphis
Percentage of Population in Urban Areas 2000	63.6%
Population Density (people/square mile) 2010	153.90

ECONOMY – 2009

Median Household Income	$42,943
Poverty Rate (Individual)	16.1%
Gini Coefficient (Perfect equality=0, Perfect inequality=1)	.467

EDUCATIONAL ATTAINMENT (25 YEARS AND OVER) – 2009

Less Than High School	18.2%
Bachelor's Degree	14.6%
Master's, Professional School, or Doctorate Degree	7.8%

RACE – 2010

White alone	77.6%
Black or African American alone	16.7%
American Indian or Alaska Native alone	0.3%
Asian alone	1.4%
Native Hawaiian and other Pacific Islander alone	0.1%
Some other race alone	2.2%
Two or more races	1.7%

HISPANIC ORIGIN – 2010

Hispanic or Latino	4.6%

NATIVITY – 2009

Foreign born	4.1%

GENDER – 2009

Sex ratio	0.951

AGE – 2010

Percentage of Children	24.0%
Percentage Over 65	12.9%

MARRIAGE – 2009

Percent Married	51.4%
Percent Divorced	10.5%
Cohabitation	4.7%

Source: See end of appendix.

★ TEXAS ★

POPULATION

Total Population 2010	25,145,561
Population Change 2000–2010	+4,293,741 (+20.6%)
House of Representatives Seats 2000–2010	32–36
Largest City 2008	Houston
Percentage of Population in Urban Areas 2000	82.5%
Population Density (people/square mile) 2010	96.26

ECONOMY – 2009

Median Household Income	$48,199
Poverty Rate (Individual)	16.8%
Gini Coefficient (Perfect equality=0, Perfect inequality=1)	.474

EDUCATIONAL ATTAINMENT (25 YEARS AND OVER) – 2009

Less Than High School	20.7%
Bachelor's Degree	17.0%
Master's, Professional School, or Doctorate Degree	8.3%

RACE – 2010

White alone	70.4%
Black or African American alone	11.8%
American Indian or Alaska Native alone	0.7%
Asian alone	3.8%
Native Hawaiian and other Pacific Islander alone	0.1%
Some other race alone	10.5%
Two or more races	2.7%

HISPANIC ORIGIN – 2010

Hispanic or Latino	37.6%

NATIVITY – 2009

Foreign born	15.8%

GENDER – 2009

Sex ratio	0.998

AGE – 2010

Percentage of Children	27.9%
Percentage Over 65	10.1%

MARRIAGE – 2009

Percent Married	51.4%
Percent Divorced	10.5%
Cohabitation	4.7%

Source: See end of appendix.

★ UTAH ★

POPULATION

Total Population 2010	2,763,885
Population Change 2000–2010	+530,716 (+23.8%)
House of Representatives Seats 2000–2010	3–4
Largest City 2008	Salt Lake City
Percentage of Population in Urban Areas 2000	88.2%
Population Density (people/square mile) 2010	33.64

ECONOMY – 2009

Median Household Income	$55,642
Poverty Rate (Individual)	10.4%
Gini Coefficient (Perfect equality=0, Perfect inequality=1)	.414

EDUCATIONAL ATTAINMENT (25 YEARS AND OVER) – 2009

Less Than High School	9.6%
Bachelor's Degree	19.5%
Master's, Professional School, or Doctorate Degree	9.2%

RACE – 2010

White alone	86.1%
Black or African American alone	1.1%
American Indian or Alaska Native alone	1.2%
Asian alone	2.0%
Native Hawaiian and other Pacific Islander alone	0.9%
Some other race alone	6.0%
Two or more races	2.7%

HISPANIC ORIGIN – 2010

Hispanic or Latino	13.0%

NATIVITY – 2009

Foreign born	7.9%

GENDER – 2009

Sex ratio	1.013

AGE – 2010

Percentage of Children	31.1%
Percentage Over 65	8.8%

MARRIAGE – 2009

Percent Married	56.9%
Percent Divorced	9.0%
Cohabitation	3.9%

Source: See end of appendix.

★ VERMONT ★

POPULATION

Total Population 2010	625,741
Population Change 2000–2010	+16,914 (+2.8%)
House of Representatives Seats 2000–2010	1–1
Largest City 2008	Burlington
Percentage of Population in Urban Areas 2000	38.2%
Population Density (people/square mile) 2010	67.89

ECONOMY – 2009

Median Household Income	$51,284
Poverty Rate (Individual)	11.0%
Gini Coefficient (Perfect equality=0, Perfect inequality=1)	.428

EDUCATIONAL ATTAINMENT (25 YEARS AND OVER) – 2009

Less Than High School	9.9%
Bachelor's Degree	20.1%
Master's, Professional School, or Doctorate Degree	12.8%

RACE – 2010

White alone	95.3%
Black or African American alone	1.0%
American Indian or Alaska Native alone	0.4%
Asian alone	1.3%
Native Hawaiian and other Pacific Islander alone	–
Some other race alone	0.3%
Two or more races	1.7%

HISPANIC ORIGIN – 2010

Hispanic or Latino	1.5%

NATIVITY – 2009

Foreign born	3.7%

GENDER – 2009

Sex ratio	0.969

AGE – 2010

Percentage of Children	21.1%
Percentage Over 65	13.8%

MARRIAGE – 2009

Percent Married	50.4%
Percent Divorced	12.1%
Cohabitation	8.1%

Source: See end of appendix.

★ VIRGINIA ★

POPULATION

Total Population 2010	8,001,024
Population Change 2000–2010	+922,509 (+13%)
House of Representatives Seats 2000–2010	11–11
Largest City 2008	Virginia Beach
Percentage of Population in Urban Areas 2000	73.0%
Population Density (people/square mile) 2010	202.61

ECONOMY – 2009

Median Household Income	$60,316
Poverty Rate (Individual)	10.1%
Gini Coefficient (Perfect equality=0, Perfect inequality=1)	.456

EDUCATIONAL ATTAINMENT (25 YEARS AND OVER) – 2009

Less Than High School	14.2%
Bachelor's Degree	19.8%
Master's, Professional School, or Doctorate Degree	13.7%

RACE – 2010

White alone	68.6%
Black or African American alone	19.4%
American Indian or Alaska Native alone	0.4%
Asian alone	5.5%
Native Hawaiian and other Pacific Islander alone	0.1%
Some other race alone	3.2%
Two or more races	2.9%

HISPANIC ORIGIN – 2010

Hispanic or Latino	7.9%

NATIVITY – 2009

Foreign born	10.1%

GENDER – 2009

Sex ratio	0.967

AGE – 2010

Percentage of Children	23.7%
Percentage Over 65	11.8%

MARRIAGE – 2009

Percent Married	51.8%
Percent Divorced	9.5%
Cohabitation	4.7%

Source: See end of appendix.

★ WASHINGTON ★

POPULATION

Total Population 2010	6,724,540
Population Change 2000–2010	+830,419 (+14.1%)
House of Representatives Seats 2000–2010	9–10
Largest City 2008	Seattle
Percentage of Population in Urban Areas 2000	82.0%
Population Density (people/square mile) 2010	101.19

ECONOMY – 2009

Median Household Income	$56,384
Poverty Rate (Individual)	11.8%
Gini Coefficient (Perfect equality=0, Perfect inequality=1)	.439

EDUCATIONAL ATTAINMENT (25 YEARS AND OVER) – 2009

Less Than High School	10.6%
Bachelor's Degree	19.9%
Master's, Professional School, or Doctorate Degree	10.9%

RACE – 2010

White alone	77.3%
Black or African American alone	3.6%
American Indian or Alaska Native alone	1.5%
Asian alone	7.2%
Native Hawaiian and other Pacific Islander alone	0.6%
Some other race alone	5.2%
Two or more races	4.7%

HISPANIC ORIGIN – 2010

Hispanic or Latino	11.2%

NATIVITY – 2009

Foreign born	12.1%

GENDER – 2009

Sex ratio	0.998

AGE – 2010

Percentage of Children	23.9%
Percentage Over 65	11.8%

MARRIAGE – 2009

Percent Married	51.8%
Percent Divorced	12.0%
Cohabitation	6.8%

Source: See end of appendix.

★ WEST VIRGINIA ★

POPULATION

Total Population 2010	1,852,994
Population Change 2000–2010	+44,650 (+2.5%)
House of Representatives Seats 2000–2010	3–3
Largest City 2008	Charleston
Percentage of Population in Urban Areas 2000	46.1%
Population Density (people/square mile) 2010	77.09

ECONOMY – 2009

Median Household Income	$37,356
Poverty Rate (Individual)	17.6%
Gini Coefficient (Perfect equality=0, Perfect inequality=1)	.463

EDUCATIONAL ATTAINMENT (25 YEARS AND OVER) – 2009

Less Than High School	18.4%
Bachelor's Degree	10.4%
Master's, Professional School, or Doctorate Degree	6.7%

RACE – 2010

White alone	93.9%
Black or African American alone	3.4%
American Indian or Alaska Native alone	0.2%
Asian alone	0.7%
Native Hawaiian and other Pacific Islander alone	–
Some other race alone	0.3%
Two or more races	1.5%

HISPANIC ORIGIN – 2010

Hispanic or Latino	1.2%

NATIVITY – 2009

Foreign born	1.3%

GENDER – 2009

Sex ratio	0.962

AGE – 2010

Percentage of Children	21.4%
Percentage Over 65	15.5%

MARRIAGE – 2009

Percent Married	53.8%
Percent Divorced	11.5%
Cohabitation	5.2%

Source: See end of appendix.

★ WISCONSIN ★

POPULATION

Total Population 2010	5,686,986
Population Change 2000–2010	+323,311 (+6.0%)
House of Representatives Seats 2000–2010	8–8
Largest City 2008	Milwaukee
Percentage of Population in Urban Areas 2000	68.3%
Population Density (people/square mile) 2010	105.01

ECONOMY – 2009

Median Household Income	$51,569
Poverty Rate (Individual)	11.1%
Gini Coefficient (Perfect equality=0, Perfect inequality=1)	.432

EDUCATIONAL ATTAINMENT (25 YEARS AND OVER) – 2009

Less Than High School	11.0%
Bachelor's Degree	17.0%
Master's, Professional School, or Doctorate Degree	8.4%

RACE – 2010

White alone	86.2%
Black or African American alone	6.3%
American Indian or Alaska Native alone	1.0%
Asian alone	2.3%
Native Hawaiian and other Pacific Islander alone	–
Some other race alone	2.4%
Two or more races	1.8%

HISPANIC ORIGIN – 2010

Hispanic or Latino	5.9%

NATIVITY – 2009

Foreign born	4.4%

GENDER – 2009

Sex ratio	0.987

AGE – 2010

Percentage of Children	23.6%
Percentage Over 65	13.2%

MARRIAGE – 2009

Percent Married	52.8%
Percent Divorced	9.8%
Cohabitation	6.4%

Source: See end of appendix.

★ W Y O M I N G ★

POPULATION

Total Population 2010	563,626
Population Change 2000–2010	+69,844 (+14.1%)
House of Representatives Seats 2000–2010	1–1
Largest City 2008	Cheyenne
Percentage of Population in Urban Areas 2000	65.1%
Population Density (people/square mile) 2010	5.81

ECONOMY – 2009

Median Household Income	$51,990
Poverty Rate (Individual)	9.6%
Gini Coefficient	.415

EDUCATIONAL ATTAINMENT (25 YEARS AND OVER) – 2009

Less Than High School	8.9%
Bachelor's Degree	15.6%
Master's, Professional School, or Doctorate Degree	7.6%

RACE – 2010

White alone	90.7%
Black or African American alone	0.8%
American Indian or Alaska Native alone	2.4%
Asian alone	0.8%
Native Hawaiian and other Pacific Islander alone	0.1%
Some other race alone	3.0%
Two or more races	2.2%

HISPANIC ORIGIN – 2010

Hispanic or Latino	8.9%

NATIVITY – 2009

Foreign born	2.8%

GENDER – 2009

Sex ratio	1.037

AGE – 2010

Percentage of Children	24.0%
Percentage Over 65	12.1%

MARRIAGE – 2009

Percent Married	55.1%
Percent Divorced	12.3%
Cohabitation	6.5%

Source: See end of appendix.

POPULATION

Total Population	U.S. Census Bureau, "2010 Census Data—Redistricting Data Map," http://2010.census.gov/2010census/data.
Population Change 2000–2010	Paul Mackun & Steven Wilson, "2010 Census Briefs— Population Distribution and Change, 2000 to 2010," http://www.census.gov/prod/cen2010/briefs/c2010br-01.pdf.
House of Representatives Seats 2000–2010	U.S. Census Bureau, "2010 Census Data—Apportionment Data," http://2010.census.gov/2010census/data/ apportionment-data-text.php.
Largest City	U.S. Census Bureau, "Statistical Abstract of the United States: 2011—Table 446. Residential Property Tax Rates for Largest City in Each State: 2008," http://www.census.gov/ compendia/statab/2011/tables/11s0446.pdf.
Percentage of Population in Urban Areas	U.S. Census Bureau, "Statistical Abstract of the United States: 2011—Table 29. Urban and Rural Populations by State: 1990 and 2000," http://www.census.gov/compendia/statab/ 2011/tables/11s0029.pdf.
Population Density (people per square mile)	Social Explorer, "Census 2010— T2. Population Density," http://www.socialexplorer.com/pub/reportdata/ htmlresults.aspx?ReportId=R10051544&Page=1.

ECONOMY

Median Income	U.S. Census Bureau, "2005–2009 American Community Survey 5-Year Estimates—Table B19013. Median Household Income in the Past 12 Months (In 2009 Inflation-Adjusted Dollars)," http://factfinder.census.gov/ servlet/DTTable?_bm=y&-context=dt&-ds_name=ACS_ 2009_5YR_G00_&-CONTEXT5dt&-mt_name=ACS_ 2009_5YR_G2000_B19013&-tree_id=5309&- redoLog=true&-_caller=geoselect&-geo_id=01000US&- search_results=ALL&-format=&-_lang=en.
Poverty Rate (Individual)	U.S. Census Bureau, "2005–2009 American Community Survey 5-Year Estimates," http://factfinder.census.gov.
Gini Coefficient (Perfect equality=0, Perfect inequality=1)	Amanda Noss, "Household Income for States: 2008 and 2009," http://www.census.gov/prod/2010pubs/acsbr09-2.pdf.

EDUCATIONAL ATTAINMENT (25 YEARS AND OVER)

Less Than High School	U. S. Census Bureau, "2005–2009 American Community Survey 5-Year Estimates—SE:T25. Educational Attainment for Population 25 Years and Over," http://www.socialexplorer.com.
Bachelor's Degree	
Master's, Professional School, or Doctorate Degree	

RACE

White alone	U.S. Census Bureau, "2010 Census Data—Redistricting Data Map," http://2010.census.gov/2010census/data.
Black or African American alone	
American Indian or Alaska Native alone	
Asian alone	
Native Hawaiian and other Pacific Islander alone	
Some other race alone	
Two or more races	

★ SOURCES (CONTINUED) ★

HISPANIC ORIGIN

Hispanic or Latino

Not Hispanic or Latino

U.S. Census Bureau, "2010 Census Data—Redistricting Data Map," http://2010.census.gov/2010census/data.

NATIVITY

Foreign born

Social Explorer Tables: ACS 2005 to 2009 (5-Year Estimates) (SE), ACS 2005—2009 (5-Year Estimates), Social Explorer; U.S. Census Bureau.

GENDER

Sex ratio

U.S. Census Bureau, "2009 Population Estimates—Table GCT-T3-R. Sex Ratio of the Total Population," http:// factfinder.census.gov/servlet/GCTTable?_bm=y&- geo_id=01000US&-_box_head_nbr=GCT-T3-R&- ds_name=PEP_2009_EST&-format=U-40Sb.

AGE

Percentage of Children

Percentage Over 65

Social Explorer, "2005–2009 American Community Survey 5-Year Estimates—SE:T9. Age (Short Version)," http://www.socialexplorer.com.

MARRIAGE

Percent Married

Social Explorer, "2005–2009 American Community Survey 5-Year Estimates—SE:T22. Marital Status for the Population 15 years and Over," http://www.socialexplorer.com.

Percent Divorced
Cohabitation
2000 National Data

Social Explorer Tables (SE), Census 2000, U.S. Census Bureau and Social Explorer. http://www.socialexplorer.com.

- indicates a value of zero or a value that rounds to zero.

Appendix II:
2010 Census
Questionnaire

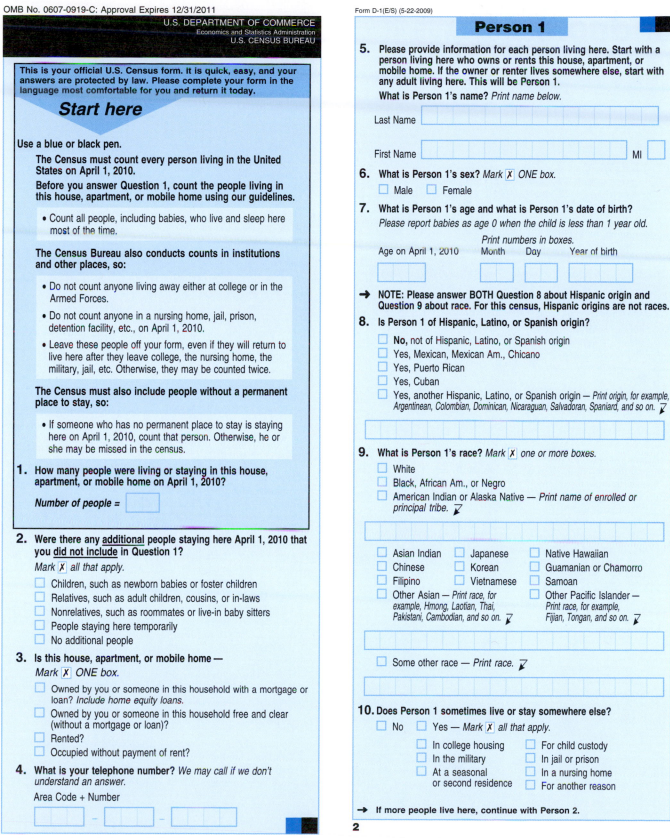

U.S. DEPARTMENT OF COMMERCE
Economics and Statistics Administration
U.S. CENSUS BUREAU

This is your official U.S. Census form. It is quick, easy, and your answers are protected by law. Please complete your form in the language most comfortable for you and return it today.

Start here

Use a blue or black pen.

The Census must count every person living in the United States on April 1, 2010.

Before you answer Question 1, count the people living in this house, apartment, or mobile home using our guidelines.

- Count all people, including babies, who live and sleep here most of the time.

The Census Bureau also conducts counts in institutions and other places, so:

- Do not count anyone living away either at college or in the Armed Forces.
- Do not count anyone in a nursing home, jail, prison, detention facility, etc., on April 1, 2010.
- Leave these people off your form, even if they will return to live here after they leave college, the nursing home, the military, jail, etc. Otherwise, they may be counted twice.

The Census must also include people without a permanent place to stay, so:

- If someone who has no permanent place to stay is staying here on April 1, 2010, count that person. Otherwise, he or she may be missed in the census.

1. How many people were living or staying in this house, apartment, or mobile home on April 1, 2010?

Number of people =

2. Were there any <u>additional</u> people staying here April 1, 2010 that you <u>did not include</u> in Question 1?

Mark ☒ all that apply.

- ☐ Children, such as newborn babies or foster children
- ☐ Relatives, such as adult children, cousins, or in-laws
- ☐ Nonrelatives, such as roommates or live-in baby sitters
- ☐ People staying here temporarily
- ☐ No additional people

3. Is this house, apartment, or mobile home —
Mark ☒ ONE box.

- ☐ Owned by you or someone in this household with a mortgage or loan? *Include home equity loans.*
- ☐ Owned by you or someone in this household free and clear (without a mortgage or loan)?
- ☐ Rented?
- ☐ Occupied without payment of rent?

4. What is your telephone number? *We may call if we don't understand an answer.*

Area Code + Number

U S C E N S U S B U R E A U

Person 1

5. Please provide information for each person living here. Start with a person living here who owns or rents this house, apartment, or mobile home. If the owner or renter lives somewhere else, start with any adult living here. This will be Person 1.

What is Person 1's name? *Print name below.*

Last Name

First Name   MI

6. What is Person 1's sex? *Mark ☒ ONE box.*

- ☐ Male   ☐ Female

7. What is Person 1's age and what is Person 1's date of birth?

Please report babies as age 0 when the child is less than 1 year old.

Print numbers in boxes.

Age on April 1, 2010   Month   Day   Year of birth

→ NOTE: Please answer BOTH Question 8 about Hispanic origin and Question 9 about race. For this census, Hispanic origins are not races.

8. Is Person 1 of Hispanic, Latino, or Spanish origin?

- ☐ **No,** not of Hispanic, Latino, or Spanish origin
- ☐ Yes, Mexican, Mexican Am., Chicano
- ☐ Yes, Puerto Rican
- ☐ Yes, Cuban
- ☐ Yes, another Hispanic, Latino, or Spanish origin — *Print origin, for example, Argentinean, Colombian, Dominican, Nicaraguan, Salvadoran, Spaniard, and so on.* ↘

9. What is Person 1's race? *Mark ☒ one or more boxes.*

- ☐ White
- ☐ Black, African Am., or Negro
- ☐ American Indian or Alaska Native — *Print name of enrolled or principal tribe.* ↘

- ☐ Asian Indian   ☐ Japanese   ☐ Native Hawaiian
- ☐ Chinese   ☐ Korean   ☐ Guamanian or Chamorro
- ☐ Filipino   ☐ Vietnamese   ☐ Samoan
- ☐ Other Asian — *Print race, for example, Hmong, Laotian, Thai, Pakistani, Cambodian, and so on.* ↘   ☐ Other Pacific Islander — *Print race, for example, Fijian, Tongan, and so on.* ↘

- ☐ Some other race — *Print race.* ↘

10. Does Person 1 sometimes live or stay somewhere else?

- ☐ No   ☐ Yes — *Mark ☒ all that apply.*
  - ☐ In college housing   ☐ For child custody
  - ☐ In the military   ☐ In jail or prison
  - ☐ At a seasonal or second residence   ☐ In a nursing home
  - ☐ For another reason

→ If more people live here, continue with Person 2.

Endnotes

CHAPTER 1

1. Sabrina Tavernise and Jeff Zeleny, "South and West See Large Gains in Latest Census," *New York Times*, December 21, 2010, http://www.nytimes.com/2010/12/22/us/22census.html?_r=1&partner=rss&emc=rss.
2. Leo A. Orleans, "1953 Chinese Census in Perspective" *Journal of Asian Studies* 16, no. 4 (1957): 565–573.
3. Walter Scheidel, *Rome and China: Comparative Perspectives on Ancient World Empires* (Oxford University Press, 2009), 8.
4. Margo J. Anderson, *The American Census: A Social History* (New Haven, CT: Yale University Press, 1988), 7–8.
5. Clara Rodriguez, *Changing Race: Latinos, the Census, and the History of Ethnicity in the United States* (New York: New York University Press, 2000), 88–91.
6. Ibid., 91–92.
7. Scott, 16–21.
8. Anderson, 18–19.
9. Scott, 28.
10. Edward Lunt, "History of the United States Census," *Publications of the American Statistical Association* 1, no. 2/3 (1888): 77.
11. Anderson, 34–37.
12. Ibid., 49–50.
13. Scott, 34.
14. U.S. Constitution, Article 1, Section 2.
15. U.S. Census Bureau, Mission Statement, 2010, http://www.census.gov/aboutus/mission.html.
16. U.S. Census Bureau, "What Is the Census?" http://2010.census.gov/2010census/about/.
17. Dough Beizer, "Census CIO Counts on Future Tech," *Federal Computer Week*, January 22, 2010, http://fcw.com/Articles/2010/01/25/QA-Brian-McGrath-Census.aspx?Page=3f.
18. Ann Herbert Scott, *Census U.S.A.* (New York: Seabury Press, 1968), 14–17.
19. U.S. Census Bureau, "1790 Census Overview," 2011, http://www.census.gov/history/www/through_the_decades/overview/1790.html.
20. Anderson, 7–8.
21. Population Reference Bureau, "The U.S. Census Tradition," 2011, http://www.prb.org/Articles/2009/censustradition.aspx?p=1.
22. Ibid.
23. U.S. Census Bureau, "Fast Facts," 2011, http://www.census.gov/history/www/through_the_decades/fast_facts.
24. Anderson, 14.
25. Ibid., 18–23.
26. U.S. Census Bureau, "Index of Questions," 2011, http://www.census.gov/history/www/through_the_decades/index_of_questions.
27. Ibid.
28. Anderson, 213–220.
29. U.S. Census Bureau, "Index of Questions," 2011, http://www.census.gov/history/www/through_the_decades/index_of_questions.
30. Ibid.
31. Population Reference Bureau, "About the American Community Survey," 2011, http://www.prb.org/Articles/2009/acs.aspx.
32. Anderson, 32–43.
33. U.S. Census Bureau, "Legislation: 1902–1941," 2011, http://www.census.gov/history/www/reference/legislation/legislation_1902_-_1941.html.
34. Anderson, 118–119.
35. Ibid., 188–190.
36. U.S. Census Bureau, "Legislation: 1989–Present," 2011, http://www.census.gov/history/www/reference/legislation/legislation_1989_-_present.html.
37. Population Reference Bureau, "The U.S. Census Tradition," 2011, http://www.prb.org/Articles/2009/censustradition.aspx?p=1.
38. U.S. Census Bureau, "Fast Facts," 2011, http://www.census.gov/history/www/through_the_decades/fast_facts.
39. Population Reference Bureau, "The U.S. Census Tradition," http://www.prb.org/Articles/2009/censustradition.aspx?p=1
40. Ibid., 197.
41. U.S. Census Bureau, "FOSDIC," 2011, http://www.census.gov/history/www/innovations/technology/fosdic.html.
42. U.S. Census Bureau, "Internet," 2011, http://www.census.gov/history/www/innovations/technology/internet.html.
43. U.S. Census Bureau, "TIGER Overview," 2011, http://www.census.gov/geo/www/tiger/overview.html.
44. Scott, 36–37.
45. Anderson, 170–182.
46. Ibid., 184–190.
47. Ibid., 201.
48. U.S. Census Bureau, "Developing Sampling Techniques," 2011, http://www.census.gov/history/www/innovations/data_collection/developing_sampling_techniques.html.
49. Jorge Duany, "The Census Undercount: The Underground Economy and Undocumented Migration: The Case of Dominicans in Santurce, Puerto Rico," 1992, http://www.census.gov/srd/papers/pdf/ev92-17.pdf.
50. Anderson, 202, 222.
51. Reynolds Farley, "Ref: Census Taking and Census Undercount: Prickly Statistical, Political and Constitutional Issues," University of Michigan Population Studies Center, June 17, 2008, http://www.psc.isr.umich.edu/dis/acs/.../Censusundercountlecture.doc.
52. Julia Preston, "Latino Leaders Use Churches in Census Bid," *New York Times*, December 22, 2009, http://www.nytimes.com/2009/12/23/us/23latino.html.
53. Wade Goodwyn, "Texas Tea Party Sues over Census Districts," *All Things Considered*, NPR, March 7, 2011, http://www6.lexisnexis.com/publisher/EndUser?Action=UserDisplayFullDocument&orgId=574&topicId=25131&docId=l:1373802837&isRss=true.
54. U.S. Census Bureau, "2010 Census: Master Address File, Issues and Concerns," 2011, http://www.census.gov/newsroom/releases/pdf/Groves_House_Testimony_10-21_Final.pdf.
55. U.S. Census Bureau, "2010 Overview," 2011, http://www.census.gov/history/www/through_the_decades/overview/2010_overview_1.html.

CHAPTER 2

1. Holland Cotter, "So What about This Record-Setting Picasso?" New York Times Arts Beat Blog, May 5, 2010, http://artsbeat.blogs.nytimes.com/2010/05/05/so-what-about-this-record-setting-picasso.
2. Hope Yen, "Income Gap between Rich, Poor the Widest Ever," CBS News, Sept. 28, 2010, http://www.cbsnews.com/stories/2010/09/28/national/main6907321.shtml.
3. Timothy Noah, "Why We Can't Ignore Income Inequality," *Slate*, Sept. 3, 2010, http://www.slate.com/id/2266025/entry/2266026.
4. Ibid.
5. Yen. "Income Gap."
6. Lydia Saad, "Vast Majority Wants Some Aspect of Bush Tax Cuts Extended," *Gallup*, Dec. 1, 2010, http://www.gallup.com/poll/144989/vast-majority-wants-aspect-bush-tax-cuts-extended.aspx.

7. "Inside the Middle Class: Bad Times Hit the Good Life," Pew Research Center, April 9, 2008, http://pewresearch.org/pubs/793/inside-the-middle-class.

8. U.S. Department of Health and Human Services, "Computations for the Annual Update of the HHS Poverty Guidelines for the 48 Contiguous States and the District of Columbia," 2011, http://aspe.hhs.gov/poverty/11computations.shtml.

9. U.S. Census Bureau, "Poverty," 2010, http://www.census.gov/hhes/www/poverty/methods/definitions.html.

10. U.S. Census Bureau, "How the Census Bureau Measures Poverty," 2010, http://www.census.gov/hhes/www/poverty/about/overview/measure.html.

11. "Manhattan Rental Report," The Real Estate Group, Feb. 2011, http://www.tregny.com/manhattan_rental_market_report.

12. J. S. Hacker, *The Great Risk Shift: The New Insecurity and the Decline of the American Dream* (New York: Oxford University Press, 2006).

13. Todd Henderson, "We Are the Super Rich," *Truth on the Market*, Sept. 15, 2010, http://truthonthemarket.com/2010/09/15/we-are-the-super-rich.

14. U.S. Census Bureau, "People Below 125 Percent of the Poverty Line and the Near Poor," 2010, http://www.census.gov/hhes/www/poverty/data/historical/hstpov6.xls.

15. U.S. Census Bureau, "Share of Aggregate Income Received by Each Fifth and Top 5 Percent of Households, All Races: 1967 to 2009," 2011, http://www.census.gov/compendia/statab/2011/tables/11s0693.xls.

16. Ibid.

17. Ibid.

18. Ibid.

19. "Superrich Americans Driving Income Inequality," National Public Radio, Sept. 23, 2010, http://www.npr.org/templates/story/story.php?storyId=130052776.

20. Andrea Brandolini and Timothy Smeeding, "Inequality: International Evidence," The New Palgrave Dictionary of Economics, March 2007, http://www.irp.wisc.edu/aboutirp/people/affiliates/Smeeding/12-Palgrave_0407.pdf.

21. Central Intelligence Agency, "Distribution of Family Income—Gini Index," *The World Factbook*, https://www.cia.gov/library/publications/the-world-factbook/fields/2172.html.

22. Brandolini and Smeeding, "Inequality: International Evidence."

23. "Supperrich Americans Driving Income Inequality."

24. Robert Putnam, *Bowling Alone* (New York: Simon & Schuster, 2000).

25. Richard Wilkinson and Kate Pickett, "Income Inequality and Population Health: A Review and Explanation of the Evidence," *Social Science & Medicine* 62, no. 7 (2006): 1768–1784.

26. G. William Domhoff, "Wealth, Income, and Power," Power in America, University of California at Santa Cruz Sociology Department, 2011, http://sociology.ucsc.edu/whorulesamerica/power/wealth.html.

27. Janny Scott and David Leonhardt, "Shadowy Lines That Still Divide," *New York Times*, May 15, 2005, http://www.nytimes.com/2005/05/15/national/class/OVERVIEW-FINAL.html?_r=1.

28. Katharine Bradbury and Jane Katz, "Women's Labor Market Involvement and Family Income Mobility When Marriages End," *New England Economic Review* no. Q4 (2002): 41–74.

29. Doyle McManus, "The Upward Mobility Gap," *Los Angeles Times*, Jan. 2, 2011, http://articles.latimes.com/2011/jan/02/opinion/la-oe-mc-manus-twous-20110102.

30. Noah, "Why We Can't Ignore . . . "

31. Willford King, *The Wealth and Income of the People of the United States* (New York: Macmillan Company, 1915).

32. Ibid.

33. John F. Kennedy, "Remarks in Heber Springs, Arkansas, at the Dedication of Greers Ferry Dam," Oct. 2, 1963, The American Presidency Project, http://www.presidency.ucsb.edu/ws/index.php?pid=9455.

34. U.S. Census Bureau, "Share of Aggregate Income."

35. Ibid.

36. Jill Littrell, Fred Brooks, Jan Ivery, and Mary L. Ohmer, "Why You Should Care about the Threatened Middle Class," *Journal of Sociology & Social Welfare* 37, no. 2 (2010): 87–113.

37. U.S. Census Bureau, "Race and Hispanic Origin of People by Median Income and Sex: 1947–2009," Table P-2, 2010, http://www.census.gov/hhes/www/income/data/historical/people/P02_2009.xls.

38. U.S. Census Bureau, "Educational Attainment—People 25 Years Old and Over by Median Income and Sex," Table P-16, 2010, http://www.census.gov/hhes/www/income/data/historical/people/P16_2009.xls.

39. Ibid.

40. Frank S. Levy and Peter Temin, "Inequality and Institutions in 20th Century America," MIT Department of Economics Working Paper No. 07–17, June 27, 2007, http://papers.ssrn.com/sol3/papers.cfm?abstract_id=984330.

41. "Poverty and Income in 2009: A Look at the New Census Data and What the Numbers Mean," Brookings, Sept. 16, 2010, http://www.brookings.edu/events/2010/0916_poverty_income.aspx.

42. Noah. "Why We Can't Ignore . . . "

43. U.S. Census Bureau, "Money Income of Families—Median Income by Race and Hispanic Origin, in Current and Constant (2008) Dollars," 2011, http://www.census.gov/compendia/statab/2011/tables/11s0696.xls.

44. Campbell J. Gibson and Emily Lennon, "Historical Census Statistics on the Foreign-Born Population of the United States: 1850–1990," U.S. Census Bureau, 1999, http://www.census.gov/population/www/documentation/twps0029/twps0029.html; Elizabeth M. Grieco and Edward N. Trevelyan, "Place of Birth of the Foreign-Born Population: 2009," U.S. Census Bureau, October 2010, www.census.gov/prod/2010pubs/acsbr09-15.pdf

45. Nicole Stoops, "Educational Attainment in the United States: 2003," U.S. Bureau of Statistics, 2004, http://www.census.gov/prod/2004pubs/p20-550.pdf.

46. Ibid.

47. George Borjas, "Increasing the Supply of Labor through Immigration: Measuring the Impact on Native-Born Workers," Center for Immigration Studies, May 2004, http://www.cis.org/articles/2004/back504.pdf.

48. Ibid.

49. Noah, "Why We Can't Ignore . . . "

50. Chris Isidore, "It's Official: Recession Since Dec. '07," *CNN Money*, Dec. 1, 2008, http://money.cnn.com/2008/12/01/news/economy/recession/index.htm.

51. Carmen DeNavas-Walt, Bernadette D. Proctor, and Jessica C. Smith, "Income, Poverty, and Health Insurance Coverage in the United States: 2009," U.S. Census Bureau, Sept. 2010, http://www.census.gov/prod/2010pubs/p60-238.pdf.

52. Ibid.

53. Elizabeth Kneebone and Emily Garr, "Income and Poverty," in *The State of Metropolitan America*, Brookings, 2010, http://www.brookings.edu/metro/MetroAmericaChapters/poverty_income.aspx.

54. DeNavas-Walt, Proctor, and Smith, "Income, Poverty, and Health Insurance . . . "

55. Ibid.

56. Steven F. Hipple, "The Labor Market in 2009: Recession Drags On," *Monthly Labor Review Online* 133, no. 3 (2010), http://www.bls.gov/opub/mlr/2010/03/art1exc.htm.

57. Ibid.

58. Bureau of Labor Statistics, "How the Government Measures Unemployment," 2009, http://www.bls.gov/cps/cps_htgm.htm.

59. Hipple, "The Labor Market in 2009 . . . "

60. Catherine Rampell, "More College Graduates Take Public Service Jobs," *New York Times*, March 1, 2011.

61. Sandra Luckett Cark and Mai Weismantle, "Employment Status: 2000, Census 2000 Brief," U.S. Census Bureau, August 2003, www.census.gov/prod/2003pubs/c2kbr-18.pdf.

62. Bureau of Labor Statistics, "Regional and State Employment and Unemployment Summary," 2011, http://www.bls.gov/news.release/empsit.nr0.htm.

63. Ibid.

64. Ibid.

65. DeNavas-Walt, Proctor, and Smith, "Income, Poverty, and Health Insurance . . . "1

66. Ibid.
67. Ibid.
68. Ibid.
69. Noah, "Why We Can't Ignore . . . "
70. Yen.
71. Kneebone and Garr, "Income and Poverty."
72. Ibid.
73. Ibid.
74. Ibid.
75. Michael Luo, "Doubling-Up in Recession-Strained Quarters," *New York Times*, Dec. 28, 2010, http://www.nytimes.com/2010/12/29/us/29families.html.
76. Hope Yen, "Another Victim of the Recession: Marriages," MSNBC, September 28, 2011, http://today.msnbc.msn.com/id/39401113/ns/today-today_news/.
77. Noah, "Why We Can't Ignore . . . "
78. U.S. Census Bureau, "Share of Aggregate Income . . . "
79. DeNavas-Walt, Proctor, and Smith, "Income, Poverty, and Health Insurance . . . "
80. Howard Wial and Alec Friedhoff, "Work," The State of Metropolitan America, Brookings, 2010, http://www.brookings.edu/metro/MetroAmericaChapters/work.aspx.
81. Ibid.
82. U.S. Census Bureau, "Gini Index of Income Inequality: Households," 2009 American Community Survey, www.census.gov/prod/2010pubs/acsbr09-2.pdf.
83. Kneebone and Garr, "Income and Poverty."
84. Ibid.
85. U.S. Census Bureau, "Household Income for States: 2008 and 2009," 2010, http://www.census.gov/prod/2010pubs/acsbr09-2.pdf.
86. Ibid.
87. U.S. Census Bureau, "Small Area Income and Poverty Estimates," 2010, http://www.census.gov/cgi-bin/saipe/national.cgi?year=2009&ascii.
88. Ibid.
89. Department of Labor Statistics, "Regional and State Unemployment" (Annual), Feb. 25, 2011, http://www.bls.gov/news.release/srgune.htm.
90. Ibid.
91. Vincent Fernando, "10 States with Ridiculously Low Unemployment—And Why," Business Insider, Aug. 23, 2010, http://www.businessinsider.com/ten-states-with-ridiculously-low-unemployment-rates-and-why-2010-8.

CHAPTER 3

1. "Times Topics: Hurricane Katrina," *The New York Times*, Aug. 25, 2010, http://topics.nytimes.com/top/reference/timestopics/subjects/h/hurricane_katrina/index.html.
2. Campbell Robertson, "Smaller New Orleans after Katrina, Census Shows," *The New York Times*, Feb. 3, 2011, http://www.nytimes.com/2011/02/04/us/04census.html.
3. Ibid.
4. Ibid.
5. U.S. Census Bureau, "2010 Census Data: Redistricting Data," 2011, http://2010.census.gov/2010census/data.
6. Steve Campbell, "Texas Population Tops 25 Million in 2010 Census," *Star Telegram*, Dec. 21, 2010, http://www.star-telegram.com/2010/12/21/2720043/texas-population-tops-25-million.html.
7. Robertson, "Smaller New Orleans."
8. Sabrina Tavernise and Robert Gebeloff, "Many U.S. Blacks Moving to South, Reversing Trend," *New York Times*, Mar. 24, 2011, http://www.nytimes.com/2011/03/25/us/25south.html?_r=1&hp.
9. Joseph L. Graves, *The Race Myth: Why We Pretend Race Exists in America* (New York: Penguin, 2004).
10. John D. Carl, *Think: Social Problems* (Boston: Pearson, 2011).
11. Ibid.
12. Ibid.
13. Louis Wirth, "The Problem of Minority Groups," in *The Science of Man in the World Crisis*, ed. Ralph Linton (New York: Columbia University Press, 1945).
14. Melissa Nobles, "History Counts: A Comparative Analysis of Racial/Color Categorization in U.S. and Brazilian Censuses," *American Journal of Public Health* 90, no. 11 (2000): 1738–1745.
15. Ibid.
16. Ibid.
17. U.S. Census Bureau, "Measuring America: The Decennial Census from 1790 to 2000," 2002, http://www.census.gov/prod/2002pubs/pol02marv-pt2.pdf.
18. Nobles, "History Counts."
19. Ibid.
20. Ibid.
21. Ibid.
22. Ibid.
23. Ibid.
24. U.S. Census Bureau, "2010 Census Data: Redistricting Data,"
25. Nobles, "History Counts"
26. Campbell Gibson and Kay Jung, "Historical Census Statistics on Population Totals by Race, 1790 to 1990, and by Hispanic origin, 1970 to 1990," in *Working Paper Series No. 56* (Washington, DC: U.S. Census Bureau, 2002), http://www.census.gov/population/www/documentation/twps0056/twps0056.html#intro.
27. Ibid.
28. Ibid.
29. Ibid.
30. Kenneth C. Davis, "The Founding Immigrants," *New York Times*, Jul. 3, 2007, http://www.nytimes.com/2007/07/03/opinion/03davis.html.
31. Southern Poverty Law Center, "Ideology: Anti-Immigrant," http://www.splcenter.org/get-informed/intelligence-files/ideology/anti-immigrant.
32. Carl, *THINK: Social Problems*.
33. Ibid.; Ruben G. Rumbaut, "Assimilation and Its Discontents: Between Rhetoric and Reality," *International Migration Review* 31, no. 4 (1997): 923–968; Min Zhou and Carl L. Bankston III, *Growing Up American: How Vietnamese Children Adapt to Life in the United States* (New York: Russell Sage Foundation Press, 1998).
34. Ibid.
35. Nasser Daneshvary, Henry W. Herzog, Richard Hofler, and Alan Schlottmann, "Job Search and Immigrant Assimilation: An Earnings Frontier Approach," *The Review of Economics and Statistics* 74, no. 3 (1992): 482–492.
36. Ibid.
37. Nolan Malone, Karri F. Baluja, Joseph M. Costanzo, and Cynthis J. Davis, *The Foreign-Born Population: 2000 Census Brief* (Washington, DC: U.S. Census Bureau, 2000), http://www.census.gov/prod/2003pubs/c2kbr-34.pdf.
38. Vicki Haddock, "President Schwarzenegger?: Some Think It's Time to Stop Excluding Foreign-Born Citizens from Serving in the Oval Office," *San Francisco Chronicle*, Nov. 2, 2003, http://articles.sfgate.com/2003-11-02/opinion/17516430_1_constitution-arnold-schwarzenegger-white-house-vic-snyder.
39. U.S. Census Bureau, *Race Data: Racial and Ethnic Classifications Used in Census 2000 and Beyond* (Washington, DC: U.S. Census Bureau, 2009), http://www.census.gov/population/www/socdemo/race/racefactcb.html.
40. Social Explorer, "1790 to Present," in *U.S. Decennial Census Files*, http://www.socialexplorer.com/pub/home/home.aspx.
41. U.S. Census Bureau, *Current Population Survey (CPS): Definitions and Explanations* (Washington, DC, 2010), http://www.census.gov/population/www/cps/cpsdef.html.
42. Social Explorer, "1790 to Present."
43. Ibid.
44. Ibid.
45. Ibid.
46. Ibid.
47. Ibid.
48. Ibid.
49. National Institutes of Health, "Native American Health," *Medline Plus*, Jan. 13, 2011, http://www.nlm.nih.gov/medlineplus/nativeamericanhealth.html.
50. Social Explorer, "1790 to Present."

51. Ibid.

52. Ibid.

53. Ibid.

54. Haya El Nasser, "Increase in Household Size Could Slow Economic Recovery," *USA Today*, May 7, 2010, http://www.usatoday.com news/nation/2010-05-06-household_N.htm.

55. Social Explorer, "1790 to Present."

56. Ibid.

57. Ibid.

58. Ibid.

59. Ibid.

60. U.S. Census Bureau, *The Foreign-Born Population: 2000 Census Brief*.

61. Ibid.

62. Ibid.

63. U.S. Census Bureau, "Nation's Foreign-Born Population Nears 37 Million," *U.S. Census Bureau Newsroom*, Oct. 19, 2010, http://www .census.gov/newsroom/releases/archives/foreignborn_population/ cb10-159.html.

CHAPTER 4

1. Sam Roberts, "So Many Men, so Few Women," *New York Times*, Feb. 12, 2006, http://www.nytimes.com/2006/02/12/weekinreview/ 12roberts.html.

2. Steve Conner, "The Equatorial Enigma," *Independent*, Apr. 1, 2009, http://www.independent.co.uk/news/science/the-equatorial-enigma- why-are-more-girls-than-boys-born-in-the-tropics-ndash-and-what- does-it-mean-1658981.html.

3. Roberts, "So Many Men . . ."

4. Ibid.

5. Theodore E. Long and Jeffrey K. Hadden, "Reconception of Socializa- tion," *Sociological Theory* 3, no. 1 (1985): 39–49.

6. J. Declareuil, *Rome the Law-Giver* (London: Routledge, 1997), 96.

7. William I. Thomas, *Sex and Society*, (Chicago: University of Chicago Press, 1918), 516.

8. Target, "Toys," http://www.target.com/b/ref=in_br_display-ladders/ 1038620.

9. American Psychological Association, *Sexualization of Girls: Executive Summary*, 2007, http://www.apa.org/pi/women/programs/girls/report .aspx.

10. Target Corp., http://www.target.com/.

11. Candace West and Don Zimmerman, "Doing Gender," *Gender and Society* 1, no. 2 (1987): 125–151.

12. U.S. Census Bureau, "The Questions on the Form," http://2010 .census.gov/2010census/text/text-form.php.

13. K. J. Navara, "Humans at Tropical Latitudes Produce More Females," *Biology Letters* 5, no. 4 (2009): 524–527; Amadu Jacky Kaba, "Sex Ra- tio at Birth and Racial Differences: Why Do Black Women Give Birth to More Females than Non-Black Women?" *African Journal of Reproductive Health / La Revue Africaine de la Santé Reproductive* 12, no. 3 (2008): 139–150.

14. Susan B. Carter, Scott Sigmund Gartner, Michael R. Haines, Alan L. Olmstead, Richard Sutch, and Gavin Wright (eds.), *Historical Statis- tics of the United States: Millennial Edition* (Cambridge, MA: Cambridge University Press, 2006), 1–48.

15. Teresa L. Amott and Julie A. Matthaei, *Race, Gender, and Work: A Multi-Cultural Economic History of Women in the United States* (Cam- bridge, MA: South End Press, 1996), 97.

16. Daniel J. Kruger, "Sexual Selection and the Male: Female Mortality Ratio," *Evolutionary Psychology* 2 (2004): 66–85.

17. "Colleges for Women," National Women's History Museum, 2007, http://www.nmwh.org/online-exhibits/education/1800s_6.htm.

18. Carter et al., *Historical Statistics of the United States*, 2–26.

19. Ibid., 2-27–2-28.

20. David S. Heidler & Jeanne T. Heidler (eds.), *Encyclopedia of the Civil War: A Political, Social, and Military History* (New York: Norton, 2000), 373.

21. Carter et al., 1-51–1-53.

22. Arnott and Matthaei, *Race, Gender, and Work*, 110–111.

23. Carter et al., *Historical Statistics of the United States*, 2–26.

24. Ibid., 2–39.

25. Ibid., 1-51–1-53.

26. Ibid., 2–39.

27. Ibid., 1-51–1-53.

28. Ibid., 1-401–1-402.

29. Mitchell Geoffrey Bard, *Complete Idiot's Guide to World War II* (New York: Alpha, 2010).

30. Carter et al., *Historical Statistics of the United States*, 1-51–1-53.

31. Ibid., 279.

32. Office of Management and Budget and the Economics and Statistics Administration, *Women in America: Indicators of Economic and Social Well-Being* (Washington, DC: U.S. Government, 2011), 5.

33. Ibid., 41.

34. Carter et al., *Historical Statistics of the United States*, 1-51–1-56.

35. PBS Independent Lens, "Maggie Growls," 2003, http:// www.pbs .org/independentlens/maggiegrowls/film.html.

36. U.S. Census Bureau, "American Community Survey: 2009," 2009, http://factfinder.census.gov/servlet/ACSSAFFPeople?_submenuId= people_2&_sse=on.

37. U.S. Census Bureau, "American Community Survey: 2009," 2009, http://factfinder.census.gov/servlet/ACSSAFFPeople?_submenuId=p eople_2&_sse=on.

38. Center for Disease Control, "10 Leading Causes of Death by Age Group, United States—2007," 2007, http://www.cdc.gov/injury/ wisqars/pdf/Death_by_Age_2007-a.pdf.

39. Seth Borenstein, "Women Drivers? They're Safer Than Men," *Sci- ence on msnbc.com*, Jan. 20, 2007, http://www.msnbc.msn.com/id/ 16698153/ns/technology_and_science-science.

40. Bureau of Justice Statistics, "Homicide Trends in the U.S.," 2011, http://bjs.ojp.usdoj.gov/content/homicide/gender.cfm.

41. Center for Disease Control, "Number of Suicides by Sex, Race, and Age in 2007," 2007, http://www.nimh.nih.gov/statistics/ pdf/CDC-2007Trend%20Numbers.pdf.

42. Office of Management and Budget and the Economics and Statistics Administration, *Women in America*, 15.

43. Ibid., 15, 28.

44. U.S. Census Bureau, Decennial Census of Population, 2000.

45. Derek Thompson, "It's Not Just a Recession, It's a Mancession!," *The Atlantic*, Jul. 9, 2009, http://www.theatlantic.com/business/archive/ 2009/07/its-not-just-a-recession-its-a-mancession/20991.

46. Pew Research Center, "Dissecting the 2008 Electorate: Most Diverse in U.S. History," April 30, 2009, http://pewresearch.org/assets/pdf/ dissecting-2008-electorate.pdf.

47. Office of Management and Budget and the Economics and Statistics Administration, *Women in America*, 39–40.

48. Yun-Suk Lee and Linda J. Waite, "Husbands' and Wives' Times Spent on Housework: A Comparison of Measures," *Journal of Marriage and Family* 67, no. 2 (2005): 328–336.

49. Nancy Folbre and Marjorie Abel, "Women's Work and Women's Households: Gender Bias in the U.S. Census," *Social Research* 56, no. 3 (1989): 545–569.

50. Office of Management and Budget and the Economics and Statistics Administration, *Women in America*, 15.

51. Ibid., 4–14.

52. Ohio History Central, "Oberlin College," http://www.ohiohistory central.org/entry.php?rec=775; Tamar Lewin, "At Colleges, Women Leaving Men in the Dust," *New York Times*, Jul. 9, 2006, http://www.nytimes.com/2006/07/09/education/09college.html.

53. Office of Management and Budget and the Economics and Statistics Administration, *Women in America*, 17.

54. Lewin, "At Colleges, Women Leaving Men in the Dust."

55. Ibid.

56. Office of Management and Budget and the Economics and Statistics Administration, *Women in America*, 20.

57. Ibid., 23.

58. Institute for Women's Policy Research, "The Gender Wage Gap by Occupation," April 2010, http://www.iwpr.org/publications/pubs/ the-gender-wage-gap-by-occupation/at_download/file.

59. U.S. Department of Labor, Women's Bureau, "20 Leading Occupa- tions of Employed Women 2009 Annual Averages," 2009, http:// www.dol.gov/wb/factsheets/20lead2009.htm.

60. Office of Management and Budget and the Economics and Statistics Administration, *Women in America*, 33.

61. Karen Datko, "It's No Longer Just a 'Mancession,'" *MSN Money*, Mar. 23, 2011, http://money.msn.com/saving-money-tips/post.aspx?post=b7651cb1-4a58-417e-9194-8df8464310ac.

62. Thompson, "It's Not Just a Recession . . ."

63. Catherine Rampell, "The Mancession," *New York Times*, Aug. 10, 2009, http://economix.blogs.nytimes.com/2009/08/10/the-mancession.

64. U.S. Census Bureau, "2007 Survey of Business Owners," 2011, http://fact finder.census.gov/servlet/IBQTable?_bm=y&-fds_name=EC0700 A1&-geo_id=D&-ds_name=SB0700CSA01&-_lang=en.

65. Office of Management and Budget and the Economics and Statistics Administration, *Women in America*, 27–28.

66. U.S. Census Bureau, 2005–2009 American Community Survey.

67. Daniel H. Weinberg, "Earnings by Gender: Evidence from Census 2000," *Monthly Labor Review* 130, no. 7/8 (2007).

68. Bureau of Labor Statistics, "Women at Work," 2011, http://www.bls.gov/spotlight/2011/women.

69. Institute for Women's Policy Research, "The Gender Wage Gap by Occupation."

70. Ibid.

71. Weinberg, "Earnings by Gender."

72. Office of Management and Budget and the Economics and Statistics Administration, *Women in America*, 32.

73. Institute for Women's Policy Research, "The Gender Wage Gap by Occupation."

74. Social Explorer, "American Community Survey 2005–2009 Census Tract Data," http://www.socialexplorer.com.

CHAPTER 5

1. Texas State Data Center, "Population Change," 2011, http://txsdc.utsa.edu.

2. Ibid.

3. Laurel Brubaker Caulkins, "Rising Young Hispanics in Texas Poised to Pick Up the Aging Tab," *Bloomberg.com*, February 18, 2011, http://www.bloomberg.com/news/2011-02-18/rising-young-hispanics-in-texas-poised-to-pick-up-aging-tab.html.

4. Ibid.

5. Ibid.

6. John D. Carl, *Think: Social Problems* (Boston: Pearson, 2011).

7. Ibid.

8. "GCT-T2-R Median Age of the Total Population: 2009," http://factfinder.census.gov/servlet/GCTTable?_bm=y&geo_id=01000US&-_box_head_nbr=GCT-T2-R&ds_name=PEP_2009_EST&-format=U-40Sa.

9. United Nations, "World Population Prospects: The 2008 Revision Population Database," http://esa.un.org/unpp/p2k0data.asp.

10. Ibid.

11. Adele Hayutin, "Global Demographic Shifts," *PREA Quarterly*, Fall (2007): 47–48, http://longevity.stanford.edu/files/PREAHayutin_0.pdf.

12. Ibid.

13. John Mirowsky, "Age at First Birth, Health, and Mortality" *Journal of Health and Social Behavior* 46, no. 1, (Mar., 2005): 32–50.

14. Steven L. Gortmaker and Paul H. Wise, "THE FIRST INJUSTICE: Socioeconomic Disparities, Health Services Technology, and Infant Mortality," *Annual Review of Sociology* 23 (1997): 147–170.

15. Ibid., 47–48.

16. Ibid., 47–48.

17. Elizabeth Rosenthal, "Europe, East and West, Wrestles with Falling Birthrates," *NYTimes.com*, September 3, 2006, http://www.nytimes.com/2006/09/03/world/europe/03iht-birth.2683302.html?pagewanted=1.

18. Thomas Cole, *The Journey of Life: A Cultural History of Aging in America* (Cambridge, MA: Cambridge University Press, 1992), 50–53.

19. Ibid., 52–53.

20. Carole Haber, *Beyond Sixty-Five: The Dilemma of Old Age in America's Past* (Cambridge, MA: Cambridge University Press, 1983) 26–27.

21. David Hackett Fischer, "Growing Old in America," (New York: Oxford University Press, 1977) 161–169.

22. Ibid.

23. Ibid., 174–184.

24. Cole, 222–227.

25. Robert Barnes, "Court Backs Workers in Age Bias Lawsuit," *The Washington Post*, June 20, 2008, http://www.washingtonpost.com/wp-dyn/content/article/2008/06/19/AR2008061901359.html.

26. Laurence J. Kotlikoff and Scott Burns, *The Coming Generational Storm: What You Need to Know about America's Economic Future* (Cambridge, MA: MIT Press, 2004)

27. Social Explorer, "Census 1850, Age," http://www.socialexplorer.com/pub/reportdata/htmlresults.aspx?ReportId=R10042400s.

28. Social Explorer, "ACS 2005–2009 Estimates, Age (Detailed Version)," http://www.socialexplorer.com/pub/reportdata/htmlresults.aspx?ReportId=R10042396s.

29. Leslie Morgan, Suzanne Kunkel, "Aging, Society, and the Life Course," (New York: Springer Publishing Company, 2011) 5–6, 11–12.

30. Julie Meyer, "Age: 2000," *Census Bureau,* October 2001, http://www.census.gov/prod/2001pubs/c2kbr01-12.pdf.

31. U.S. Census Bureau, "Selected Characteristics of Baby Boomers 42 to 60 Years Old in 2006," 2006, 3, http://www.census.gov/population/www/socdemo/age/2006%20Baby%20Boomers.pdf.

32. Leslie M. Harris, *After Fifty: How the Baby Boom Will Redefine the Mature Market*, (Ithaca, NY: Paramount Market Publishing, 2003), 37–38.

33. Laurence J. Kotlikoff and Scott Burns, *The Coming Generational Storm: What You Need to Know about America's Economic Future*, (Cambridge, MA: MIT Press, 2004).

34. H. Michael Zal, *The Sandwich Generation: Caught Between Growing Children and Aging Parents*, (Cambridge, MA: Da Capo Press, 2001).

35. William Strauss and Neil Howe, *Generations: The History of America's Future: 1584 to 1629* (New York: William and Morrow, 1991), 324–325.

36. Ibid.

37. "Questions About Generation X/Generation Y: A Sloan Network & Family Research Network Fact Sheet," *Sloan Work & Family Research Network*, 2006, http://www.fourhourworkweek.com/reports/sloan-genxyfactsheet.pdf.

38. Ibid.

39. Ibid.

40. Melinda Crowley, "Generation X Speaks Out on Civic Engagement and the Decennial Census: An Ethnographic Approach," *U.S. Census Bureau*, June 17, 2003, 10–24, http://www.census.gov/pred/www/rpts/Generation%20X%20Final%20Report.pdf.

41. "Millennials: A Portrait of Generation Next," *Pew Research Center*, February 2010, 9–12, http://pewsocialtrends.org/files/2010/10/millennials-confident-connected-open-to-change.pdf.

42. Ibid.

43. Ibid.

44. Ibid.

45. Ibid., 25–29.

46. Laurence J. Kotlikoff and Scott Burns, *The Coming Generational Storm: What You Need to Know about America's Economic Future*, (Cambridge, MA: MIT Press, 2004).

47. Matilda White Riley, Robert L. Kahn, Anne Foner, *Age and Structural Lag: Society's Failure to Provide Meaningful Opportunities in Work, Family, and Leisure* (New York: John Wiley and Sons, 1994), 15–19.

48. "The State of Aging and Health in America: 2007," (Whitehouse Station, NJ: Centers for Disease Control and Prevention and the Merck Company Foundation, 2007), iii, http://www.cdc.gov/Aging/pdf/saha_2007.pdf.

49. Ibid.

50. Ibid., 4–5.

51. John D. Carl, *Think: Social Problems*, (Boston: Pearson, 2011).

52. Yvonne Gist and Lisa Hetzel, "We the People: Aging in the United States," U.S. Census Bureau, December 2004, 1–2, http://www.census.gov/prod/2004pubs/censr-19.pdf.

53. Ibid., 3–4.

54. Ibid., 3–4.

55. Ibid., 4–5.

56. Ibid., 6.

57. "Older Americans 2010: Key Indicators of Well-Being," *Federal Interagency Forum on Aging-Related Statistics* (2010), http://www.agingstats.gov/agingstatsdotnet/Main_Site/Data/2010_Documents/Docs/OA_2010.pdf.

58. Ibid.

59. Grayson Vincent and Victoria Velkoff, "The Next Four Decades The Older Population in the United States: 2010 to 2050," May 2010, 8–9, http://www.census.gov/prod/2010pubs/p25-1138.pdf.

60. Ibid.

61. Vincent, Velkoff, 4–8.

62. U.S. Census Bureau, "U.S. Census Bureau, Current Population Survey, Annual Social and Economic Supplement, 2009," Table 11: Educational Attainment of the Population 55 Years and Over by Sex and Age, 2009, http://www.census.gov/population/www/socdemo/age/older_2009.html; Yvonne Gist, Lisa Hetzel, "We the People: Aging in the United States," *U.S. Census Bureau* December 2004, 1–2, http://www.census.gov/prod/2004pubs/censr-19.pdf.

63. U.S. Census Bureau, "The 2011 Statistical Abstract: Table 16: Resident Population by Age and State: 2009," 2011, http://www.census.gov/compendia/statab/cats/ population.html.

64. U.S. Census Bureau, "Statistical Abstract of the United States: 2001," 22, http://www.census.gov/prod/2002pubs/01statab/pop.pdf.

65. U.S. Census Bureau, "The 2011 Statistical Abstract: Table 18: Resident Population by Age and State—Projections," 2011, http://www.census.gov/ compendia/statab/cats/population.html.

66. Ibid.

67. Kirsten J. Colello, "Where Do Older Americans Live? Geographic Distribution of the Older Population," Congressional Research Service, March 5, 2007, 9–12, http://aging.senate.gov/crs/aging5.pdf.

68. Colello, 12–13.

CHAPTER 6

1. Sabrina Tavernise, "Parenting by Gays More Common in the South, Census Shows," *New York Times*, January 18, 2011.

2. Ibid.

3. Ibid.

4. National Conference of State Legislatures, "Same-Sex Marriages, Civil Unions, and Domestic Partnerships," Feb. 2011, http://www.ncsl.org/default.aspx?tabid=16430.

5. Ibid.

6. Human Rights Campaign, "Respect for Marriage Act," Mar. 15, 2011, http://www.hrc.org/issues/13530.htm.

7. Tavernise, "Parenting by Gays . . ."

8. Rose M. Kreider and Tavia Simmons, "Marital Status: 2000, Census 2000 Brief," U.S. Census Bureau, October 2003.

9. U.S. Census Bureau, Current Population Survey (CPS), Definitions and Explanations, 2010, http://www.census.gov/population/www/cps/cpsdef.html.

10. National Conference of State Legislatures, "Same-Sex Marriage, Civil Unions and Domestic Partnership," 2011, http://www.ncsl.org/default.aspx?tabid=16430.

11. Stephanie Coontz, *Marriage, a History: From Obedience to Intimacy, or How Love Conquered Marriage* (New York: Viking Adult, 2005); Stephanie Coontz, *The Way We Never Were: American Families and the Nostalgia Trap* (New York: Basic Books, 2000).

12. Andrew J. Cherlin, *The Marriage-Go-Round: The State of Marriage and Family in America Today* (New York: Knopf Publishers, 2009).

13. K. C. Smith & Christie Schuler Smith, "U.S. State Laws," http://www.cousincouples.com/?page=states.

14. Stephanie Coontz, *Marriage, a History: From Obedience to Intimacy, or How Love Conquered Marriage* (New York: Viking Adult, 2005); Stephanie Coontz, *The Way We Never Were: American Families and the Nostalgia Trap* (New York: Basic Books, 2000).

15. U.S. Census Bureau, "Current Population Survey (CPS)–Definitions and Explanations," 2010, http://www.census.gov/population/www/cps/cpsdef.html.

16. U.S. Census Bureau, "America's Families and Living Arrangements: 2009," http://www.census.gov/population/www/socdemo/hh-fam/cps2009.html.

17. Valerie Kincade Oppenheimer, Matthijs Kalmijn, and Nelson Lim, "Men's Career Development and Marriage Timing During a Period of Rising Inequality," *Demography* 34, no. 3 (Aug., 1997): 311–330.

18. Larry L. Bumpass, James A. Sweet, and Andrew Cherlin, "The Role of Cohabitation in Declining Rates of Marriage," *Journal of Marriage and the Family* 53, no. 4 (1991): 913–927.

19. U.S. Census Bureau, "America's Families and Living Arrangements: 2009," Table A1, http://www.census.gov/population/www/socdemo/hh-fam/cps2009.html.

20. Ibid.

21. Jane Lawler, "Current Population Reports: Fertility of American Women: 2006," U.S. Census Bureau, 2008, http://www.census.gov/prod/ 2008pubs/p20-558.pdf.

22. Ibid.

23. U.S. Census Bureau, "America's Families and Living Arrangements: 2009," http://www.census.gov/population/www/socdemo/hh-fam/cps2009.html.

24. Ibid.

25. U.S. Census Bureau, "American Community Survey: 2008," http://factfinder.census.gov.

26. U.S. Census Bureau, "The 2011 Statistical Abstract," Tables 1334–1336, 2011, http://www.census.gov/compendia/statab/2011/tables/11s1335.pdf.

27. Sheryl WuDunn, "Stigma Curtails Single Motherhood in Japan," *New York Times*, Mar. 13, 1996, http://www.nytimes.com/1996/03/13/world/stigma-curtails-single-motherhood-in-japan.html.

28. U.S. Census Bureau, "Estimated Median Age at First Marriage, by Sex: 1890 to the Present," http://www.census.gov/population/www/socdemo/hh-fam.html#ht.

29. Ibid.

30. Ibid.

31. Jay D. Teachman, "Stability Across Cohorts in Divorce Risk Factors," *Demography* 39, no. 2 (2002): 331–351.

32. Ibid.

33. Ibid.

34. U.S. Census Bureau, "The 2011 Statistical Abstract," Tables 1334–1336, 2011, http://www.census.gov/compendia/statab/2011/tables/11s1335.pdf.

35. Rose M. Kreider and Tavia Simmons, "Marital Status: 2000, Census 2000 Brief," U.S. Census Bureau, October 2003.

36. Ibid.

37. U.S. Census Bureau, "Survey of Income and Program Participation: - Introduction to SIPP," 2006, http://www.census.gov/sipp/intro.html.

38. Rose M. Kreider, "Current Population Reports: Number, Timing, and Duration of Marriages and Divorces: 2001," U.S. Census Bureau, Feb. 2005, http://www.census.gov/prod/2005pubs/p70-97.pdf.

39. Ibid.

40. Ibid.

41. Ibid.

42. Ibid.

43. Ibid.

44. Ibid.

45. Ibid.

46. Ibid.

47. Ibid.

48. Ibid.

49. Rose M. Kreider and Tavia Simmons, "Marital Status: 2000, Census 2000 Brief," U.S. Census Bureau, October 2003.

50. Ibid.

51. Ibid.

52. Rose M. Kreider, "Current Population Reports: Number, Timing, and Duration of Marriages and Divorces: 2001," U.S. Census Bureau, Feb. 2005, http://www.census.gov/prod/2005pubs/p70-97.pdf.

53. Ibid.
54. Ibid.
55. Ibid.
56. Ibid.
57. Ibid.
58. Ibid.
59. Ibid.
60. Ibid.
61. Ibid.
62. Ibid.
63. Ibid.
64. Ibid.
65. Ibid.
66. Ibid.
67. Tavia Simmons and Martin O'Connell, "Married-Couple and Unmarried-Partner Households: 2000," U.S. Census Bureau, Feb. 2003, http://www.census.gov/prod/2003pubs/censr-5.pdf.
68. Ibid.
69. Ibid.
70. Ibid.
71. Ibid.
72. Ibid.

73. U.S. Census Bureau, "2005–2009 American Community Survey 5-Year Estimates," http://factfinder.census.gov/servlet/Dataset MainPageServlet?_program=ACS&_submenuId=&_lang=en& _ds_name=ACS_2009_5YR_G00_&ts=.
74. Ibid.
75. Ibid.
76. Ibid.
77. Ibid.
78. Ibid.
79. Ibid.
80. Ibid.
81. Ibid.
82. Ibid.
83. Ibid.
84. Ibid.

CHAPTER 7

1. U.S. Census Bureau, "Simpler path to 2010 Census data," *Census Bureau Director Groves says* (2011), http://www.census.gov/newsroom/releases/archives/miscellaneous/cb11-13.html
2. Ibid.

Index

A

ACS. *See* American Community Survey
African Americans, 3
    gender and, 52
    race and, 41–44
Age, aging, 15
    Age Discrimination in Employment
        Act, 70
    baby boomers, 72
    birthrate and, 69
    demographic change, U.S., 71–73
    Generation X, 72
    geographic distribution, 76–77
    health care and, 73
    historical trends, 69
    life expectancy, 69
    millennials, 72–73
    national impact, 68
    in recent censuses, 74–77
    Social Security and, 74
    Texas Hispanics, 68
    20th century, 71
    U.S., 70–73
    worldwide trends, 69
Age Discrimination in Employment Act, 70
Ageism, defined, 70
AHS. *See* American Housing Survey
American Community Survey (ACS),
    8–9, 90
American FactFinder, 98–108
American Housing Survey (AHS), 99
Asian Americans
    gender and, 52
    race and, 42, 44, 52
Asylum, defined, 39

B

Baby-boom generation, defined, 70
Beveridge, Andrew, 104
Birth cohort, defined, 85
Birth dearth, defined, 69
Birthrate, defined, 69
Blood quantum laws, defined, 3

C

Census Bureau, 2, 5–6
Census, changes over time, 6
    ACS, 8–9
    age and, 15
    changing country, 7
    costs, 10
    economic changes, 14
    gender, 14–15
    legislation, 9
    marriage, family, 15
    philosophy evolution, 8–10

    politics, 2
    questionnaires, 10
    race, racial changes, 14
    technology, 10
Census, data use
    ACS, 8–9, 98
    AHS, 99
    American FactFinder, 98–108
    CPS, 98
    historical data, 102
    IDB, 102–103
    international programs, 102–104
    MySocLab, 104
    NCVS, 99
    Social Explorer, 104–105
Census, historical origins, 2–4, 12–13
Changing country, 7
Cohabitate, defined, 84
Cohorts, defined, 70
Costs, 10
Current Population Survey (CPS), 98

D

Davis, Kingsley, 21
Decennial, defined, 2
Decile ratio, defined, 22
Defense of Marriage Act, 80

E

Economic changes, 14
Economic trends, employment, 23–24
    gender, 24–25
    immigration, 25
    income and, 26
    income inequality history, 23–24
    inequality, 29
    median household income, 26
    occupations, highest median
        earnings, 62
    race, 25
    state-by-state comparison, 29–30
    unemployment rate, 27–28
    women, 58–62
Education, 25, 59–60, 76
Entrepreneurial immigrants, 39
Enumeration, defined, 2
Ethnic enclaves, defined, 39
Ethnicity, defined, 35
Extended family, defined, 83

F

Family, defined, 83
Film Optical Sensing Device for Input to
    Computers (FOSDIC), 10
First Census Act, 3
Foreign-born residents, 39–40

G

Gender, 14–15. *See also* Sex ratio; Women
    concept, 52–54
    defined, 52
    economic trends, employment and, 24–25
    gap, 52
    patriarchy and, 52–53
    state-by-state comparisons, 62–65
    wage gap, 24–25
Gender bias, defined, 59
Gender gap, defined, 58
Gender roles, defined, 53
Generation, defined, 71
Generation X, defined, 71
Gerontology, defined, 68
Gini index, 22
Graves, Joseph, 35

H

Hispanic, Latino, 13
    gender and, 52
    race and, 40–45
    Texas population, 68
Householder, defined, 41

I

IDB. *See* International database
Immigration, 4–5, 13
    asylum, 39
    economic trends, employment and, 23–24
    entrepreneurial immigrants, 39
    foreign-born residents, 39–40
    history, U.S., 38–39
    labor immigrants, 39
    migration types, 39
    refugees, 39
    undocumented immigrants, 13–14
Income, 19
Income inequality, 18–20
    attitudes, 23
    defined, 21
    distribution across quintiles,
        1967–2005, 24
    Gini index, 22
    history, 23–24
    social classes, outcomes, 20–23
    social mobility and, 23
    U.S. *vs.* industrialized nations, 22–23
International database (IDB), 102–103
Involuntary immigration, defined, 39

L

Labor immigrants, 39
Latino. *See* Hispanic, Latino
Leading-edge boomers, defined, 72
Legal basis, 4–6

Legislation, 9
Life expectancy, defined, 69

M
Majority group, defined, 35
Mancession, defined, 61
Marriage cohort, defined, 86
Marriage, family, 15
    age of first marriage, 82–83
    changing American family, 80–81
    cohabitation, 89, 93
    Defense of Marriage Act, 80
    defined, 83
    divorce, 83, 84–86
    marital history, ages 15 and older, 85
    new American family, 80
    parenting, 93
    population characteristics, 87–90
    race and, 85–87, 92
    Respect for Marriage law, 80
    SIPP data, 83, 85–86, 88, 91–93
    state-by-state differences, 93–95
    2000–2001 Census findings, 83–90
    2005–2009 ACS, 90–93
    unmarried adults, 81–82
    unmarried couples and race, 89–91
    unmarried parents, 82
Matriarchies, defined, 53
Median age, defined, 68
Meritocracy, defined, 21
Methodologies, 3–4
    early census methods, 11–12
    immigration and, 13
    purposive sampling, 11
    random sampling, 12
    sampling frame, 12
    sampling science, 11–12
    2010 Census, 13–14
    undercounts, 12–14
Migration types, 39
Millennials, defined, 72
Minority group, defined, 35
Moore, Wilbert, 21
Mulatto, 36
MySocLab, 104

N
National Bureau of Economic
    Statistics, 26
National Crime Victimization Survey
    (NCVS), 99
Native Americans, 2–3, 42, 44
Near poor, defined, 20
Nuclear family, defined, 82

O
Obama, Barack, 35
Octoroon, defined, 36
Old-old, defined, 74

P
Parenting, 93
Patriarchy, defined, 53
Pensions, defined, 70
Politics, 2
Population changes, New Orleans,
    post-Katrina, 34
Population, geographic center, 5

Population projections, defined, 103
Poverty, defined, 19
Poverty line, defined, 19
Purposive sampling, defined, 11

Q
Quadroon, defined, 36
Questionnaires, 10
Quintiles, defined, 20

R
Race, 14
    census race categories, 1790–2010, 37
    census racial definitions, historical
        variances, 37–38
    concept of, 35
    defined, 35
    economic trends, employment and, 25
    historical background, America, 34–38
    marriage and, 85–87, 92
    state-by-state racial population
        changes, 45–48
    unmarried couples and, 89–90
Race, census definitions over time
    1790–1840, 35–36
    1850–1920, 36
    1930–1960, 36
    1970–2010, 36–37
*The Race Myth: Why We Pretend Race Exists
    in America* (Graves), 35
Race, 2000 Census findings, 40–43
    Asian, 42
    black, 41–42
    foreign-born population, 45
    Hispanic, Latino, 42–43
    Native American, Alaska Native, 42
    non-Hispanic White, 40–41
Race, 2010 Census findings
    Asian, 44
    black, 43–44
    foreign-born population, 45
    Hispanic, Latino, 44–45
    Native American, Alaska Native, 44
    non-Hispanic White, 43
Random sampling, defined, 12
Real median incomes, defined, 26
Reapportion, defined, 2
Refugees, defined, 39
Relative poverty, defined, 20
Respect for Marriage law, 80

S
Sampling, defined, 11
Sampling frame, defined, 12
Sandwich generation, defined, 72
Sectionalism, defined, 9
Sex, defined, 65
Sex ratio
    by age, 58
    aging population and, 57
    application in census, 54
    Civil War impact, 56
    defined, 52, 74
    Great Depression impact, 57
    immigration, industrialization and, 56
    over time, all ages, 55–56
    state-by-state comparison, 64
    women and, 55

women in workforce and, 56–57
    World War II impact, 57
Sexism, defined, 53
Sexualization, defined, 53
SIPP. *See* Survey of Income and Program
    Participation
Social class, 18. *See also* Income inequality
    Davis and Moore *vs.* Tumin, 20–21
    defined, 19
    income outcomes and, 20–21
Social Explorer, 104–105
Social mobility, defined, 23
Social Security Act, defined, 70
Social Security funding, 74
States, 4–5
    county-by-county census data, 101
    economic trends, employment, 29–30
    geographic age distribution, 76–77
    marriage, cohabitation patterns, 93–95
    median incomes, 65
    sex ratio, 64
Stratification, defined, 18–19
Structural lag, defined, 73
Survey of Income and Program Participation
    (SIPP), 83, 85–86, 88, 91–93
Surveys, defined, 11

T
Technology, 10
Topologically Integrated Geographic
    Encoding and Referencing
    (TIGER), 10
Trailing-edge boomers, defined, 72
Transgendered, defined, 54
Tumin, Melvin, 21
2010 Census, methodologies, 13–14

U
Undercount, defined, 13
Undocumented immigrants, 13–14
Unemployed, defined, 26
Unemployment rate, 27–28
Universal Automatic Computer
    (UNIVAC), 10

V
Voluntary immigration, 38

W
Wage gap, defined, 24
Wealth, 19
Women
    business ownership, 61
    common occupations, 2009, 60
    education and, 59–60
    employment and, 59–62
    gender bias and, 59
    at home roles, 59
    income inequality, 61–62
    mancession and, 61
    21st century, 58–62
Works Progress Administration, 9

X
Xenophobia, defined, 38

Y
Young-old, defined, 74